YOU DON'T KNOW WHO YOU'RE DEALING WITH!

A BIOGRAPHY
Rescuing Colleen from Acquired Brain Injury

Bernadette's story as told to

JEANETTE A. TILLEY

First published by National Biographic Australia

Copyright © Jeanette Tilley 2011

Email: jeanette.a.tilley@gmail.com

The National Library of Australia
Cataloguing-in-Publication Data

Tilley. Jeanette
You Don't Know Who You're Dealing With!

ISBN: 9-780980-7796-5-3 (pbk)

1. Clancy, Colleen–Biography
2. Brain damage/Stroke–Patients

362.197481092

All rights reserved. No part of this publication may be reproduced, stored in a retrieval system, or transmitted, in any form, by any means, electronic, mechanical, photocopying, recording or otherwise, without prior permission from the author.

Typeset in Garamond 13 pt

Printed by TB Books
P.O. Box 8138,
Seymour South Victoria 3660
www.tbbpublishing.com.au

CONTENTS

Author's Note 7

Preface 11

Chapter 1 : Growing Up 17

Chapter 2 : The Event 29

Chapter 3 : Just coping 39

Chapter 4 : Bedside Vigil 49

Chapter 5 : On the Ward 57

Chapter 6 : Early Days at Royal Talbot 75

Chapter 7 : Christmas 1998 87

Chapter 8 : Ongoing Therapy 95

Chapter 9 : Excursions 111

Chapter 10 : Appropriate Accommodation 121

Chapter 11 : Pirra Lodge 127

Chapter 12 : The Fun Run 143

Chapter 13 : Emotional Times 151

Chapter 14 : Kidnap from Pirra Lodge 163

Chapter 15 : Back into Society 169

Chapter 16 : Busy Times 179

Chapter 17 : Back to the Alfred 191

Chapter 18 : The Granny Flat ……......................... 203

Chapter 19 : AFL Sportsready ………………….. 215

Chapter 20 : A Traineeship ………….................... 231

Chapter 21 : New Experiences ………………….. 245

Chapter 22 : Trouble on the Horizon 257

Chapter 23 : Marking Time ………………............... 271

Chapter 24 : Living a Distinctive Life 289

Chapter 25 : Independence 303

Postscript ……………………………………….. 313

PHOTOS

Page 47 : Colleen : Second week in Intensive Care at Alfred Hospital

Page 64 : Grueling physiotherapy with the staff at Alfred Hospital

Page 68 : Decked out for the footy : Colleen with Peter

Page 73 : Time to say goodbye to the staff at the Alfred Hospital

Page : 93 : Home for Christmas : Paul and Shaun with Colleen

Page 201 : Colleen celebrating her 27th birthday in Alfred Hospital with Suzanne

Page 202 : Colleen with Christine – wheelchair helps with broken ankle

Page 214 : Shaun commences work on the granny flat

Page 214 : The completed granny flat

Page 312 : Christmas 2010.

AUTHOR'S NOTE

At 22 years of age, Colleen was fit and happy. Then she suffered a cerebral aneurysm. She had only a .06 chance of survival.

Nationally, there are some 6,700 young (under sixty-five years of age) Australians residing in aged care nursing homes. A percentage of this number consists of the very young, under thirty years of age, and some as young as early teens. Disabilities arrive without warning and can require intensive and immediate responses. This presents a conundrum for different areas of community services, and disability and health systems which are unable to deliver the services desperately needed.

Young people across Australia are forced to live in nursing homes because they have nowhere else to go.

Acquired brain injury (A.B.I.) may arise from a work place injury, a road traffic accident, or as in Colleen's case from illness.

Stroke affects 53,000 Australians per year and is the second single greatest killer. Whilst two-thirds of stroke victims are over sixty-five, young people in the peak of life can also be struck down.

The Clancys were advised that there is no specific facility to cater for young people with a medically acquired brain injury, that the only option was a nursing home. They queried, why should young people struck down by accident, stroke or other illnesses leaving them with an A.B.I. be limited to the choice of an aged care facility for their ongoing care?

Colleen's siblings were passionate about helping not only their sister, but other young people with an A.B.I. This came from their exasperation at the lack of support for people who suffered a brain injury caused by illness, in comparison to accident or work place injuries leading to a brain injury. They planned to lobby the Government and raise awareness of this disparity. With the vision of a ten year plan, they hoped sufficient funds would be raised in the first year to help Colleen, and then in successive years to help others. They talked about where they could buy land and build a home for young people with medically acquired brain injuries. They thought.......if only we had an endless pot of money........

It would appear the chronic underfunding and the rapidly rising unmet demand have meant that existing disability systems have focused on a demand management approach where services are delivered according to availability of funding rather than the immediate needs of consumers.

Council of Australian Governments' five year funding initiative which commenced implementation in 2006 has been but a drop in the ocean in addressing the overwhelming need in the community.

Satisfying the growth in demand for disability supports and services has been an enduring challenge for governments at state and federal levels for many years. Nowhere has this been more evident than in the movement of very young disabled Australians into a residential aged care system ill-equipped to meet their needs.

I would like to thank the Clancy family for entrusting me with their story and Bernadette in particular for baring her soul during the course of this project.

Diary records of the first several critical years helped me reconstruct the remarkable progress of Colleen's rehabilitation. Meetings and casual interviews with

Bernadette, Peter and their family have provided an insight into this family's resolve to restore Colleen to health and provided me with firsthand knowledge to write this book. I have been amazed at the resilience of this family and touched by their support for and devotion to not only Colleen but each other.

Bernadette's determination to leave no stone unturned in her quest for quality of life for Colleen is amazing and her willingness to retrain in her endeavour to help Colleen is awe-inspiring. The many people who have encountered Bernadette during the incredible journey the Clancys travelled with Colleen soon found out with whom they were dealing; a mother determined to secure the best possible future for her daughter.

As each day passes and it is seen how Colleen's "Circle of Friends" assists her to lead a distinctive life I think of all the other ABI sufferers who would also benefit from the structures which have been put in place for Colleen. Society has a responsibility to see that all medically acquired brain injury people receive adequate first class care to assist them lead fulfilling lives and to enable them where possible to integrate into our communities.

Initially I did not set out to raise awareness of the inappropriate incarceration of very young people with A.B.I. in nursing homes, but I hope that ultimately this is what my book might achieve and that funding will come from somewhere to provide alternatives and to enable the quality of their lives to improve.

Colleen did not have to go into a nursing home. She is one of the lucky ones.

This is Bernadette's story: the anguish of rescuing Colleen from acquired brain injury as told to me.

Jeanette A. Tilley

PREFACE

I didn't usually do the afternoon shift. My time was 7.00 a.m. until 11 a.m. at the Southern Cross Homes for the aged in Newport. But on Tuesday the 24th June, 2003, I had been on the job since late afternoon and at 7.30 p.m. was heading home. It was so convenient living next door, but that was soon to change. Enjoying the cold evening air after the stuffy heat of the nursing home, I walked the short distance to the gateway of our small rented house, resolving to confront head on the muddle I suspected awaited me. Little did I know just how much of an ordeal I would have to contend with that night and in the coming days.

Anyone who has moved house will appreciate the enormity of the task. The house in Melbourne Street which had been our home for eighteen months, was a single fronted, brown brick with a carport in the front, plain, unattractive but functional. To our delight though, on Saturday my husband Peter was to start the shift to our newly purchased house in Ashburton, a south eastern suburb of Melbourne. I had hoped over the coming week the transition would be complete, and we could finally settle into our own home once again, but more importantly, be able to set up accommodation for Colleen in a granny flat at the rear of the house.

The front door had clicked shut behind me, and I was surprised to find the lounge room empty. Colleen had the use of this room and the adjoining bedroom and would spend hours there playing her music. I navigated through packing boxes scattered across the room, and went down the hallway into the kitchen and little family room at the back of the house. There I had found Colleen with her leg propped up on the couch.

'What have you done?' I asked.

'I fell over, Mum. I've hurt my ankle,' Colleen said.

I flung my bag onto the table spilling its contents and asked, 'How did you do that? What shoes did you have on?' I was unsuccessful in keeping the accusing tone out of my voice.

'Umm. Not my runners.' Colleen avoided looking at me.

'What do you mean not your runners?' I said. 'Why are you going for a walk without your runners?'

Peter had looked up from where he was squatted in front of Colleen adjusting a cold pack to her ankle.

'Take it easy, Bernadette,' he said.

'That means you didn't have you're A.F.O. on did you? You know you can't go anywhere without your foot support,' I said.

'Yeah, I know,' Colleen replied. 'We were just going around the block,' she mumbled.

'How did you fall?' I enquired.

After a bit more questioning I learnt how the accident had occurred. Colleen and her carer had set off on a three kilometre walk, but unfortunately ill prepared. Colleen had not worn her artificial foot orthotic (A.F.O.) which fits in her right runner and straps around her ankle and calf giving her leg necessary support. A tree root was protruding through the footpath and over she had gone. I had bit back the recriminations and set about trying to relieve the discomfort she was experiencing.

'It's her good leg,' Peter had said. 'She can't bear any weight on her ankle.'

I was concerned too. 'I can't believe her carer has let this happen.' I rattled the ice-tray angrily as I prepared another cold pack.

'It certainly shouldn't have happened,' Peter replied. 'I think it's only a sprain,' he added hopefully.

At any time it was difficult for Colleen to get up off the lounge with her gammy leg. But now her good leg had a suspected sprained ankle so it was almost impossible. Getting Colleen's seventy kilogram weight to the toilet was challenging. She tried a tippy toed sort of hop with Peter and I on either side, but the space was so tiny it was just a nightmare.

'I know, tomorrow I'll borrow a pair of crutches and a wheel chair from next door,' I declared.

We managed to get through that night continuing to apply ice in an endeavour to reduce the swelling. She did not appear to be in a great deal of pain. Funny thing is, even now Colleen complains loudly about a little cut on her finger, but she just seems to endure real pain. For her it is just a trauma.

The next morning I left Peter in charge while I did my morning shift. I felt I had a responsibility to the oldies, getting them up and out to breakfast. Peter was on late shift at the Alfred Hospital where he was an orderly, so he continued with the ice packs. When I returned home before lunch with a wheel chair we found it helped, but it could not be maneuvered to the toilet in the tiny space and Colleen could not manage the crutches I had borrowed.

'Try and put a little weight on the ankle Colls,' I had coaxed her as Peter tried to shunt her foot around and I twisted her body. But by then it was more painful for her than it had been previously. Also we were in danger of twisting her knee and doing a whole lot of damage.

'I can't, it hurts Mum,' she yelled.   My husband and I were in danger of hurting our backs too.

'Nah, Peter, we need help here,' I had declared as I collapsed onto the box labelled bathroom gear.

'Don't muck around, Mum, get the physiotherapist to call.'   Christine had been quick to help make decisions regarding her sister's well being when she called in a short time later.

And so the physiotherapist visited later that day.

'It may be broken,' she suggested when we told her Colleen was not asking for pain killers. 'Breaks are sometimes less painful than sprains.'

So on Thursday, off to Williamstown Hospital. After x-rays and four hours in the hospital's casualty department, diagnosis confirmed a fracture and the ankle was in plaster. The break where the tibia and fibula join would have to be pinned.

'I'm going to give you a referral to the Alfred,' the doctor said, and we were so lucky, being able to book in for the coming Saturday. We were no strangers to the Alfred Hospital.

Back home we managed to get through the night, Colleen helped to sleep with a herbal preparation.

The next day we continued maneuvering the wheel chair around the packing boxes.   The impairment of her left leg and the weight of the plaster boot meant we had no success with the crutches. Besides, she could not co-ordinate.

'Oh, you're joking aren't you,' I exclaimed when the three of us nearly fell on one of Colleen's expeditions on crutches.

We called Colleen's occupational therapist and eventually she had Colleen doing transfers from the chair to the bathroom with the crutches.

'It's going to be difficult,' she had said doubtfully, 'but if we keep going, perhaps with practice we'll get there.'

When she was leaving she had decided to ring the other physiotherapist to make sure we were doing the right thing.

'No,' had been his unequivocal answer. 'Take her straight to hospital and get referred to the right guy to sort it out.'

So at 11.00 a.m. on Friday morning we took her to the Alfred Hospital and at 6.00 p.m. she was admitted, waiting to have the fracture pinned.

Surgery was ultimately to take place at 4.00 p.m. on Saturday 28th June, 2003, Colleen's twenty-seventh birthday. We were advised she would need six weeks rehabilitation, and then have respite care before returning home.

And why all this fuss for just a broken ankle you might ask? Well, you see, Colleen has special needs. She has a medically acquired brain injury.

We were once again faced with a challenge in the incredible journey we were travelling with Colleen. I guessed there would be many more.

Chapter 1

GROWING UP

Our third daughter Colleen Louise Clancy was born on the 28th June, 1976 weighing seven pounds five ounces (approximately three and a quarter kilograms). She was thirteen days late and arrived with a little egg shaped lump on her head to the left side of the crown. My goodness I thought, what is this? But we were assured it was quite common, just a swelling which would subside within about six months, which it did. My little girl was perfect.

Peter and I shifted our family to Broadford on the 31st January, 1981. We had been living and operating a newsagency at Pascoe Vale in suburban Melbourne. My brother John at that time also owned a newsagency. For as long as I could remember my family had been involved with newsagencies. My father was a teacher by profession but then turned his hand to running a newsagency business before going into real estate. He died aged sixty-one from a massive heart attack in 1972 shortly after retiring. I was the second youngest of a family of seven children, and felt the need to cut the family apron strings, gain our independence and do things our way.

Broadford seemed ideal geographically to suit our purpose. The township situated just off the Hume Freeway seventy-two kilometres north of Melbourne, was surrounded by sheep and cattle properties. It had developed over many years more because of the northbound traffic from Melbourne rather than the needs of the local farmers. The town's huge paper mill built in 1890, along with the wool scourers gave employment to a great many of the town's residents. Smaller industries also contributed to the commerce. So in the main street which boasted the regular range of country shops, we purchased the newsagency business and shifted north. Not I might add, without a twinge of guilt.

At sixty-four years of age in 1975, my mother had had a stroke and at the time of our move had been living with my sister Pat for about twelve months. I remember writing a letter to Pat apologizing for shifting to Broadford and thereby placing a greater burden of responsibility on her. I felt I was deserting Mum. Still, with only an hour's drive back to Pascoe Vale, Broadford did not seem like the end of the earth and I soon got into the routine of regular visits to see Mum.

We settled into our new cramped environment. The residence we lived in at the rear of the shop with our four children was tiny. The children bunked in together.

'I reckon we'll only last six months here,' Peter predicted.

Our three eldest children were primary school age, and Colleen at four and a half, would attend kindergarten. After seeing her sisters, Suzanne ten, Christine eight, and brother Paul seven, off on the school bus each morning, I would walk Colleen around the corner to kinder. In a very short time we knew everybody. Colleen would help us in the shop every afternoon, especially if I had been down to the warehouse and brought toys back which had to be priced and put on the shelves. She had a wow of a time, because she would always score something for her day's work, a little click clack toy or other small tokens that would probably be broken in five minutes. It was all so exciting for her. Her eyes would become round in wonderment. A shop that had lots of toys and lollies was a small child's paradise.

I remember one hot night before Christmas the kids and I had been to the warehouse and were traveling home from Melbourne in our old Valiant with parcels stacked up everywhere around them. No-one could move.

'Let's have an ice-cream,' I suggested.

Happily on our way again licking our treats, I was horrified to see red and blue flashing lights in the rear view mirror and was pulled over and breathalized.

'I've had a rum and raisin ice-cream,' I guiltily confessed, before being allowed to continue on our way without prosecution.

The kids couldn't wait to spill the beans to Peter. I was just so amazed I had not been booked for being overloaded.

Colleen loved her kinder teachers and all the mums would come into the shop and see her there and sometimes take her away. Come home and play – can I have Colleen for a couple of hours? Sometimes I would feel a little bit guilty, not being able to return the favour. She was very lucky with her kinder group.

True to Peter's prophecy, half way through Colleen's kindergarten year we shifted to the Presbyterian Manse just a short distance from the shop. About this time I remember over the Sunday roast making an announcement which was greeted by the children with great excitement, and at the end of that year our fifth child Shaun was born.

Then came the dilemma of deciding what school Colleen should attend. Our other three children were travelling to St. Patrick's Catholic Primary School in Kilmore, but it did not seem appropriate to send a little tot on a bus journey each day.

Seventeen kilometres south of Broadford, Kilmore is the centre of a rural community although many people commute to Melbourne for employment. Catholic primary education had existed in the parish for over 100 years prior to St. Pat's School opening in 1968. We never thought of sending the kids to a non catholic school, you just followed suit. I think the reason for this was all a part of the non thinking process of a bigoted Catholic upbringing. Still we wondered, can we send this little five and a half year old to school on the bus? But after due consideration we did. After all she did have three siblings also travelling who could look out for her.

In later years the children would refuse my offer to collect them from school. The bus trips gave them great entertainment and were indeed an education. When each of them in turn progressed to year twelve and the back seat of the bus, they thought they were just the best. Although often in trouble Paul, and more regularly Christine, would be shifted to the front seat as punishment.

What excitement on Colleen's first day at St. Pat's. Four other Clancy children started in the same prep grade with Colleen, and we weren't related to any of them. The parish priest made a great fuss about this presenting us with an engraved 'welcome' glass at the school Mass. It was a good feeling and made us feel special and welcomed. I still have the photo of these five little preppies taken on the first day, Colleen with her cheeky grin and distinctive row of freckles under her left eye.

Despite the long bus journey which took a very circuitous route between Broadford and Kilmore, Colleen settled in well. She was a conscientious young student and loved doing everything, especially drawing and colouring in. As it happened, her time there that year was short lived.

My work was cut out for me in the first few months of that year. I had a new baby, was taking an active roll in the management of the shop, organizing four primary aged children and then in the January my invalid mother came to stay for a holiday. Pat needed a break and at last I felt I could do something to assist my sister. The stroke had left Mum completely paralyzed down her left side. She could not move from bed to chair without assistance. Although she had minimal verbal communication due to the loss of all her throat muscles, her mind was as sharp as ever. She loved Colleen as she did all our other children. Mum was such an accepting person, did not whine about her lot and was very patient. The other children would get down in the dumps about Mum's condition. They would try and understand, but I think it was just too hard, because they remembered her as she had been. Colleen on the other hand had only known Mum as she was and accepted the situation. She would get busy with paper and scissors making cards.

'Nan will like this one, Mummy,' she would say proudly holding up the efforts of her labours.

At the time of Mum's visit Colleen was only attending school for five half days a week, as is the custom with all prep children, which necessitated my having to pick her up at lunch time. Not a problem until one blistering hot day when the routine was interrupted. I had to ring the school to say I was sorry for the inconvenience but I was going to be late. The washing machine had overflowed, it was too hot to put baby Shaun in the car, and I was arranging for a neighbour to mind him so I could collect Colleen. When I got there Colleen was very upset and told me when we arrived home that the teacher had smacked her on the leg and told her to stop sooking.

I rang the school and challenged the teacher's actions saying how disappointed I was, and even if Colleen was misbehaving, thought it unnecessary to hit her. Perhaps the teacher was having a really bad day, but I didn't believe little kids should be hit. It was probably a bit of a storm in a tea cup. But then, when the bus morning time table changed to seven thirty, it was too early for a little tyke, so we swapped her to Broadford Primary School.

It was shortly after this we commenced building a new shop, and it became necessary to use the front bedroom of the manse as the toy's lay-by room, up to and beyond the following Christmas. Colleen thought that it was wonderful. Originally the bassinette for Shaun was in there, but now it was like another shop at home except all the goods were wrapped (thank goodness). Colleen was right into whatever we were doing, spending all her time out of school in the shop when I was there. She would always say 'can I come?', her brown eyes large with a pleading look on her round freckled face.

After completing her prep year at Broadford she went back to St. Pat's for grade one and continued on there for the rest of her primary years. She did not show any particular attributes, but she had the ability to get on with all sorts of different people. She wasn't a great scholar, just middle of the road for her tests, but her sporting ability was above average. She loved music lessons and when she reached grade six we started piano lessons much to the annoyance of her siblings who thought they had missed out.

Scholastically, none of our children excelled. Oh, they made it all right and are now very successful in their chosen fields, but each approached school differently to achieve their goals. Sport was another matter.

It always amazed me the amount of energy all of our children expended on sport. Winter it was football and netball, and swimming in summer. Colleen loved netball and in particular when St. Pat's played Broadford at

Broadford. On these occasions Peter would sneak away from the shop to watch. I coached her team for a couple of years and being members of the Kilmore-Broadford Netball Association, we travelled north to Seymour, and south to Wallan and Wandong for matches. Colleen played all the way through, the under eights, under tens and under twelve year olds in either the wing or goaler position. She wasn't tall enough for defence, but she was a good little runner. When playing in A grade we were delighted when she was made Captain.

Being five minutes from the local pool, all the kids joined the Broadford swimming club. They just went like fish. Colleen loved it and was very good at butterfly. They would train four nights a week, and with Broadford being affiliated with the Goulburn Valley Swimming Association, go to swimming meets, again at Seymour and at the more distant towns of Yea and Alexandra. Colleen would always come home with ribbons. She was swimming champion for six years. It didn't just end with the training and the meetings either, there may also be trials on a Sunday morning. You could not say you would not front up because they were all so keen.

Peter and I would compete with the children in the parent-child races. Having taught himself to swim at forty, Peter struggled to keep up.

'Kick your legs, Dad,' the kids would shout their encouragement. At the pool every night after work he would practice kicking on his stomach and back.

'I'm trying,' he would say taking enormous gasps when he was breathing.

Pete has always adored the kids and would do anything for them. He was a bit of a soft touch where the girls were concerned.

'I'll do the paper round this morning, the girls must be tired, I could not wake them,' he would occasionally say.

Over the years, it was a different matter with the boys, and rain, hail or shine they were expected to pull their weight. I don't think the girls were that heavy sleepers!

We always expected the children to do their fair share. Shaun was a great distraction.

'Christine, your turn to peel the potatoes.'

'But Mum, I have to look after the baby, Paul can do it,' she'd reply, whisking Shaun away to change him.

Completing grade six at St. Pat's, the natural progression was for Colleen to attend Kilmore's Assumption College. Our second eldest daughter Christine, was in the first intake into the completely integrated co-educational system at Assumption, the younger ones following her.

Suzanne our eldest also attended Assumption. She loved school work, the challenge of projects and essays, and was a keen debater. She enjoyed being in the shop and would spend time before school and Saturday nights helping Peter. She loved being the mother figure to her siblings, so it was a very comfortable transition from primary to secondary school for Colleen.

All the Clancy kids won swimming competitions at Assumption, and we were very proud when Colleen was made swimming captain, not only at school but for the home town team. She continued to enjoy her music, but she did not do particularly well scholastically. Unfortunately she found it difficult to buckle down to piano practice and was devastated when we stopped her lessons because we thought she was not putting in enough effort. We looked for an alternative, and as taking up a musical instrument was compulsory at school, she commenced learning the flute, which was supplied by the school. She took to it very well, eventually progressing through to grade five. She did not put up any objections when practice for all the school concerts and productions would take her out of class. Nothing ever ruffled Colleen. She would get up at all the school assemblies and performances, do solos and never bat an eye. Even in the shop if Peter was running around in a bit of a flap, she would stay calm and handle more than one customer at a time, and keep them all happy without turning a hair.

Christine on the other hand did not like the shop. She struggled with school but hid the fact. She was not one to take discipline and is even now not shy of speaking her mind and bucking the system. She has always been extremely caring and has an amazing rapport with Colleen. She was always looking for fun and excitement whereas Colleen would just cruise along and not overstep the mark.

In addition to helping in our shop, Colleen was employed by Aussie Swag Jewellery in the shop assistant role in which she was so comfortable. She was also able to earn pocket money by babysitting around Broadford. I often wondered where her reserves of energy came from.

Family meal times were special. I encouraged the children to talk after I had ensured their plates were empty, and the boys' broccoli or cauliflower which they hated was finished. Peter would come in from the shop and unsuccessfully try and contribute to the conversation. Even today he still struggles to get a word in.

Paul had trouble with Colleen's exuberant nature.

'For goodness sake, keep it down Colleen, we're in the same room,' he would complain when she would be competing for attention relating some story or other in a very loud voice.

In year eleven she was school athlete of the year. She ran in every race. She wasn't a trained runner, but because she competed, she won the prize. We were amazed.

Like Colleen, Shaun was born for sport. He never liked school and would use every excuse to avoid scholastic tasks.

Colleen had a large circle of friends with whom she spent her spare time. There was always a birthday party or get together to attend. If she had been as keen on her studies as she was in socializing, she may have had better school results. Still she successfully completed year twelve. Her score determining the future direction her life would take.

Tertiary education required Colleen to take up residence in Melbourne while she attended Swinburne University of Technology, situated at Hawthorn, one of Melbourne's eastern suburbs. Leaving the confines of her country home to reside in a city, opened up a whole new world to her which had previously been denied. She took every opportunity to discover all Melbourne had to offer. Many of her friends from Broadford also shifted to Melbourne and together they explored the social scene and the delights of a capital city.

During her first year she did waitressing for Spotless Catering at the Melbourne Cricket Ground and also at Flemington Racecourse. Although I applauded her enterprise in her attempts to support herself, I was concerned about how she was coping. She continued to take an active interest in sport and was elected vice-president of the Swinburne University Netball Club.

Not one to let her skills lie idle, Colleen also found part time employment with a local newsagency. Again I believe the organizing of her social calendar took precedence over her studies. The small flat in inner suburban Brunswick which she shared with a girl friend, had a constant stream of visitors. I often wondered how her conscientious flat mate coped with all these comings and goings. Despite these social activities, by the end of 1996 Colleen had successfully completed a Diploma in Community Services in Child Care. We were pleased to see that during the time that she was studying, the strong family ties often brought her home to visit us at the home we had purchased in Fleming Drive, Broadford.

In January 1997 she commenced employment with Dunstan Reserve Child Care Centre Co-operative. Initially Colleen was in charge of the six month old babies but then she changed to the three year olds. She loved her job and was always trying to think of activities to amuse the children. I remember in her second year there she conned me into being the Easter bunny.

I had had a beautiful Easter bunny outfit made for the Broadford shop's Easter celebrations which was gathering dust at home. Peter and I had sold the newsagency business in the February of that year and I had a bit more time on my hands. I was helping Peter with his new enterprise, marketing, drumming up business, and knocking on doors. He had taken on a Tucker Tub round and was delighting all the neighbourhood canines with his wares.

I think we both missed the customers and the contact with people, but certainly not the demands of a seven day week business. I thought it was wonderful for Peter not to have to climb out of bed at 5.00 a.m. for the early morning paper delivery. Anyway I thought the bunny suit may as well be used by someone.

'Would you like to have it for the child care centre, Colls?' I had asked.

'Sure, but I think it would be better if you were in it,' came her quick retort.

'Do you really think that would be a good idea?' I asked.

'Well I can't, the kids would recognize me,' Colleen replied.

So on the appointed day I climbed into the suit, stuck on the nose and whiskers, adjusted the pink floppy ears, picked up the basket of goodies and off I went. What a laugh. Hop, hop, hop. I hid all the chocolate Easter bunnies and eggs and was a great hit with the children, once they got over their initial shyness. I thought I would probably become a regular feature at Easter time. But fate had a different idea. Soon all our lives would be turned upside down and things would never be the same again.

Chapter 2

THE EVENT

It was Sunday 2nd August, 1998.

'Do you need to be quite so cheerful this early in the day?' Paul said clasping his head in his hands as I bustled around his kitchen.

'Looks like you could do with a strong cup of coffee,' I said, clattering the kettle onto the stove without consideration for his sore head. 'Anyway,' I continued, 'it is nearly afternoon.' Paul winced.

We had left Broadford for Melbourne in time for Peter and Paul to get to the football game at the MCG. I planned a shopping expedition after dropping them at the ground. We would meet later for tea at Paul and Rachel's.

'Looks like you enjoyed your birthday celebration too, Rachael.' I laughed as she dropped onto the couch next to Paul and cuddled up to her partner.

'I suppose Colleen will be nursing a sore head too,' Peter said chuckling.

'Actually she didn't drink. She had a headache before we started and elected to drive,' said Paul sipping his coffee.

'Is her head still bothering her?' I asked frowning. 'She was complaining when I spoke to her a couple of nights ago.'

I looked at my watch. 'She and Trina are going to a Melbourne High School fundraiser today. It's too late to ring her now. I'll give her a call tonight.'

'Come on Paul. We'd better get going. I don't want to miss any of the game,' Peter said heading for the door.

'See you later today Rachael,' I called as we drove away.

'That looks lovely on you, mam,' the young sales assistant gushed.

I knew it didn't. Everything I tried on was so tizzy. If only one of the girls had been able to come with me today. I needed presents for three forthcoming weddings and of course at least one new outfit and one I could add to or change somehow to make it look different.

Suzanne was out of town for the day, Christine was overseas and Colleen attending the social function. I sobered as I thought of my youngest daughter and wondered if in fact she had been able to attend The Melbourne High School Old Boys Football Club '1000 Draw Day' that day as planned.

She had taken a really high catch at netball earlier in the week, had fallen and landed on her tailbone and was suffering the effects. But knowing Colls I thought she would make the effort even though she had been celebrating Rachael's birthday last night. I sighed. I would have to make the decisions myself.

The gifts did not prove too much of a challenge. The outfits were another matter. Dress after dress was taken off racks and trooped into the small curtained change rooms. I was looking increasingly disheveled as I whipped off my clothes and pulled each new garment over my head. Some were dismissed as unsuitable as they did not fit quite right, the colour was wrong or they did not enhance my shape. Finally, as it was near closing time, I decided I needed a second opinion before making a decision, and abandoned the task for another day. Peter and Paul would probably be home by now.

It was getting dark as I headed up the front path of Paul and Rachael's rented house. Before I reached the front door it was flung open.

'At last, thank goodness you are here,' Rachael said dragging me in through the door, grabbing the parcels and dumping them on the floor.

'What ever is the matter?' I said, alarmed by her treatment of me and my parcels.

'Colleen has had a bleed to the brain and they need to operate.' She turned me around and propelled me back through the front door and bundled me into the car.

'What do you mean a bleed to the brain? What happened? Where's Peter?' I asked bewildered. My heart was racing.

'That's all I know. Shaun rang. Peter and Paul arrived home half an hour ago and have gone to the hospital,' Rachael replied.

'Bleed to the brain, bleed to the brain,' I kept repeating over and over as we made the journey to the Alfred Hospital. What could this mean? In my mind the word 'stroke' struggled to be heard but I silenced it. Besides Colleen was only young, you couldn't have a stroke at twenty-two. The trip to the hospital seemed to take forever, but I did not want it to end. What was I to find when I got there?

We went in through the self opening glass doors and found our way to the triage nurse. Checking his books, we were then directed to intensive care. Back through the main entrance to the lifts and up to the first floor. By the time the lift doors opened I had trouble getting my legs to work. I walked down the corridor in a daze. It was all so strange. And then there were Paul and Peter. Paul was crying. My husband pulled me into his arms.

'She's in theatre, Bern,' he managed to say, in a strangled voice. 'She's had a bleed to the brain called an aneurysm. It's touch and go. They will do the best they can.

She may not live.' Peter buried his face on my shoulder. Locked in a tight embrace, we cried.

After a while I managed a choked whisper. 'Oh no! I didn't realize it was this serious.' I was numb. I broke from Peter's grasp. Nearby Paul and Rachael stood clutching each other. I drew them into the circle of our arms. We clung together crying.

It was difficult to piece together the circumstances of the incident. Peter and Paul told me the little they knew through their tears. But I was able to gather that the outlook for Colleen was very grim. It was over the next few days I was able to find out what had happened. Trina, Colleen's friend had been with her and relayed to me what she could remember of that fateful day.

They had arrived at the Melbourne High School fundraiser at about 11.00 a.m.

'Colleen was complaining of a major headache,' Trina told me. Apparently she had had it for a couple of days, but not one to pass up a social function, had said she would be all right. They had been there for a couple of hours when Colleen walked up to a couple of girls to introduce herself and fell over backwards. She appeared to be having some sort of a fit. She had wet herself.

People gathered around at a loss to know how to help. Fortunately there were two doctors at the function as well as a nurse who had just come off night duty. The nurse took out her little torch and started relaying Colleen's vital signs to the doctors. One of the doctors ordered a MICA (Medical Intensive Care Ambulance) be summonsed.

'I was told to get on my hands and knees and yell out anything that may get a reaction from Colleen,' Trina said. She had called out nicknames, and other funny comments that Colleen might respond to. But Colleen just lay there motionless as Trina held her head in her hand and stroked her back.

Trina said to me it was only moments before the ambulance arrived.

'They took off all Colleen's jewellery, gave it to me and told me to hop in the front seat of the ambulance,' Trina said. They had gone only about one hundred metres when there was a chilling noise from the back of the ambulance.

'It sounded as if all the air was getting sucked out of Colleen,' Trina said, and the ambulance attendant had called for the vehicle to stop immediately.

'Is she going to be OK,' Trina had fearfully enquired.

'If she is going to make it she will make it with us,' the ambulance driver had replied. 'She is in the best hands now.'

The all clear came from the back of the ambulance and they continued on. 'It was lucky the doctor requested a MICA. If a normal ambulance had arrived she wouldn't have had a chance,' the ambulance driver had said.

When they reached the Alfred Hospital, Colleen was rushed away and Trina was left to give the desk clerk all Colleen's personal details. She was then asked to try and contact the family.

'I called directory assistance and got the family number in Broadford. It rang out,' Trina said. She tried Paul and kept trying Broadford. Still no answer.

'The head surgeon explained to me that they would have to operate and wanted my permission. I advised I wasn't family', Trina said. 'It was just awful Bern,' she whispered. The surgeon had told her he would try Broadford one more time. Shaun answered the phone.

'Your sister has suffered a cerebral aneurism. Colleen is young, fit and healthy. There is only a slim chance she will survive but we must operate immediately. We need permission,' Trina heard the surgeon say. As he hung up the phone he said, 'We're on,' and hurried away.

Trina went out and phoned Shaun back.

'You all right?' she asked. Too much dramatic information for a sixteen year old to hear over the phone she told me she had thought.

Peter and Paul arriving home from the Collingwood/Essendon football match were told by Rachael to rush to the Alfred Hospital. A signature was needed to operate on Colleen. Peter told me they were dumbfounded.

'We have to operate,' Dr. Laidlaw had told them when they arrived at the hospital. 'She is too young, we have to give her a chance.'

All this time Peter was wondering where I was, and was asking himself why isn't Bernadette here? It was only later after I had arrived at the hospital that my husband told me he remembered saying 'Good luck!' to the doctor as they wheeled Colleen past on the trolley. By the time I did arrive at the hospital at 6.30 p.m. our daughter was in theatre.

The Alfred Hospital is beautiful now. Then it was archaic. We were in the corridor outside the intensive care waiting room. The nurses' station was behind a window with a sort of shop counter affair. They poked a phone through the window and we just stood there, exposed. We were intensely conscious of the nearby closed surgery doors.

I thought, I needed to be strong now more than ever before in my life. My heart was breaking. I could not still the trembling of my cold sweaty hands. There were people I must contact.

Paul had already made some calls. I needed to ring my sisters living interstate. But first my biggest worry was Shaun. I picked up the receiver and dialed the Broadford number. I do not remember much of the conversation I had with him. I spoke to friends in Broadford, Barry and Margaret King, who offered to bring him to Melbourne. But our Shaun has always been very practical.

'I'll stay here Mum and wait and see,' I do remember him saying. 'I will be needed at home for Dad.'

I worked my way through the pages in my telephone note book, (I never could remember the kids' mobile numbers, so I always carried it with me). First I rang my sister Pat, then my two sisters interstate and Peter's sister at Romsey. There were so many questions. I could not answer them. No-one had given me the answers.

'Just pray like you have never prayed before,' I remember telling them. Each time I hung up I struggled to control my sobs before ringing the next number.

Some thirty minutes later we went back to the Intensive Care Waiting Room.

I was confronted by a sea of anxious faces. Paul had finally contacted Suzanne and my eldest daughter hysterically threw herself into my arms. Family and friends had arrived and were continuing to arrive. I was stunned by this demonstration of solidarity. Peter and I hugged each one of them in turn and shared tears. The hours dragged by. My sister Pat and her husband Graeme had arrived and were saying the rosary.

At about 11.00 p.m. the doctors came out. One of them took Peter and I into a tiny office adjacent to the intensive care ward. He had very dark hair, was thick set and very serious. In a matter of fact manner he tried to explain the procedure Colleen had undergone and the risks involved. The tears ran unchecked down my face. I gripped Peter's hand tightly.

'Many of us may have the makings of an aneurism but will take it to the grave without incident,' he said. He went on to say that he could not give a reason why this had happened to Colleen. 'She has youth on her side and is a very strong girl,' he continued, no doubt trying to be reassuring.

As we listened we were told the medical details of the procedure Colleen had undergone. We were too stunned to ask questions.

When we did not respond he continued. 'We've got a lot of work to do. We've got to keep the cranial pressure as low as we can. She has had a very intensive bleed. We've clipped it and she will be left with disabilities. We do not know what.'

Neither of us spoke. I wanted to be with my family, to be anywhere but there. To be released from the fear that was gripping me.

Over the coming weeks we were to understand a little better the intricacies of the procedure which was gently being explained to us, but not then. No matter how considerate this doctor was in the manner in which he tried to convey the gravity of the situation, there was no hiding the truth.

'It's not very good,' the surgeon said. 'Colleen has only a very slim chance of survival, maybe thirty per cent. But because she is so very young, because she looked very young, we gave it our best shot.'

He went on, 'The pressure in the brain will cause expansion. Colleen will not look normal coming out of theatre. It will be quite disturbing.'

Then Peter and I were led in to see her. The warning was not adequate. Her head, with about fifteen tubes leading to and from various machines, was enormous. We were told the fluid causing the swelling presented the immediate danger. My heart was pounding and I grabbed Peter's arm to try and stop myself from shaking. Her freckled face was so white. The curved line of freckles under her left eye, strikingly pronounced.

We stood there motionless. The nurses competently going about their work were calm, reassuring, comforting. What do we say, what do we do? We were speechless. Colleen looked as cold as ice. Was she still alive? Reluctantly, but with a degree of relief at perhaps escaping from the nightmare, we tiptoed out.

Looking back now it is difficult to remember the details of how we all continued to function. Everyone who had congregated no doubt dispersed after we reported back to them. I remember my brother Peter, pressing the keys of his East Melbourne apartment into my hand.

'As long as you need it, it's yours,' he said.

I silently mouthed, 'Thank you,' as the tears which I had been struggling to control choked me again.

We had no clothes, no provisions and no idea what the next day would bring. We stumbled out into the cold night. Sporadic traffic swished along the wet road in front of the hospital. The scene looked so normal.

We found our way to my brother Peter's apartment.

I pulled a chair out from the table and collapsed onto it.

'Why, Pete. My little girl, my little girl. What are we going to do?'

I put my head on my arms and sobbed.

Little had we known as we quietly shut the door of the apartment on that first night, that this was to be our home for the next two years.

Chapter 3

JUST COPING

I lay with my eyes closed. Could I by some miracle, open my eyes and find myself in the quiet familiar surroundings of my bedroom at Broadford? No. The unfamiliar hum of early morning traffic confirmed the events of the day before were real. I knew the nightmare would continue.

It was very early, my eyes gravelly from fitful sleep. Peter and I made our way to the hospital, each lost in our own thoughts. Unsure of which way to go to find Colleen we stood uncertainly in front of the hospital directory. 'Chapel' came into focus and suddenly I had a purpose.

'I need to go, Peter. Will you come with me?' I asked.

We made our way through the corridors following directions until we reached the sanctuary behind inconspicuous doors. The sounds of the hospital disappeared in the quiet.

'Why Lord?' I asked as I knelt with my face buried in my hands. I felt hot tears spilling over my cold hands. Peter's arm across my shoulders drew me to him. We wept.

Gradually our tears subsided. Peter blew his nose and whispered he would wait for me outside.

'Dear God, I don't know why this has happened, but I pray you will give me the strength to cope,' I whispered into the silence that enveloped me.

By the time I joined Peter I had composed myself. I slipped my hand into his and said, 'Let's go and find Colls.'

Even at that early hour of 6.00 a.m. there was activity all around us as we made our way to Intensive Care where staff had confirmed we would find her. The curtains were partially drawn around Colleen's bed, partitioning her off from the rest of the ward. As we drew near, one of the nurses checking the multitude of monitors turned as we hesitated, not sure whether to proceed.

'Mr. and Mrs. Clancy? It's all right, you can come closer,' she said with a little smile which did not quite reach her eyes, and continuing to make notes on the clipboard she held, moved to the other side of the bed to allow us to approach.

Cautiously, so as not to disturb the mass of wires and tubes leading from various apparatus to Colleen, I tentatively cupped my hand around her fingers.

'She's so cold,' I fearfully whispered. I had never been so scared in all my life.

'We must keep her temperature and her pulse down to help stop the swelling of her brain,' the nurse said in a low voice. She went on to say that Colleen was packed in ice, lying on an ice sheet, and showed us the monitor which recorded her very low pulse. I shivered despite the heat of the room.

One by one the functions of the various tubes and wires which led from her swollen head and other parts of her body were explained to us. Most of the ones from her shaved head were drain tubes, just horrible. Her beautiful auburn hair was all but gone.

We stood looking at her for what seemed like just a few moments, observing the methodical tasks the nursing staff was performing until Peter drew my attention to the clock on the wall.

'We must call the Child Care Centre and get back on the phone to Christine,' he said.

Reluctantly, I allowed him to steer me away. I did not want to leave. My youngest daughter needed me now more than at any other time in her life. In fact her very life depended on my bedside vigil, or so I thought. Hang in there Colls I said to myself, I will return as soon as I can.

Back at the apartment we were grateful for the basic supplies with which the pantry was stocked. Not only fully furnished, the beds in the two bedrooms were made up. The unit was fully self-contained.

The call to Colleen's employer dealt with, we dialled through to Scotland where we knew Christine would be waiting for our call. We had broken the news to her the night before. Now we could tell her Colleen had survived the night, but was gravely ill.

'I've got to come home, Mum,' she said. I didn't argue with her. It was her decision to cut short her working holiday.

'We'll deposit some money into your account,' I said. I wanted her home.

I tried to get through to Shaun at Broadford. I was really pining for him, thinking of him all alone at home while we were all together in Melbourne. I wanted him with us. When eventually I spoke to him he said he was best off in Broadford where he could organize Tucker Tub for Peter. Again our friends Barry and Margaret offered to bring him to Melbourne but he was adamant. It was not until a couple of days later that we found out he had embarked on Peter's Tucker Tub run by himself. At sixteen he had passed his driver's licence test in Queensland and he did not even query whether it was legal for him to drive in Victoria. In the months to come we would chuckle at his pluck, and I, wonder what the local policeman would have made of his adventure had it been known. I remember at the time thinking 'God can take care of that one, I'm not going there.'

Nearing eighty years of age, we knew we would have to visit Peter's parents to tell them about Colleen. They had just moved into a respite, low care facility.

"We can't just phone them Pete. We must go and see them." I cringed at the thought of having to convey this news to them. The two of them were tucked into a tiny bedroom. It was awful trying to comfort them being so distressed ourselves. We knew they would wear out their rosary beads in the coming days. Meanwhile we had returned to Colleen's bedside.

The bedside vigil of that day passed in a blur. Suzanne and Paul took it in turns with Peter and I to be with Colleen. She was deathly pale, motionless, not even a flicker of life. In between, I had brief phone conversations with immediate family. Some family and friends turned up at the hospital and we were able to report first hand the gravity of Colleen's condition.

Exhausted and emotionally drained, in the evening we finally returned to the unit. Paul headed off to Broadford to collect some clothes and personal effects for Peter and I and to be with Shaun.

I was anxious to return to the hospital the next day, so concerned something would happen in my absence. Nothing had changed.

During that morning the waiting room of the Intensive Care Unit overflowed with family and friends. This was to become the pattern over the coming weeks. Some would sit for hours waiting for news, just being there, supporting us. Only two people were allowed at Colleen's bedside at a time, and visitors tip toed in for a few minutes, and then many of them distressed, came out again to be comforted by the others in the waiting room. Flowers and cards were delivered. The flowers, not allowed in the Intensive Care Ward, I guiltily took to the Unit. It looked like a florist shop. We were overwhelmed by the support of family and friends.

We tried to understand what the nursing staff told us about what had happened to Colleen. We didn't know what questions to ask. The most frightening one we dared not ask. Not 'when will she regain consciousness', but 'will she ever wake up'. We just drifted around in and out of Intensive Care where Colleen lay, trying to stay calm, each coping the best we could.

Towards the end of Tuesday torn between the need to be at Colleen's side and the frustration of not being able to do anything constructive to help her, I caught the tram down St. Kilda Road into the city and visited Myer Department Store just on closing time. I rushed in, made my purchase, and was back at the hospital within the hour. I sat the signature bear I had bought on the shelf in Intensive Care. It became the symbol of the caring and love which surrounded Colleen during her stay in hospital, as each visitor signed it.

Paul had returned from Broadford with Shaun, and the next morning Christine was due to fly in. We would all then as a family see this through together.

When Christine immerged from customs at 5.30 a.m., we were waiting for her; Paul and Shaun who would return to Broadford later that day, Suzanne anxiously awaiting her sister's arrival, and Peter and I. Christine's face lit up when she saw us.

'Hey guys, you must be absolutely exhausted. What are you all doing here?' she asked. 'I expected to take a taxi.'

Much later she told me of her thoughts as she had made the long flight home.

'I'd said goodbye to Colls on the way over, Mum, just in case,' she said. She went on to say that she thought that if Colleen was alive when she got home then she'd be there for the long haul. She had had a long time to prepare herself mentally for either eventuality. She said it was really quite bizarre, feeling so happy to be home but having to say to herself, now cool it, let's see what the situation is here, is Colls still with us? Through our tears and hugs we filled her in on Colleen's condition.

It was still very early when we arrived at the hospital. Breakfast was being organized. There were trolleys being wheeled everywhere and I remember thinking that we were probably in the way. But Intensive Care is quite separate and we were able to come and go as we pleased. Christine was advised to have counseling before seeing Colleen.

'No way,' she declared. She then went on to convince us that she was fine. She thought she'd had it easier than us because she was distanced from the drama whereas we were living though it first hand. From that moment it was very clear to me that the reason she had come home was that she thought she had a role to play and that was to do everything in her power to see Colleen though this crisis, and by her will power alone secure her recovery.

Christine's bravado was shaken though when she walked into Intensive Care.

'Oh no,' she whispered. There were tears on her face. I could see she was horrified at what had befallen her little sister, but as I watched I saw her square her shoulders and say, 'We'll pull you through this Colls.'

That afternoon, as a family, we saw the neurosurgeon and tried to be receptive to what he told us about Colleen's condition.

'Colleen has suffered a cerebral aneurysm,' he said. He went on to explain what that meant. An artery in her brain on the front left hand side of her head had ballooned or bulged. The headache she had experienced was a symptom caused by the growth of the aneurysm. The aneurysm had then ruptured causing extensive bleeding in the brain more commonly known as a stroke.

'But she is so young,' Peter declared.

'Strokes are more common in adults than in children, and strangely enough are slightly more common in women than in men,' he replied.

'Both my mother and brother had strokes,' I said. 'Is there any connection?'

'Well, it has been found that there may be a genetic predisposition to the development of intra-cerebral aneurysms, the existence in some families runs as high as ten percent,' he replied.

We listened in bewilderment as these facts were revealed to us.

'Usually the condition does not present itself until patients are between forty and sixty years of age. Approximately only half survive,' he continued.

'And what about Colleen,' Peter said, asking the question we were all afraid to address.

'We have clipped the aneurysm and now we will have to wait and see. I don't need to tell you that Colleen is gravely ill. But she is young, healthy and we were able to operate quickly to give her the best chance of recovery,' he replied.

It wasn't until weeks later that we learnt just how severe Colleen's bleed (subarachnoid haemorrhage) had been. These events are measured on various scales, one of which is the Hunt-Hess Scale, grading from one to five. Patients presenting with grades one to three who can be operated on in a relatively short period of time have a good chance of recovery with minimal or mild neurological problems and mortality is less than five percent. Colleen's bleed was a grade five. She was at the point of death.

'Will she wake up?' Paul asked.   The knuckles of his hands were white as he gripped his knees. His voice broke as he went on to say, 'What I mean is will she be a vegetable?'

He had asked the question that was burning in all our minds but were too afraid to put into words.

'We just don't know in what way Colleen's brain may have been damaged,' the neurosurgeon said gently. He went on to say again that Colleen was young and fit and there was every chance that she would recover, but to what extent he could not say. 'There is every chance that she will be left with disabilities. We will have to wait and see,' he concluded. We had to be satisfied with that.

Stunned, we stumbled out into the fresh air, each absorbed in our own thoughts. Paul was the first to speak.

'Should they keep her hanging around?' he said through his tears.

'Colls will get better. I just know she will,' Christine said fiercely.

Suzanne slipped her arm around Shaun's waist and drew him to her.

I dared not look at Peter.

'As the doctor said, Colleen has every chance of recovering, it is up to us to be there for her, now and in the future,' I said.

Little did we know how long a journey we would all have to travel with Colleen.

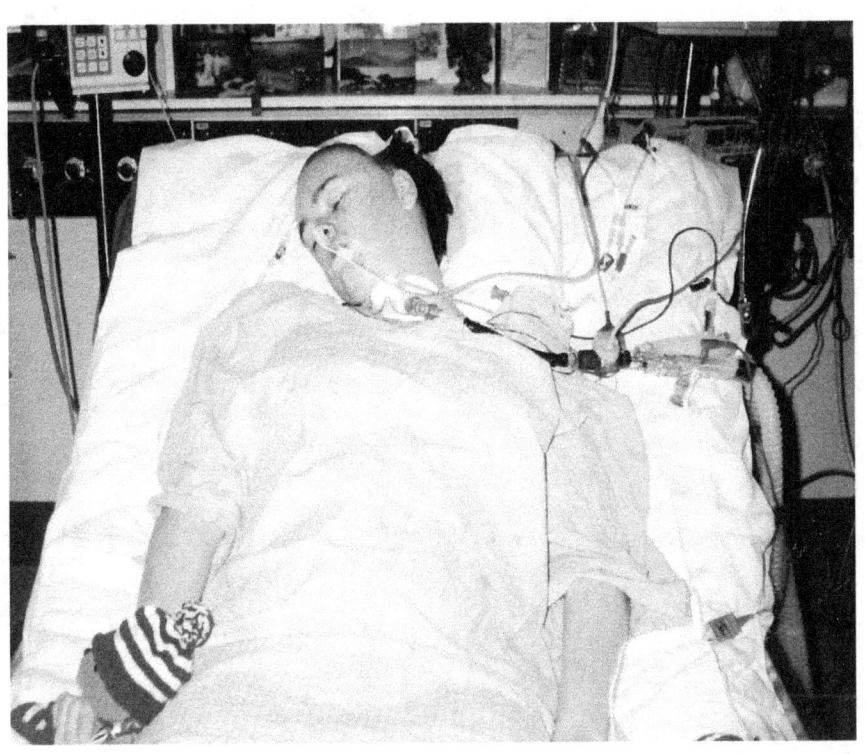

Colleen : Second week in intensive care at the Alfred Hospital

Chapter 4

BEDSIDE VIGIL

During the next few days we fell into the routine of being at Colleen's bedside during our waking hours and returning exhausted to the flat at night.

We were encouraged to talk softly to her. Hearing is the last sense to go and the first to return. There was no response. Not a flicker of life.

Paul and Shaun had returned to Broadford and continued with the Tucker Tub run for Peter for the rest of that week. Rob, the previous owner of Tucker Tub had assisted Shaun earlier in the week. The boys returned briefly on Thursday night with boxes of casseroles and other meals which had been delivered to the Tucker Tub freezer in Broadford. The support we received from community and friends was amazing. I don't think I cooked for about six weeks.

The following day Peter and I returned briefly to Broadford to collect some clothes, then hurried back to Colleen's bedside. We were anxious to be with her all the time, concerned something would happen in our absence.

Cards and flowers continued to arrive at the hospital, and there was a constant stream of family and friends in and out of the hospital. Their support at this time was immeasurable. Some would arrive as early as 10.00 a.m. All these young people, they were so beautiful. At times the waiting room resembled a bus stop. The visitors would go in two at a time, stay for ten minutes and then tip toe out. I believe just their presence helped us keep our sanity during those dreadful couple of weeks. We were kept nourished with fresh sandwiches, slices and cakes brought in by well wishers.

The second week Peter returned to Broadford to resume his Tucker Tub run. It was horrendous for him. He told me he spent most of his time crying as he drove from place to place. When questioned by the people he rarely encountered, he tearfully told of Colleen's plight.

Then on Wednesday of that second week, Colleen had a visitor who caused a buzz and gave us all the lift we so desperately needed, Peter especially. He arrived back in Melbourne unexpectedly.

'David King is visiting from Broadford this afternoon,' Peter said. I was surprised to see a little smile crease the corners of his eyes.

'That's nice,' I remarked mildly. As pleased as I was that our friend was planning a visit, I failed to see why it would cause Peter such unconcealed pleasure.

'You'll never guess who he's bringing with him,' Peter continued.

Now my curiosity was aroused.

Colleen had always been an enthusiastic North Melbourne supporter. David King, had arranged to bring Wayne Carey, Colleen's football team idol to visit her that afternoon.

Wayne Carey during his career was known as the 'King of Australian Rules Football', some thought him one of the most gifted players the game had ever known. Unfortunately an indiscretion put a scar on a brilliant career and ended his association with North Melbourne Football Club. Continuing controversy surrounding his conduct ensued in the coming years. At this time though, I was aware he was at the height of his profession.

I excitedly rang my sister Pat, and she and other relations came to the hospital. Peter had told one of the nurses and she must have told dozens of staff who all happened to be 'in the vicinity' when Wayne arrived. I was extremely embarrassed.

So there we all were around Colleen's bedside, Peter and I, my sister Pat, Christine, David King and our very special visitor Wayne Carey, quietly chatting and trying not to talk about football.

David said. 'Colleen, I have brought the skipper to see you.'

Then Wayne said 'If you reckon I'm here Colleen, I want you to blink your eyes.' And I would have sworn her eyelids moved. We all had to stop ourselves from laughing out loud. The visit lasted only about ten minutes. It was a real highlight. A grin did not leave Peter's face the whole time.

But our euphoria was short lived. That night our daughter was returned to surgery.

The pressure in Colleen's head had become so great the surgeons had decided to remove the bone flaps from her forehead. Seeing Colleen being wheeled out through Intensive Care, down the corridor and through another door to theatre was sheer hell. There were tubes all over the bed connected to different parts of her body. I thought to myself how much can her body take? I silently prayed to God asking him to be with the doctors whom I thought were all so clever. If ever I had doubts, it was that night.

There were still visitors in the waiting room and I had to tell them they would not be able to see Colleen. It was about 8.00 p.m. I was so scared. It was all so incomprehensible. We were exhausted. There was nothing we could do. We returned to the unit to wait.

'She's in good hands. They know what they are doing.' I said trying to be reassuring. I knew I had to keep it together or we would all fall apart. At the unit we had dinner, Peter and I, Paul and Rachael, Suzanne and her partner Jim, Christine and Shaun. It was a very subdued meal.

Also with us that night was a friend of Colleen's. They had been good mates over recent years. He had attended Coll's twenty-first birthday and we had met him on several occasions. That was the last time we saw him. Like some other of Colleen's friends he obviously found her condition too confronting. I find this so sad, although I can appreciate how difficult some would find Colleen's situation. On the other hand there have been friends who have stuck with her all along the way, aiding her in her recovery and supporting us, her family.

Late that night we rang the hospital. Colleen had survived surgery and was back in Intensive Care. She was still in a coma. To this day I am amazed by the mysteries of medical science. Would her head not cave in without her forehead? But she looked no different.

There were one hundred and thirty staples across the front of her head securing the incision where the doctors had removed her forehead. This was placed in a solution and stored in refrigeration. Although it could safely be kept in storage for twelve months, it ultimately was replaced a month later.

The day following Colleen's surgery, I was telling my sister Pat about this latest drama.

'We need to have a mass said for Colleen,' Pat said. 'Let's arrange for it to be said at St. Francis' in the city.'

And so the word went out, and at ten o'clock on Sunday 16th August, 1998, more than one hundred family and friends gathered at the church. All my family was there. Sisters, brothers, uncles and aunties and their families and so many friends from Broadford. Unfortunately Peter's family did not seem to realize the importance we were putting on the occasion and were not present. Peter was disappointed but was philosophical regarding the situation, after all no one was compelled to attend.

We went to see the priest before the service and explained about Colleen and requested he make special mention of her in the prayers. We showed him the basket in which we had special little church candles we had purchased, to be handed out and lit for Colleen.

The priest did say prayers for Colleen and then following the service we congregated in the St. Francis' community hall for a cup of tea.

The whole occasion was a beautiful experience. There was a feeling of solidarity and a very special time of togetherness for everybody. We were going to pull this kid through.

I don't think I could have endured the heartache during these first couple of weeks without my faith to sustain me.

Not only that but also the outpouring of love which was displayed by the many friends and family who visited Colleen during that time and left messages in the notebook beside her bed helped us all to cope.

From that point on Colleen's condition started to improve. The first progress was when tubes and wires started to be removed as all vital signs and pressures commenced to return to normal.

First there were infinitesimal movements.

'Look, her fingers moved,' Christine said excitedly. Sure enough there was a twitch in her fingers followed the next day by a flutter of her hand. Then very gradually a few days later her eyelids started to open.

'Colls, we are here, can you see us?' But at this stage there was no response.

Christine's entry in the note book beside Colls' bed expressed how we all felt.

'I feel so helpless seeing you lying there. I wish I could just do something, but babe, I hate to tell you it's all up to you. You're so precious to me and I love you with all my heart. Please wake up soon. I really miss you.'

Messages of encouragement were also left by friends.

'If anyone can fight this and beat it, it would have to be you. You are one of the sweetest most selfless people, always thinking of others. But now it's time to think of yourself and get through this. This is your biggest challenge yet, so imagine how good it will feel in the end when you win, which of course you always love to do. Please wake up soon.'

Then on Thursday the 20th August, 1998, without warning, a fantastic announcement was made when we arrived at the hospital.

'We are moving Colleen from Intensive Care onto the ward,' one of the nurses told us. 'Her pressure levels are fine, although we are a bit worried about the congestion on her lungs.' Actually we were to learn the pneumonia was quite severe and the staff was very worried about it.

I could not believe we had come so far. I thought back over the last few weeks remembering the enormously long stream of visitors visiting the comatose Colleen, some waiting for hours to spend ten minutes at her bedside. Bending the rules, some even called at eleven o'clock and midnight. But now there was this ever so slight improvement and we could take a step forward.

So with tubes still in her mouth because of the amount of phlegm on her lungs, and a turban on her head, Colleen's cot was wheeled out of Intensive Care and onto ward 3D. Her half opened eyes followed our progress.

Now I thought, we are on our way to Colleen's full recovery. It had been three weeks since she had been admitted to hospital.

Chapter 5

ON THE WARD

'The pneumonia will kill this girl you know,' the registrar said. He was standing at the end of Colleen's bed.

Colleen had been on the ward for a few days. We had been delighted to see the ever-so-slight improvement in her condition. Her eyes were starting to focus. She had even squeezed the sponge when I was washing her. What a star! Peter, feeling more encouraged than when Colleen had been in intensive care, had even spent a day at her bedside; a rare occurrence.

'Her beautiful brown eyes kept on looking at me,' he had said.

Now here I was at Colleen's bedside waiting for the physiotherapist to come and commence therapy. We were all so thrilled to have her out of Intensive Care and on the ward. It was wonderful, a miracle. The only way now was forward. The registrar had called in on his morning rounds; the same doctor we had seen on the first night. Then we had thought him really nice. This retort was the last thing I expected when I greeted him.

My smile faded. My knuckles went white as I gripped the side of the cot bed. I could feel the pulse beating at my temples. He continued.

'It's quite severe you know. You're wasting your time here. You may as well pack your bags and go home.'

'How dare you!' My voice shook as I replied. 'We've just come out of three weeks in Intensive Care and you're telling me to go home? Why would you have such an attitude? We've come over a huge hurdle. Surely we'll beat the congestion.' It was not a question. I thought, how could you say that to anybody?

Angrily I grabbed my bag, threw it over my shoulder, and started for the door. I stopped and turned.

'You don't know who you're dealing with,' I cried before I fled.

I don't know how I found my way to the lifts. I was blinded by the tears which were pouring down my face. Having been in check over the last few weeks, now all the pent up emotions were released and out of control. The lift doors opened and I stumbled into the arms of Suzanne who was with her friend Louise.

Alarmed, Suzanne asked, 'Whatever has happened?'

She held me tightly as I told her as best I could through my tears what the doctor had said. Finally my sobs subsided.

'If he thinks we're going to give up now he has another think coming,' I said through clenched teeth. 'Let's get out of here and get some fresh air,' I concluded.

To this day I cannot understand his appalling attitude. Colleen proved him wrong. But it was to be some eight months before we saw him again and could tell him so.

After that encounter, I was more determined than ever that we were not going to give up on Colleen. We did everything we could to help. Taking instruction from the physiotherapists we massaged her legs, feet, neck, back, arms and fingers with almond oil and orange drops. Even the staff seemed to be putting in extra effort. Patrick told me of his care of Colleen when I arrived one morning as he was coming off night duty

'I did the face cream thing, bit hard to suss for a fella. I hope I got it right,' he said laughing. He continued, 'Colleen seemed happy with the outcome. I asked her to close her eyes if she understood me, and she did! So it means the message is getting in.'

'That's fantastic,' I said. 'Is she doing OK?' I asked.

'Well her temperature is down a bit and her oxygen saturation is up. Actually, she has quite a bit of movement in her left arm, so it's all good news,' he said.

We had told the nursing staff of the incident with the Registrar. Although reluctant to criticize their colleague, they were enormously reassuring. They still had no idea of Colleen's prognosis, but were confident things would start to happen with the physiotherapy treatment and therefore they were optimistic about Colleen's ultimate recovery.

We found this to be the situation all through Colleen's hospitalization. The doctors would present the worse case scenario and we would be shattered. The nursing staff would then prop us up and help us cope on a day to day basis. They were marvellous.

A course of antibiotics was prescribed to combat the pneumonia and Colleen had a tracheostomy, a surgical procedure where a hole was made at the base of her neck and a tube inserted into her windpipe, in order to create a clear airway. This was a bit horrendous, noisy and scary, but certainly helped her breathing. She was still being fed intravenously.

Fluid was drained from her spinal column with a lumbar puncture and from then on she appeared to be more awake.

Physiotherapy became regular and amazingly they soon had Colleen vertical with the help of a tilt table. She was strapped to a table which was slid under her body and gradually over a period of a few days she was elevated to increasing levels for short periods. We meet with the physiotherapists and were taught simple exercises we could help with. The girls and I did what we could to cater for Colleen's physical well being. We plaited her hair and Suzanne even painted her toe nails.

Her right lung had collapsed and the other was not too good but with unrelenting physiotherapy this improved and she was able to progress to being placed in a big recliner chair. Exhausted, she would then be returned to her bed where she would sleep through the visits of friends and extended family who left messages of love and encouragement in a diary we had placed at her bedside.

At this time Coll's eyes were open but she was not responding to us. Her unblinking stare was quite chilling. Paul and Shaun found Colleen's stare disturbing.

'It looks like she's looking at me Mum, but she just does not seem to be there,' Paul said. 'I wish she would wake up properly.' Shaun had made it his business while Colleen was in intensive care to find out the function of each machine attached to her and keep us informed. Now he was at a loss. He and Paul's visits were short.

'I'm sorry Mum, I just can't bear to see her like this. I'm going. I'll be in touch,' Paul said.

Then at the end of August the stare went. Christine excitedly rang Paul.

'You've got to come and see this,' she said excitedly. 'Colls is smiling.' At last Paul and Shaun felt more at ease when they visited.

'I do believe you are flirting big time with the male nurses, Colls. You tart!' Paul said, with a big grin. I excused his comment as I did his pastry cook gear and the smell of the bakery he had brought into the hospital with him.

The improvement in just one week was amazing. Colleen's temperature returned to normal. She had started to swallow and I arrived one day to see her enjoying a thickened blue milk shake. Then the first unintelligible sounds indicated that she was trying to talk.

Early in September Suzanne, who at this time was working at Australian Consolidated Press, would sneak out at different times during the day to visit. Even one night after she had been out, she had called in 11.30 p.m. to say goodnight to her little sister. When Christine had gone overseas, Suzanne began spending more time with Colleen and the girls had become very close. On this occasion when she visited she found Colleen very agitated.

'It was awful Mum, she was thrashing around, I just felt so helpless,' Suzanne said as we shared a meal a couple of nights later. 'I massaged her right leg like we were shown and it seemed to calm her a little. The nursing staff came and attended to her and by the time I left at 1.00 a.m. she was sleeping peacefully.'

Colleen's agitation continued and we were told it was a sign that she was fighting her unconscious state. She was desperately trying to speak and she seemed anxious and uncomfortable. The nursing staff advised us that Colleen's behavior also indicated that she was suffering from post traumatic amnesia. She was shifted from the four bed ward into a private room near the nurses' station. Visitors were strictly limited, the room was darkened and lots of quiet times were scheduled. When visiting we would just sit quietly and hold her hand.

Another time when Suzanne visited, Colleen became really distressed.

'Tears trickled down her cheeks when I went to leave Mum, so I stayed,' Suzanne said. 'It was magic to feel needed instead of being so helpless, but I cried too.'

Peter and I sponged her down on another occasion when she was agitated and this seemed to have a calming effect.

Peter was still having difficulty doing hospital visits.

His escape continued to be football as it had been while Colls was in Intensive Care. Christine wasn't impressed. I returned to the unit one evening to be greeted by her anger.

'I've just spoken to Dad,' she said. Roughly she took the brown paper bag from my hand and rummaged around in the drawer looking for a cork screw.

'He's going to the footy again this weekend. It's ridiculous Mum, he can't do this, you need him. We need him, and I told him so.' The wine spilt as she pushed the glass across the bench top towards me.

Travelling down from Broadford at the weekends, Peter would attend one, sometimes two football matches.

'Cool it Christine, your Father seems to find it difficult to be at Colleen's bedside,' I said. I desperately wanted him with me more often, but knew this was his way of coping. He had recommenced the Tucker Tub run by himself, having had the support of friends Laurie Balmer and Garnet Wilcox initially, and was now finding it very tough going. I knew how lonely he was without me. As I sipped my drink I thought that perhaps I was relying too much on alcohol to help me cope. I had resisted getting a prescription for sleeping pills, but would detour on the way home from the hospital to keep up the wine supply. It made me maudlin. Most nights I would be in tears, but at least I was able to sleep.

Also I was feeling guilty. Rightly or wrongly I spent my time in hospital with Colleen. But was that wrong? She was safe where she was. Would my being there make a difference? I thought it would. Perhaps Peter and Shaun needed me more. I would sometimes get this overwhelming feeling that I had deserted my husband and youngest son. And was I giving my other children the support they needed? I felt I was being torn apart and each night my pillow was wet as I drifted off to sleep.

At this time it was a great comfort for me to know that Shaun's schoolboy friendship with Laura was blossoming and she was there for him. They were both very young, but seemed genuinely fond of each other.

The phone rang constantly, at the unit and at Broadford. Everyone we had contact with wanted an update on Colleen's progress. Every waking moment was consumed with Colleen's progress.

'I find it difficult to be all the time talking about Colleen,' Peter said to me.

'People are so kind. The cards are still coming in,' I replied.

'I know, but sometimes I want to talk about how I feel,' he said.

Many months later he told me what he meant.

'I always make a point of asking a person how they are feeling, how they are coping with what is happening in their lives,' he explained.

Christine was bursting with suppressed energy. She had commenced some part time agency work, but the rest of her waking hours she spent at the hospital. She was so anxious to assist and watched keenly every move of the physiotherapists, helping when she could.

She went with Colleen when she was taken to the physiotherapy room. There Colleen was placed on a mat and had her arms and legs manipulated. She would scream.

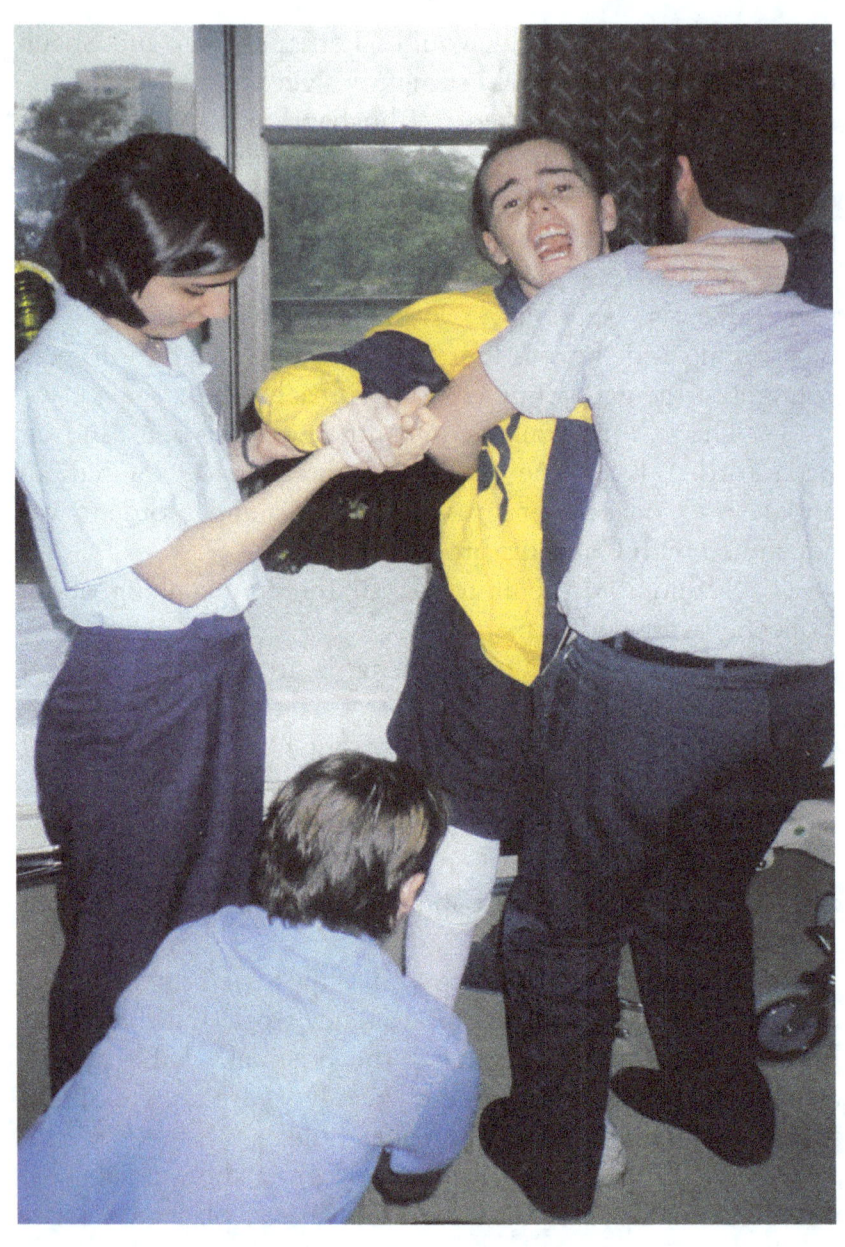

Gruelling physiotherapy with the staff at Alfred Hospital

When an attempt was made to have her stand without the help of the tilt table, she would scream.

'I don't think I need to be here to observe this Christine,' I said. I then chose to visit outside of physiotherapy treatment time.

'At least you know the therapy is over by lunchtime Mum,' Suzanne said. 'The physiotherapist told me Colls is more receptive in the mornings. That makes a change,' she said chuckling.

But physiotherapy sessions were not the only times we witnessed Colleen's distress. She would lie in her bed and scream. We would hear her long before we reached her room. It was awful. She seemed scared. Perhaps she was screaming in fear, not knowing what was happening to her. Perhaps she was in pain.

Still, we took this period of returning to a conscious state as being encouraging. At this stage none of us doubted for a moment that having come so far and shown such courage and determination, that Colleen would fail to recover completely.

Although she was being given some food orally, she was still receiving sustenance intravenously, and on one occasion we spent the entire visit preventing her from pulling out the tube.

On the 14th September, 1998, nearly five weeks after it had been removed, the bone flap was replaced in Colleen's forehead. It was surprising how quickly her hair had developed a spikey re-growth. This was to be removed and the original incision which extended across her forehead from behind one ear to the other was reopened.

I had spent a couple of days working for my sister Pat, and was grateful for this distraction, generally from the hospital routine and particularly on the day of surgery.

'She'll be OK, Mum,' Christine said. 'The nursing staff said it is quite a simple procedure.' She had come into my room as I was on my knees praying.

'How can you do that?' she said. Christine had always been skeptical of my faith. I don't know how I would have coped without it.

'Perhaps you could visit the Chapel and say a prayer for your sister too,' I suggested.

'I just can't do that Mum,' she replied.

'I know Colleen will be all right, but she's been through so much already,' I said. There was just this sea of emotion which was sweeping over me, pain, hurt, lack of understanding. 'I'm glad she is not aware that she is going under anesthetic again. It is bad enough that I am worrying about it,' I said. 'We'll just have to put her in God's care again.'

With a turban nearly covering her eyes, the morning following surgery, Colleen was sitting up while Suzanne fed her breakfast of berry yoghurt. We were told a close watch would be kept for the next forty-eight hours. Hydrocephalus (fluid on the brain) was likely to develop which would require a further lumbar puncture. This did not eventuate.

Within a few days the tracheal tube was removed. To this day the scar from this incision is visible.

The agitation persisted, but each day we witnessed improvement in Colleen's alertness and capabilities. We bought a whiteboard and texta and soon she was attempting to write answers to our questions.

'Dad, Colleen is left handed, swap the texta over,' Christine said laughing. Peter had forgotten that Colleen was left handed and had been encouraging her to write with her right hand. As her right side was affected by the stroke, her attempts had not been encouraging.

'That's better Colls, isn't it?' Christine held the whiteboard steady and to our amazement, Colleen managed a wobbly 'Y' trailing down the page. At last Colleen had a way of communicating with us. We spent visiting time playing naughts and crosses with her. We were not able to understand her attempts at speech.

Peter was disturbed by a doctor's attitude to the minuscule achievements Colleen was accomplishing. To him each step was a milestone.

'Look doctor, isn't that great,' he enthused. The doctor looked on devoid of emotion. I watched as Peter's eyes filled with tears at Colleen's feeble attempts to do a basic kindergarten jigsaw puzzle.

We tried to make visiting times fun times, not appearing as though we were always examining her progress.

'Isn't that nurse a spunk, Colls,' we would whisper, and wait for a wobbly reply to appear on the whiteboard.

Soon we were able to make excursions with Colleen in a wheel chair, just very occasional little trips into the park for a few minutes. How wonderful it was to be out of the confines of the hospital ward and in the fresh air. Our longest excursion was when we were given permission to take Colleen in the wheel chair to the hospital lounge room.

North Melbourne had made it to the grand final. We decked Colls out in a Kangaroo's beanie and scarf, tied streamers and balloons to the wheel chair and spent the afternoon in front of the telly. I don't think she was really aware of what was going on but she did give us some smiles in answer to our comments about the game. North lost, but for us just being able to share something of the outside world with Colls gave us a lift.

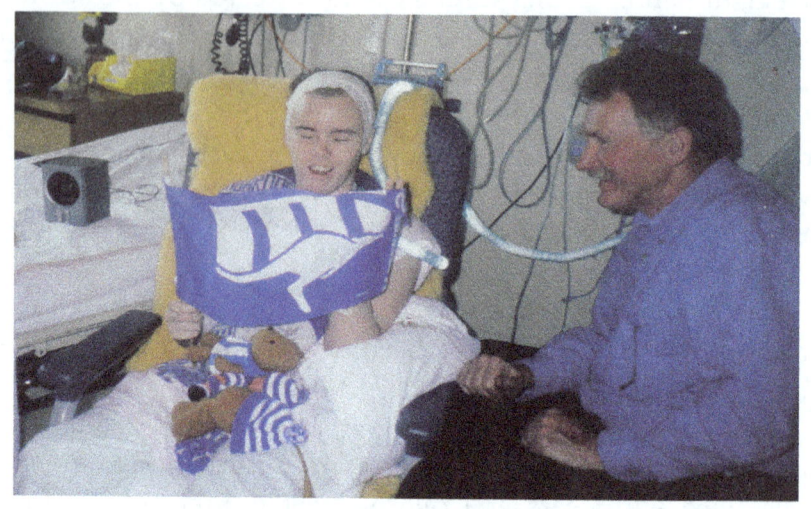

Decked out for the footy : Colleen with Peter

    To our amazement, although unable to talk, she started to sing. I had taken a tape recorder into the ward, thinking the music would soothe her.

    'Let's put on Celine Dion, Mum, she was always Coll's favourite,' Christine suggested.

    The music started. Colleen's eyes lit up and her face became animated. She commenced singing along, at the top of her lungs. Then when we turned it off, she would regress to her former state. It was bizarre.

    Gradually Peter became less daunted by the hospital atmosphere. Most visits he would just stay quietly in the background, watching and listening. He was mostly limited to weekend visits as Tucker Tub took up the work week. Sometimes he would come down mid week or Thursday and then stay until the weekend. During this phase of Colleen's recovery, he would sometimes find himself alone with his daughter and I would come in and find him talking quietly to her.

He was a bit nonplussed at one of the staff member's treatment of Colleen.

'That male nurse paused in the doorway and gave Colleen the finger,' he told me one day when I arrived.

I laughed and asked, 'How did Colls react?'

'She smiled,' Peter replied. 'I guess that is the reaction he was wanting.'

Sure enough, one of the advantages of being near the nurses' station was that Colleen was able to observe the bustle of the hospital, and the nursing staff was able to stimulate her interest in their activities.

Not only was Colleen smiling, but we were all treated to some filthy looks. The yelling continued, especially when she was moved, but the biggest break through was when she commenced greeting us with a hello, then recognized visitors and actually spoke their names. Visiting hours were less tedious as we were able to interact with her. Her favorite pastime was playing snap. We did not mind when she cheated.

Although she could not read, and her speech was limited, the white board became invaluable as a source of communication for Colleen. As her control of the texta improved we would decipher little words like 'why' and 'angry' and other words indicating her frustration. We thought it best to move on from there.

It was now mid October and although we had settled into a routine around hospital visits, we were trying to get on with our lives. With talk of Colleen being moved to rehabilitation, we could look positively to the future and her ultimate recovery. We did not count on Pete being hospitalized.

Peter and I had been delighted to be invited to a wedding. We were getting ready at the unit.

'Look at my leg,' Peter said.

'Heavens! How long has it been like that?' I'd exclaimed. He had this great big fat leg.

'A couple of days now, I didn't think it was much. Now it's bothering me,' he replied.

'Oh, your timing's terrible. We're just about to walk out the door.' I sank down on to the bed wondering what to do. Finally, 'Well let's go to the church and see how you go,' I said. One step at a time, I thought. 'Then we'll see how you manage the reception. Tomorrow we'll deal with your leg.' Well, wasn't that the most practical thing to do?

After the church service we walked around the corner to the reception. During the speeches Peter disappeared.

'Do me a favour,' I asked a friend. 'Pete's been gone for ages and I can't find him. Could you check the men's room?' He wasn't there.

Eventually I found him by himself in a little lounge room, bawling his eyes out. He was in a great deal of pain. We made a quiet exit.

The next morning we went to a medical clinic.

'It's hospital for you. You need x-rays and tests,' the doctor advised.

'If I have to go to hospital I'll go to the Alfred,' Peter declared.

X-rays revealed a clot in Peter's leg.

There we were. Colleen and Peter on the same floor at the Alfred Hospital. I couldn't believe it.

So for two fun days I excelled as Mrs. Tucker Tub. After arriving home at Broadford at 8.00 a.m. on Monday morning an elderly Broadford friend who had offered to drive and I, left home for Seymour to explore the streets looking for the houses where we had to deliver the orders. How grateful I was to have a companion even though we never exceeded forty-five kilometres per hour and arrived home very late. The next day with a different and speedier driver, another wonderful friend from our home town of Broadford, I travelled to Pyalong, then on to Heathcote on our way to Puckapunyal. That was the plan. It wasn't until we passed the Nagambie sign post that we realized we were well off track. Another long day by the time we had finished.

With warfarin blood thinning injections twice a day, Peter was able to resume the Tucker Tub run for the rest of the week with the help of yet another wonderful Broadford friend. It was an anxious week but the thrombosis eventually cleared. How we valued the support of the people of Broadford. During the initial horrendous first weeks when we were in Melbourne, and all during the time when Colleen was in Intensive Care, not only were our physical needs catered for with copious amounts of food being delivered in our absence to the Tucker Tub freezer at our home in Broadford, but the moral support given with the many phone messages and the cards and letters we received, helped us enormously as we fumbled our way through each torturous day.

Colleen's speech improved; she would recognize staff and call them by name. Then came an expedition. Aided by two physiotherapists one holding each of her legs, and supported by a nurse and Suzanne on either arm, she managed to walk across her room to the nurse's desk. It was a huge effort. The look on her face in the mirror as she caught sight of herself standing was priceless.

Then it was time to say goodbye to all the wonderful staff at the Alfred. We had come to know them so well and each member visited over the last few days with words of encouragement and good wishes for the future.

'Look forward to seeing you walk back in here in a few months, Colleen,' nurse Paul said.

'It's been an absolute delight working with you, even if you did do an awful lot of yelling. Good luck,' said George, laughing.

I hugged each of them in turn, fighting to keep back the tears. We were thrilled that Colleen was moving on, but lost for words to express our gratitude for all that had been done for her and the support that had been given to us.

On the 26th October, 1998, nearly three months since she had been hospitalized, Colleen was transported by ambulance to Royal Talbot Rehabilitation Centre.

It was to be one of the worst days of my life.

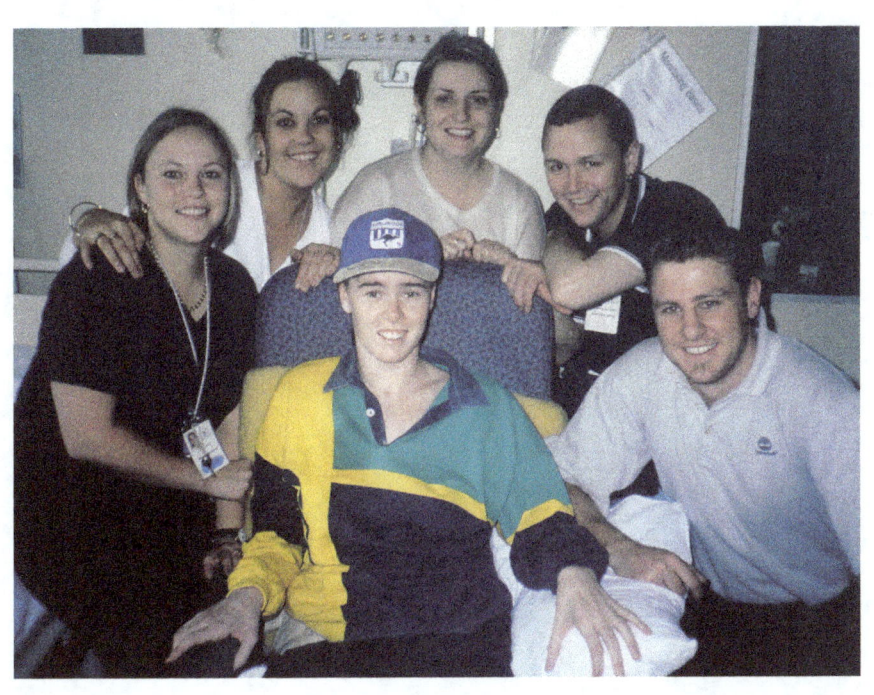

Time to say goodbye to the wonderful staff at the Alfred Hospital

Chapter 6

EARLY DAYS AT ROYAL TALBOT

During the drive to Royal Talbot I had time to get my emotions under control. Or so I thought.

Arriving, I lugged Colleen's suitcase to the door of reception. Christine had travelled in the ambulance. She had already been let in with Colleen. I rang the bell with a shaking hand and the door was opened by a woman who did not greet or speak to me.

And there was Colleen strapped into a special wheelchair, her head supported against the headrest to prevent it from lolling forward; her right leg was in a caliper. She looked petrified.

I looked around uncertainly. I could see a patient through a partition. He was walking around banging on the glass, a vacant expression on his face. Just banging and banging. How could we leave Colleen here?

'Oh God, is this really this bad?' I said quietly to Christine who was standing anxiously next to Colleen. My heart was breaking.

We were led to a quite large room. We presumed the woman who was there was in charge of the shift at the time. Still no-one spoke to us.

'Could someone please speak to me!' I could not keep the tremor out of my voice, but it was loud and decisive. 'I have just brought my daughter in here, we've all arrived and nobody can be bothered to speak to us.' I was shaking and trying not to cry. 'I reckon we're in the loony bin here Christine,' I said in a whisper.

The reception we received did nothing to dispel our first impressions of Royal Talbot, gained when we had visited previously. We had been told to go and have a look at the unit prior to Colleen's admittance. On that occasion we were meet by a balding guy who seemed to be in charge; about forty odd, with an aggressive attitude.

'Give us a minute and I'll show you around,' he said by way of greeting before bustling off, leaving us standing awkwardly not knowing quite where to look. He returned a short while later.

'This guy's as camp as a row of tents,' I heard Christine mutter to Paul when our guide was out of earshot. I gave her a withering look. The idea was to discuss with him how the acquired brain injury department at Royal Talbot worked, the type of patients Colleen would be mixing with, and when we would be able to be with her.

My sister Margaret was visiting us from Queensland, and she had come with me, along with Suzanne and Christine, Paul and Rachael.

As we were on the tour of inspection with our guide we asked questions and answered queries regarding Colleen's progress to date.

In addition to his explanations of how things worked this fellow said, 'You realize that after Colleen's finished here she'll be going into a nursing home.'

We all looked at one another, speechless. I was the first to recover. 'Oh, we don't think she's nursing home material,' I said with a shaky laugh.

'Well, I think you'd better realize she is,' he retorted.

We were all appalled by his attitude. But there was more to come.

His next remark was directed at Paul. 'Well, what's wrong with you, haven't you got a tongue?'

Paul who was as shell shocked as the rest of us, and had been quietly listening to all that was being said, was quick to reply, 'I don't need to speak when there are five very capable women to answer your aggressive questions.'

We could not wait to leave. As we made our way to the cars Suzanne expressed what we were all feeling, 'What a cold, formidable atmosphere,' she said with a shiver.

'I've nothing against gays, but what a rude, obnoxious man,' said Christine, 'and a horrible, daunting place.'

But we had no option. Colleen had to go into a closed unit. She was yelling all the time, and would throw things. Perhaps she was at a stage where frustration was starting to kick in. She needed the special care that only this place could give.

So there we were. Colleen's room was quite big. All the patients had private rooms. They were all within a large secured area which was accessed by a code to get in and out. Further on down the corridor behind a locked door, the dementia patients were housed. These were people with extreme behavior problems.

Being left on our own, we unpacked Colleen's things. Eventually we plucked up courage and went out and asked what the routine was for patients. We were shown a large communal room with a sort of kitchen and there were two lounge rooms with a television, piano and some board games. There was a microwave and tea and coffee making facilities for the use of visitors.

'Colleen will have her meals in the dinning room with the other patients, and her physiotherapy and other treatments will be scheduled at different times during the day,' we were told.

It was time for us to leave. Colleen exhausted by the transition, was settled down to sleep.

'Get your act together, Bernadette,' I admonished myself as Christine and I walked to the car park. 'We have to be here, this is the process, and we'll never get out if we don't do this process.' I was determined not to cry for Christine's sake. But she was, not surprisingly, philosophical.

'We'll have Colls out of here in no time Mum, just you wait and see.' And she draped her arm across my shoulders and gave me a squeeze.

Apart from these initial impressions of Royal Talbot, we now have nothing but admiration for the work the staff does. They were fantastic. Their care for Colleen was wonderful despite her pretty awful behavior.

Many years previous to Colleen's admission, I had had occasion to visit Royal Talbot.

Some twenty odd years ago, at age forty-six years, my brother John had a very serious stroke, and spent some time in Royal Talbot for his rehabilitation. He was the second eldest of my six siblings, whereas I was the second youngest. John did recover to a reasonable level and was able to resume part time work in his newsagency business much to the relief of his wife and four teenage children. But he had had the grueling task of re-learning to walk and talk, and then required the help of a manager to run the shop. Unfortunately his recovery was short lived because four years later he had a series of strokes, the last leaving him totally incapacitated.

I really admired my niece Louise, John's youngest daughter on her wedding day. It was planned that my youngest brother Terry would collect John from the nursing home, but for one reason or another they were half an hour late arriving at the church.

'I'm not walking down the aisle until my Dad arrives,' Louise had declared. So the proceedings did not start until John was installed in the church in his mobile bed. He cried all the way through the ceremony. It was a very emotional time for us all.

Sadly, a few years later he had a massive heart attack and died. His wife and children have been a wonderful support to us during Colleen's illness.

First Mum, then John and now Colleen, I thought. What is it with my family and strokes? But no. I would not go down that path. Colleen was young and healthy. There was no reason why she would not, given time, make a full recovery. So it was with that resolve that I entered Royal Talbot the next day.

But on that day and in the days that followed the only thing that got me through one day and into the next was the way Colleen's eyes lit up when I walked in. Apart from saying the odd word, she just made noises and stared. I was anxious for physiotherapy to commence and we were told she would receive occupational therapy and speech pathology too, but nothing seemed to be happening. I was very frustrated. I wasn't the only one who found this time difficult. I arrived one day to find Christine in tears.

'I've just changed Colleen's nappy, Mum,' she said. 'Can you believe it she was laughing the whole time. Here was I crying at the humiliation of my twenty-two year old sister having to have me administer to her basic needs, and she was laughing. She looked at me as if to say what's there to cry about.'

At the end of the first week I retreated to Broadford for a couple of days and returned for Melbourne Cup Day when we had the opportunity to explore the grounds of the rehabilitation centre with Colleen in her wheelchair.

Previously I had done some investigation regarding this establishment. First opening in Clayton, a Melbourne suburb in 1907 as a facility for epileptics, Talbot, half a century later, had approval from Queen Elizabeth II for the prefix Royal to be used in the title. A State Government land swap shifted what was to become Royal Talbot Rehabilitation Centre, from Clayton to another Melbourne suburb, Kew, on the site where it is presently located, the first building being opened in 1970. Over the next twenty or so years additional facilities were added, including the Acquired Brain Injury Unit in 1992. The Centre on twenty-five acres, now caters for among other things, orthopaedic, neurological and respiratory cases, has a convalescent ward, a rehabilitation building housing physiotherapy, gymnasium, occupational therapy, speech pathology, social work, hydrotherapy, and ancillary services, as well as a spinal rehabilitation unit which was relocated from the Austin Hospital.

On Cup Day we arrived just before the running of the big race. We were surprised to see the patients dressed up with scarves and hats giving the place a festive atmosphere. In glorious weather Paul, Coll's friend Danny and I sat with Colleen, a hat on her head and a colourful feather boa wound around her neck, outside under a large golden oak tree. After Colleen's horse ran second in the big race, pushing the wheelchair, we went exploring. To me the grounds appeared no different than when we had visited my brother John. Why haven't they planted any more trees, I thought. All the patients were in a pretty bad way and the environment should be bright and cheerful, inside and out. At the entrance door there was a full ashtray, in my opinion, not very welcoming. Over the months I kept on asking the staff about it, but nothing was ever done. It was never moved. This day on our journey, we found the swimming pool and were more impatient than ever for Colleen's rehabilitation to commence.

But first, a couple of days later, Colleen was taken to Austin hospital for a bone scan of her right side ribs, hip and leg to ascertain why she was experiencing so much pain with movement. We had a grueling day, traversing a labyrinth of corridors in the dungeons of a very old part of the hospital, and then after seven hours arrived back at Royal Talbot. Colleen was exhausted, so thin and with a ghostly white face looked so fragile. The scan showed calcification in her groin caused through inactivity when she was unconscious, and this was making her scream when moved.

Once she had been properly assessed for treatment, therapy commenced. When I arrived in the mornings, Colleen was usually dressed in the new track suit pants and tops I had purchased for her. Sometimes she would have breakfast before her shower. From the outset she was encouraged to be independent with her ablutions, and even though she made a terrible mess she fed herself. She was given painkillers to help her through the physiotherapy sessions.

Those early days were horrendous and a real eye opener.

'This is horrible Peter, and we're going to be here for a long time,' I said on the phone to him trying not to cry. That day I had been listening to Colleen scream while she was encouraged by the physiotherapists to do her exercises. 'The kids are freaking out when they visit. They find the patients very confronting. They can't believe the dedication of the nursing staff.'

I was trying to be positive about the situation and Paul couldn't fathom my attitude.

'Lucky! How can you say we are lucky?' he challenged me one day. 'It's the most depressing place.'

'Well Paul, Colls could be sitting in the corner in a wheel chair being drip fed. One day we are going to leave here. There are some people who never will. I just think we are lucky.'

But having said that, I also was having trouble adjusting to Colleen's surroundings. I was heartened by the positive attitude of the parents of tall, redheaded Mark who occupied the room next door to Colleen.

Mark had suffered severe injuries when his father Terry, lost control of the car he was driving on the family farm.

'We're going to take him home one day, no matter what,' his mother Fay confidently announced. This was hard to believe when I saw him thrashing about on his mattress on the floor. But ultimately they did.

Because at this stage I could not be of much assistance with Colleen's therapy, I decided I would make her surroundings as pleasant and homely as I could.

Having sought permission I set about transforming her room. On returning from a trip home to Broadford, I took Colleen's doona cover into her along with some photos and other personal things. What a difference it made.

'Oh, what a great idea, Mum. Awesome. It looks like home,' Paul said giving me a bear hug. When he finally released me I saw the tears which he hastily wiped away with the heels of his hands.

Grinning I said, 'Yes, I'm blown away too.'

Not only did the things I installed make the room look different from the sterile hospital atmosphere, I thought having familiar items around her may help bring everything back to Colleen. This wasn't the only change.

'What do you think?' Barbara the main nurse asked with a laugh when I arrived one morning. She had given Colleen a crew cut. Hair washing had always been traumatic. The damage done to the nerve endings on Colleen's scalp caused her considerable distress and any contact was very painful. Now her hair did not have to be washed so often.

Gradually her body movements improved, more so than her speech. She would look at me as if to say 'Look, I can do more things with my arms, I can lift myself out of my chair and I can pick up things.' The looks she gave us said more than words. You would swear she was saying, 'don't do that to me' or I don't know what you think you are doing'. These looks would be accompanied by a very stern 'no'.

She was unable to concentrate on conversations going on around her. On a one to one basis she would begin fiddling and after about five minutes you would know you had lost her.

At first physiotherapy was only in the mornings. Then as days turned to weeks, therapy began in earnest. It was nothing for Colleen to have morning and afternoon physiotherapy interspersed with speech pathology sessions. She would need a rest in the middle of the day to prepare her for the afternoon's activities. Sometimes when I arrived, the door to Colleen's room would be shut.

These were occasions when she had been worked particularly hard and needed complete quiet in which to rest. With the intense therapy, we began to see improvement in her condition almost immediately. By mid November she stood, aided, for increasingly long periods, and her speech was improving. We received very definite, yes and no responses to our questions.

'Now we're getting somewhere Mum,' Christine said after I joined her following one of the physiotherapy sessions. Checking on Colleen's routine, she would organize her visits around her work commitments so she could assist with the physiotherapy.

'I really feel I am contributing for the first time in the whole process. I told you. We will have Colls out of here in no time,' she said, but continued wistfully, 'I just wish she was not in so much pain when she is moved.'

Lots of friends continued to support Colleen by visiting regularly as they had while she was in the Alfred.

We found support of another kind came from Melbourne City Mission. A leader in the provision of services to the community, this non-denominational organization established by the Churches of Melbourne in 1854, gives assistance to thousands of Victorians, regardless of faith or culture, by providing financial assistance for a variety of disability services. Its aim is to improve the quality of life of people with different kinds of disabilities, be they intellectual, physical, acquired brain injury or a combination of these conditions.

The head nurse at Alfred Hospitals' Neurology Department had submitted Colleen's name on a list of candidates who had disabilities appropriate to be considered for funding. Colleen was one to be chosen to go on the 'Slow to Recover' programme. Although the connotation that this name evoked was a little shattering, we were so grateful that Colleen was chosen and queried why we should be so lucky. We were told that being young was certainly in her favour, and because she had come so far in her recovery since the stroke, there was hope of a good recovery. So funding commenced. We thought we had won Tattslotto. It soon became apparent how beneficial the funding would be in facilitating our care of Colleen.

With Christmas only a few weeks away, we were told we were to take Colleen home for a week. Where possible, patients are discharged over Christmas time to allow the staff time off then too.

'My God, how am I going to manage, Peter. The thought terrifies me.' I gripped his hand, thoughts racing through my mind'

'Don't worry Bern, you always do. We all will have to manage,' he said pragmatically.

So preparations for the visit began. Firstly a major expedition from Royal Talbot to Broadford was embarked upon on the 11th December, 1998. Colleen in a vehicle catering for her wheelchair, was transported with two Royal Talbot Staff members and two physiotherapists. Our house had to be assessed. A couple of hours after their arrival, I had a long list of modifications which would accommodate Colleen's special needs. A ramp would have to be constructed over the back door steps. The steeper ones at the front could not even be contemplated. All the sliding doors throughout the house had to be removed for wheelchair access. The shower door was to be taken off to allow room for the shower chair they had brought with them. We were to hang a curtain in its place. I laugh when I come to think of it, none of the doors were replaced until we sold Broadford. Colleen's bed was to be placed on blocks to make it easier to get her in and out, as was the kitchen table to enable the wheelchair to be pushed right in. With these alterations to be carried out over the coming week or so, we would be ready for Colleen's Christmas visit.

A couple of days later the next stage in preparations, was to practice a transfer of Colleen from her wheelchair into a car.

I watched as Paul slipped his arms under Colleen's armpits and slowly got her vertical. Then holding her to his chest he swiveled around and as gently as he could lowered her into the front passenger seat while, having moved the wheelchair away, I helped move her legs.

'I'm sorry Colls. I'll try and get better at doing this,' Paul said as Colleen cried out with pain.

My eyes pricked with tears. Paul looked so miserable with this first attempt. Colleen's friend Jo-anne who was studying to be a physiotherapist had been helping too. She and I climbed into the back seat and Paul put the keys in the ignition.

'Look out shops, here we come,' I said, and the tension was broken as we all laughed, even Colleen.

With Christmas only ten days away, I wondered again how we would all cope. Quite frankly I was scared.

The thought of that first Christmas was horrendous for all of us. Our emotions were topsy turvy. I was determined to make the best of a difficult situation. That Christmas was one that will live in our memories forever.

Chapter 7

CHRISTMAS 1998

It was about midday on Christmas Eve. I was leaning over the bed shuffling through photos.

'Come on Mum, leave that, Colleen's here,' Shaun said impatiently. 'Dad, Colleen's here,' he called.

We followed Shaun out the front door. Nervously raking my fingers through my hair dragging it back off my damp forehead, I smiled, opened the door of the front passenger seat, and said to Colleen the line I had been rehearsing all morning, 'Wow, look at you sitting up there like Jacky.'

It was blistering hot. We had six cars in the family, five with air conditioning. Paul's didn't but he was the one who had brought Colleen home. Neither she nor Paul seemed to be concerned with the heat. They were both grinning broadly.

Peter and I thought it best to let the boys move Colleen.

'Let's get you inside Colls,' Paul said. 'You get the other side Shaun and we'll make a chair with our hands to carry her in.'

He lifted her carefully under the armpits and I supported her while the boys got in position to take her insubstantial weight.

'Gently fellas,' I whispered as Colleen cried out in pain.

During the time she was visiting us, this became the preferred manner of moving her. The wheel chair was cumbersome. Colleen loved every minute of this attention, although it was very painful for her to be moved.

I had been working hard before Colleen arrived to have everything ready for Christmas Day so I could devote as much time to her as possible. I knew I could rely on Suzanne and Christine to pitch in and I was looking forward to having all my family at home together again.

I was so disappointed though that I had not been able to complete the picture storyboard I had been working on over the past weeks. It was on the bed three-quarters finished and I had been frantically trying to get the last of it together when Paul and Colleen arrived. Perhaps the kids would help me finish it before tomorrow I had thought. It was a very large beaded picture frame and I had overlaid a patchwork of photos cut from the many I had to choose from.

Over the time that Colleen had been in hospital, we had collected numerous photos of her progress along the way. They showed all the people who had been involved in the process of her care and recovery. There was so much to tell, from the initial incident up until the present. It seemed to me to be important that Colleen's journey be recorded, a journey we had all travelled together, and this collage was to be a present to all of us for the way in which we had all contributed to arriving at this point in her recovery.

'What do you think Paul?' I asked showing him my handiwork. We had settled Colleen in bed for a rest after lunch to recover from the trip home.

'Looks good, Mum, but aren't there more important things to be done?' he queried.

'I wanted to get it finished,' I said wistfully. 'Perhaps you and Shaun could give me a hand this afternoon before the girls come home,' I suggested.

'We have the lawns to mow and the garden to do,' he replied. 'We'll leave you to it.'

Not quite the enthusiastic response I had hoped for. Never mind, I thought as I busied myself with last minute Christmas Day preparations, the girls will be here soon and they can help.

How special it was that night to have my family together around the kitchen table. I watched as Suzanne cut up Colleen's food into bite size pieces, and Colleen commenced to spoon the diet of soft vegetables awkwardly into her mouth.

'Here Colls, try the fork instead,' Christine suggested. It took a long time for the food to get from the plate to Colleen's mouth. Looking around the table at my family, I was amazed at the resilience of my children. There they all were, talking and laughing as though it was the most natural thing in the world for Colleen to be sitting there in her current state. Colleen, although monosyllabic was able to laugh, and was joining in the fun. How proud I was of them all. I swallowed hard, and blinking rapidly adjusted the napkin in my lap. Looking up I saw Peter watching me. He grinned and gave me a conspiratorial wink. How well my husband knew me.

We settled Colleen into bed early. The next day was going to be a big day for her.

'Come and have a look at this girls,' I said and ushered them into the bedroom to see my handiwork. 'What do you think?' I asked proudly showing them the storyboard. 'I just need a bit of help to finish it off before tomorrow.'

'Sorry Mum, we have to wrap our presents,' Suzanne said off handedly.

'But this is a present for all of us. Oh, can't you just spend a bit of time with me? I want to finish it before tomorrow,' I said.

'Let it go Mum,' said Christine.

'It's not important,' Suzanne agreed.

'But it is to me. This is a way of expressing my thoughts. It is some sort of closure to the last few dreadful months.' I could not understand their apathy.

'Well that doesn't mean we have to share your project. It is your therapy. Go to it. We have other things to do,' Christine said brutally, and she and Suzanne left the room to attend to their own tasks.

I could not believe it. This was something for the whole family to share in. And what was that I detected in their body language? Anger? First Paul and Shaun's indifference, and now Suzanne and Christine turning their backs on me. Well the storyboard would not be finished, not today anyway. I swallowed my disappointment and went to set the table for Christmas dinner the next day.

What a wonderful day it was. Putting aside my hurt feelings I determined I would not let anything spoil the occasion. The mood was the same as it had been the night before around the dinner table. There was great hilarity as the kids reminisced about other fun family occasions we had shared. And even though the atmosphere was one of exuberance, every now and then I saw each of her siblings glance surreptitiously at Colleen checking to see if she was all right or if there was anything she needed.

Later that day, Colleen in her wheelchair had joined us after her nap and we were lolling around outside in the late afternoon shade, when we heard a heavy vehicle coming up the drive, its horn tooting.

The kids exchanged knowing glances and Suzanne and Christine pulling me out of my chair, propelled me around the corner of the house while Paul steered Colleen's chair down the drive to where a Greyhound bus was parked, a stream of passengers spilling from its door.

There was my family, all forty-eight of them. My brothers and sisters and their families, even some nieces and nephews from Queensland, had arrived with copious quantities of food and drink for our evening meal. I was speechless.

'Well you couldn't come to us this year, so we're up here to see you,' said my brother Peter as I, in tears, hugged each one in turn.

Every year my family would get together for the evening meal on Christmas Day. Very low key, just all of us together. We would usually travel from Broadford to one of their houses in Melbourne. It was always easier for us to go to Melbourne than for everyone to come up to Broadford. But this year for obvious reasons we had decided to stay home.

Pat my sister and her husband had organized it and he said, 'I reckon you have travelled down from Broadford for about twenty years, and I though it's time we made an effort and came up here.'

It was magical. Colleen was overawed, in fact I think she was a bit spaced out by the whole performance. These were the people who loved her. This was a reinforcement of their determination that with their love they were going to see her through her illness and help her to recover.

Within minutes the table was spread with a banquet. Everyone pitched in and there was a babble of talk and shouts of laughter. I sat letting it all happen around me. Someone poured me a wine and placed it on the bench beside me. It remained there untouched. It was such a shock to see everyone and it took me some considerable time to adjust to this invasion before I could join in the festivities. It was one of the most memorable meals of my life.

Regretfully everyone piled back on the bus at 10.30 p.m. By that time I had had the opportunity to speak to each one of my family in turn and thank them for their support, not only that night but during the last anxious months. It was some hours before I could settle down to sleep that night.

Over the next couple of days people popped in to see Colleen and on the Sunday some of her friends joined us for a barbeque, a very special time.

Generally we were pleased with the way we coped with Colleen's needs during the time she was visiting, barring her showering and toileting which we found gruelling because it caused her so much pain to be moved.

It was with sadness that we returned Colleen to Royal Talbot after lunch on Monday 28th December, 1998. Regretfully we left her tucked up in bed in her room. Christine guessed what was going through my mind.

'Colleen needs therapy to improve, Mum,' she said. 'This is the place she has to be.'

'I know Christine,' I said tearfully. 'But wasn't it good having her home with us?'

'There will be other excursions Mum. Now we know we can give her the care she needs, we can take her out more often.'

I knew Christine was right and in the coming months as Colleen's condition improved we were able to take her out of the confines of institutional life.

Home for Christmas

Paul (left) and Shaun lend a helping hand

Chapter 8

ONGOING THERAPY

'I'm hungry! Can't you cook?' Colleen challenged Jim. 'Start the barby!'

'OK Colls,' said Jim with a grin, and obligingly went to flick the switch.

It was Friday 15th January, 1999. Peter and I had returned a few days earlier from a short holiday firstly at Ocean Grove on the Bellarine Peninsula and then Torquay and Apollo Bay along the Great Ocean Road . Suzanne had arranged a surprise birthday party for Jim. We had collected Colleen from Royal Talbot and the family had gathered at Suzanne and Jim's place waiting for the 'surprise guests' to arrive.

'It's a bit early to start cooking yet, Jim,' Suzanne said anxiously flashing me a glance seeking my assistance. She had been so concerned that someone would spoil the surprise, and of course we had not let Colleen into the secret. This party was very important to Suzanne. She wanted everything to be perfect for Jim. When she had first told me of her plans for the party she had confided in me.

'Jim has been great, Mum. I know I've been dreadful to live with over the months since Colleen was first admitted to hospital. I don't know how he's put up with me. He's so patient and understanding,' she said, her eyes bright with unshed tears. Now I knew I would have to come to her rescue.

'Don't let Colleen boss you, Jim,' I said with a laugh. 'It's a bit early to start the barbeque yet. Shaun's not arrived. He will be dark on you if you start cooking without his help.'

Smiling, Jim shrugged his shoulders. 'Yeah, but it's great to be bossed by her,' he said meaningfully. 'How about we wait for Shaun, Colls? I need a hand with this new barbeque and I don't want to get in his bad books,' he said with a laugh.

'I'm hungry,' said Colleen plaintively looking imploringly at me from her wheelchair. Although her speech was limited she was now having no trouble giving orders. Then the doorbell rang and Shaun and his girlfriend Laura arrived bringing with them the other guests; the party was underway.

Colleen's programme was in full swing by this time and the improvement we had seen in her since Christmas was remarkable. To think she was able to join in the fun of the party gave us great expectations for her ultimate full recovery. When we took her out we would have to return her to Royal Talbot by 8.00 p.m. This was in time for her normal bedtime of 8.30 and for her to have her medication. She needed a regular dose of pain killers. This and another drug used as a precaution against the chance that she may have a fit was her only medication. We had been able to administer these while she was with us at Christmas time. It was wonderful to take her out of the institutional routine and have her with us.

So we became a little more adventuresome with her outings. That same month on Sunday the 24th, we took her to a James Morrison concert at the Sidney Myer Music Bowl.

I have always liked this outdoor venue which is set in the parklands of Kings Domain Gardens on the outskirts of Melbourne's central business district. The stage, surrounded by a large grassy amphitheatre is a perfect setting for hosting summer events.

James Morrison had visited Assumption College a couple of times and of course Colleen thought she knew him personally. She was a great fan. In fact we were all very excited about the outing.

Despite being very early, when we arrived we were not able to secure front row seats in the allocated seating section at The Bowl. So Peter and I aided by my sister Pat and her husband Graeme, managed to get Colleen out of the wheelchair and into a seat in about the third row. In great anticipation we settled down to enjoy our picnic lunch while waiting for the show to begin. I had taken Colleen to the toilet before we left Royal Talbot and by limiting her fluid intake, I crossed my fingers hoping she would not need to go before we returned.

It was a marvellous show. At the end the people around us stood clapping for an encore. And so did Colleen. She managed to pull herself up by holding on to the chair in front of her. We were amazed. She had been standing before, but only with a lot of help from the physiotherapists. Now she had managed to stand up unaided, if only briefly before she plonked back down.

'What a miracle worker James Morrison is!' I said laughing, and we clapped a little harder.

Our next excursion, not quite so enjoyable, was a trip to the dentist four days later. The staff at Royal Talbot told me Colleen had toothache. There was no question as to whether or not we should take her to the dentist. With the other pain she had to endure, we could not have her suffering with toothache. It would have to be investigated. I rang ahead to the dentist's to forewarn them of her disability and advise that that they would have to give her clear instructions. I thought it would be belittling and undermining to say it in front of her. It was very cumbersome getting the wheelchair into the surgery, and as we chose to take her back to the dentist she had always visited, necessitated a journey to the western suburbs of Melbourne, a long way from Royal Talbot. In more recent times we have had Colleen placed on a registry for people receiving a disability pension and we have had her dental needs attended to by a dentist close to where we are living. We have found this much more satisfactory than this first expedition. On this occasion x-rays found nothing out of the ordinary. There was a bit of movement in her mouth from the head surgery and some wisdom tooth activity but no cavity. We returned to Royal Talbot, thankfully without having to visit the toilet. I think my greatest concern when we went anywhere was, where are the toilets? I don't think she ever had an accident. Colleen was not fazed by this particular outing. She knew she had to open her mouth and all went well.

At this stage, I was still giving Colleen my full attention. I was thinking, perhaps I should get a job and work Colleen around it, but I did not want to be committed. I wanted to be available to assist with her recovery in any way I could. I thought too Peter could use some help.

Tucker Tub was slow. We needed to drum up some business. I started door knocking in Broadford. People would ask how Colleen was going and I would brightly reply that she was doing fine and try to move on to my marketing strategy. I had bagged up all this doggy stuff in cellophane and tied it off with a business card attached with red curly ribbon. Most of the places I visited, no-one was home so I would leave a note saying I would call again. I extended my campaign to Seymour, marked out the streets and houses I visited and the response I received on a map on the computer. It was February, blistering hot and very unsatisfactory as the few customers I was successful in recruiting were a long way apart. This is crazy I thought to myself. Why aren't you people home?

It was after this that I decided to train as a Vic Swim teacher.

'Colleen always loved the water,' I said to Peter. 'When she gets in the pool this will be a practical way to help her.'

I went on to tell Peter I had enrolled in an Austswim Course, one that would train me to be a teacher of aquatics for people with a disability. Austswim, a National Organization formed in 1979, has developed a quality programme for people wishing to enter the aquatic industry as a teacher of swimming and water safety. The course I had chosen would cover awareness and philosophy, principles of movement in water, and safe entry, supports and exits from the water.

'Who knows, it may even give me employment down the track,' I said enthusiastically.

'Good for you,' he replied. 'But at Geelong, have you thought this through?'

'It will only take me about an hour to drive there from Melbourne and it's just a one weekend course,' I replied. 'Paul has arranged for me to stay at his friend Nathan's house at Ocean Grove. He will not be there that weekend and I will have the place to myself.'

'One weekend! Is that all?' Peter asked.

'It doesn't end there I have to do follow-up hours in a pool to put the theory into practice and to get my qualification,' I replied. 'I will have to do an examination after I have completed all the theory and practice, then I will receive a 'Teacher of Swimming and Water Safety

Certificate'. I'm really looking forward to doing it all. It will be fun.'

It was, but exhausting. Commencing Friday night the thirty or so people in the class were introduced into what was to be an intensive series of lectures over the coming days. Our reasons for being there differed. Some were hopeful of obtaining employment and others like me were involved with someone with a disability. On the Saturday night I returned to my accommodation exhausted. It was deathly quiet. No phone, no radio, and the television didn't work. I thought I may as well make the most of my environment, so in the rays of the setting sun I sat on the beach and read the paper. Then after attending mass at the Ocean Grove church, I enjoyed fish and chips with a glass of wine before falling into bed. Sunday early I again drove to the Geelong Aquatic Centre, and spent the morning attending lectures before an afternoon session in the pool to see how much we had learnt. By the time I arrived home at Broadford at 7.00 p.m. I felt great, going over in my mind all I had been taught and anxious to put it into practice, but I was bushed.

'So what's next Mum?' Suzanne asked.

The family had all been invited to Christine's place for tea to be introduced to Gavan whom she had meet on New Year's Eve. I had been telling the family about the swimming course.

'I'm off on Friday to Dandenong Valley Special School to learn more about teaching water safety swimming to people with a disability,' I said excitedly. 'I have to do approximately forty hours hands on experience and then an examination before I qualify as a Vic Swim teacher.'

'What qualifications will you end up with?' Shaun asked.

'I will be eligible to instruct infants, children, adults and people with a disability,' I replied. 'Who knows what it may lead to.'

'So where do you get your 'time in the pool' experience?' Paul asked.

'I've been so lucky. I've been accepted as a volunteer to work at the Northcote pool in the Broadway. They do special needs teaching. Just the training I need to be able to get in the pool and help Colleen,' I said eagerly. 'I can't wait.' So it was with this enthusiasm that I commenced what turned out to be a horrifying, scary experience.

People travelled by bus from Kew cottages to the Northcote pool for water therapy. Kew Cottages, dating back to 1887, was Australia's largest and oldest institution for people with an intellectual disability. Whereas nearly five hundred people were there at the time I was a volunteer, housed in institutional style accommodation, in recent years it has been redeveloped as Kew Residential Services. The one large establishment has been replaced with over ninety facilities which have been built in the community to cater for residents, most across suburban Melbourne with some in regional areas. Whereas the one old facility was inadequate to provide quality of care for residents, today the new housing provides standards of privacy and dignity to which people with disabilities and their families are entitled. So it was that from this antiquated facility, residents were transported to the Northcote pool for therapy.

Once a week I would meet the bus, and with the bus driver, the one carer from the Cottages, and the teacher, I would help the six residents stagger inside, into the change room (most had their bathers on) and then hopefully into the pool without mishap. The first day I was petrified by what confronted me. Here were severely disabled people, some from birth, some self mutilators, badly distorted bodies, one with a missing arm, some dribbling, but all extremely excited and trusting me. Once in the water they would have a wonderful time. We would join hands and go round in circles, then break into smaller groups throw balls or do some kicks. The look on their faces was precious. You could see how they were enjoying themselves, well most of the time. Sometimes one would get upset and you would have to deal with them. The teacher, he was absolutely brilliant. All the time I was thanking God that I didn't have a child like this, that Colleen hadn't been born like this, and praying to God to bless the families of these people and those who have to cope with them.

As time went on I found I was getting a bit depressed and not managing as well as I'd hoped with the swimming sessions at Northcote pool. So the teacher suggested I take on two private patients, one a forty-five year old male stroke victim, and the other a woman with multiple sclerosis. I would spend my time with the Kew Cottage people, have a break, and then I would have the two sessions with my private clients who were lifted into the pool by hoist. I loved these two clients and found it less threatening being with them. I was at the pool for about three hours, and after all it was all about getting my hours up to become qualified. To this end I became a volunteer teacher's assistant, helping with the juniors at the Kilmore pool after school.

During this time I also did a swimming course at the Narre Warren special school. This entailed helping very, very disabled children in and out of the water. I felt totally incompetent and unable to cope with their disabilities. It was frightening. I only continued with this course for a short time.

I was still visiting Colleen every day and would call in after swimming before traveling home to Broadford. I was spending less time at the East Melbourne apartment now, preferring to be at home with Peter in Broadford. Christine had rented a unit and so I only stayed in Melbourne maybe one or two nights a week and weekends when Peter could be with me to save travelling up and down.

Colleen's therapy was continuing and she was making great progress. Her speech was improving as was her mobility. She was given menial jobs to do, like folding tea towels, just little tasks, every day occurrences that we all take for granted. Towards the end of February when I called in for my regular daily visit, I was greeted by an excited Paul.

'You'll never guess what! Colleen has just walked from the physiotherapy room to the door of the Acquired Brain Injury (A.B.I.) Unit with this,' he said pointing to a three wheeled walking frame. 'I just can't tell you how I feel Mum. Isn't it fantastic?'

'Yeah, Mum!' Colleen chimed in, with a big grin.

'You star, Colleen,' I said giving her a big hug. 'What a pity we can't open a bottle of champagne!' I fought back the tears. This was the start of a very emotional time for all of us watching her use the frame. It was marvellous to see her walk unaided except for the walker. She was fitted with a leg support known as an artificial foot orthotic (A.F.O), and she would move forward slowly and tentatively with great concentration, dragging her right leg. Someone had to be close at hand in case of mishap. We were all a bit nervous, but it was fantastic to see her progressing. She was still yelling. We always heard her before we saw her. She was very loud all the time. She would draw attention to herself, sort of her way of saying 'Look at me!'

Pain in her right knee was still bothering her enormously. We thought this may have been caused by a netball injury, but tests at the Austin Hospital failed to find any old damage. She also repeatedly had urinary tract infections and trouble with thrush. For this we were referred to a doctor at the Heidelberg Repatriation Hospital, a strange man, rather like an absent minded professor. We felt we were wasting our time as well as his. At this visit Colleen gave me a look as if to say 'Well, he's a bit queer.' I had this overwhelming thought; she's going to be all right, she hasn't lost that perception. It was uncanny.

Prior to this at the beginning of February, we had been invited to attend a meeting at Royal Talbot. This was the first of bimonthly meetings during the time Colleen was there. The purpose was to keep us informed of her progress, and discuss the therapy programmes and how they all worked. In particular we were advised how she was managing and what intense assistance was required, and most importantly to report on any inappropriate behaviour and how we could assist in curbing unacceptable outbursts that were embarrassing. We certainly could not complain about the treatment Colleen was receiving. There was always something going on. In addition to daily physiotherapy and speech therapy sessions, we arranged for her to have massage. A friend, Jackie Lawler is a massage therapist.

'Jackie could bring in her portable table,' Suzanne suggested.

'What a great idea. It will be something for Colleen to look forward to,' I said. 'I'm sure it will be beneficial and help with her recovery.' We would put some music tapes on and in spite of the difficulty Colleen had of getting on and off the table we were sure she enjoyed these quiet times. This was an extra curricular activity for which we paid.

Visitors were encouraged to help with her speech therapy. In addition to immediate family members, my sister Pat, my wonderful friends, Marie Tehan and her sister Angela, and Jane Lechelle, would regularly aid her with her lessons. They would each visit once a month, which meant that once a week one person would come in to do therapy with Colls. These sessions needed to be structured and the speech therapist at Royal Talbot explained how to work through the exercises in the books. I was a bit embarrassed instructing these marvellous people in the manner in which they should work with Colleen, but it was really important that it was done correctly and not haphazardly if Colls was to progress. And although the family would also perhaps do a page from her book, we did not want our visits to be therapy based. We would encourage her to show us what she could do rather than instructing her on what she should do. Colleen's reading needed a lot of patient attention. She would say the words in a sentence backwards or maybe jump from the first or second word to the last word and leave out the middle bit. But all this attention she was receiving was working wonders.

Unfortunately, physiotherapy sessions were still extremely painful for her. The stretching would make her scream.

'We have decided to put Colleen's leg in a plaster cast,' said one of the physiotherapists. 'We have to try something different to stretch the calf muscle, we can't have her experiencing all this pain.'

So now the leg had to be covered at shower time and this was an additional element we had to cope with when she came home to visit. But it was worth it. The first cast was so successful in lengthening the muscle and helping her to get her heel to the floor, that another was fitted. We were so grateful that the staff was aware of Colleen's problems and consistent with her treatment. The cast did not prevent her from walking with the frame, and she was now independently travelling from her room to physiotherapy and speech therapy sessions.

I was anxious to get Colleen in the pool and put my skills to practical use in helping my daughter, but this would have to wait until the cast was removed. Meanwhile I had sat my Austswim examination and felt good about how I had performed.

We were still organizing excursions for her. Mid March Suzanne and Christine brought her home to Broadford for the weekend. The girls all attended a kitchen tea on the Saturday, and on Sunday we all went to see Shaun play football at Assumption College. It was a great weekend and we were all looking forward to Easter when she would be home for four days. What an improvement there had been in her condition since Christmas.

Her friends were also amazed by how she was progressing. It was fantastic the way they continued to visit and would delight in her improvement. On occasion, Colleen was collected and taken out for tea. The Clancy cousins arriving one wet day transported her to the local pub and they all had a great time. By now her speech was improving to the stage where she was starting to put sentences together.

One day a group of friends had gathered at Royal Talbot for a picnic. No longer was Colleen restricted in her diet. I was told in this one sitting she had demolished a couple of salad rolls, a hot cross bun, chocolate mint biscuits, a banana and several pieces of caramel slice, a favorite. Her friend Naomi announced that she was pregnant and rang her partner Aaron for Colleen to offer her congratulations. Colleen, very excited, took the mobile phone.

'Thanks for the pregnancy, Aaron,' she animatedly called into the receiver. The gathered company was in fits of laughter in which she joined. Having had drawn what was purported to be Wayne Carey's face on the knee of her plaster cast, her friends departed. I meet them on the way out.

'Boy, we wish we'd had a video camera to capture all the expressions on Colleen's face today. She was priceless,' Belinda's Mum, who was with the young people, said after she had told me about the day's activities. I was so grateful to these young people, Jackie, Belinda, and Naomi, for spending time with Colleen. I'd had a few days relieving work in a Tattslotto Agency with the prospect of a couple of weeks after Easter. This work together with getting my Austswim assignment ready to hand in had kept me very busy. It was lovely to know Colleen had had company in my absence.

Then on the 23rd March, 1999, the second plaster cast was removed so Colleen was able to be taken into the pool for her water therapy to commence.

As it turned out, I was not much use to Colleen in the pool. She responded to her therapist but was not inclined to take instruction from me. The times I was in the pool with her were just fun occasions and gave us an activity we could enjoy together.

Her friends Belinda and Jackie continued to be an enormous support. On Colleen's request Jackie blonde tipped her hair.

'You should have seen her Bernadette,' Belinda said to me. 'She looked such a trick with the silver foils pointing out of her head. She laughed and laughed when she looked in the mirror.'

Singing sessions were organized for the patients, not so much as part of the therapy programme but just for the social interaction. They really enjoyed these sing-a-longs.

Christine was doing agency work now but would still be there for Colleen's therapy sessions and would visit regularly.

Although initially Christine had been hesitant to expose Gavan in the early days of their relationship to the family's involvement in Colleen's rehabilitation, as their friendship advanced I observed how his quiet nature was the perfect balance for Christine's exuberance. Rather than being overwhelmed by the way we all seemed to be in each other's pockets, he helped her tremendously with his calming attitude. This flowed through to her handling of Colleen.

'The other day Mum, I watched Colls putting things to right in her room,' Christine said to me when the family was all home for Easter. We were in the kitchen quickly cleaning up after lunch before heading out to the footy. 'It was so hard not helping but I realized how important it was for developing her independence,' she continued. 'What wonderful progress she has made in the last few months'

'I know,' I'd replied. 'Jim was saying the same to me after his visit to her last week. He said apparently she had stood for fifteen minutes unaided. He was so impressed with her determination and her level of comprehension when he talked with her. He said she seems to have a real conviction to succeed with her rehabilitation.'

Christine stopped loading the dishwasher and gazed out into the backyard. Then she swung around to look at me. 'I'm going to get my little sister back. We're going to have so much fun. I'm so proud of her. I love her heaps,' she said, her brown eyes shinning.

Chapter 9

EXCURSIONS

We were becoming increasingly concerned about Colleen's diet, in particular the amount of food she was consuming and what she was choosing to eat.

Christine had called to see me one evening after being with Colleen.

'I visited Colls in time to be with her for her evening meal,' Christine said. 'She was very difficult; it was embarrassing.'

'What happened?' I'd asked and she relayed the incident to me.

Colleen had finished her main meal and rudely demanded more.

'Not so loud Colleen. And anyway you've had plenty,' Christine had said firmly to her.

'But I'm still hungry,' Colleen replied a little less stridently.

'Here, why don't you have some fruit to finish off with,' Christine encouraged her.

'I want more potato,' Colleen said her voice rising once again.

'Stop that!' Christine said. 'You won't get anything if you don't lower your voice.'

Colleen was able to choose what she liked from the smorgasbord of food which was on offer. It was simple fare, but plenty of it. Colleen could help herself at will. We had numerous discussions with the staff in an endeavour to regulate her food intake. Unfortunately with shift changes, it would depend who was supervising whether our instructions were carried out. The staff was inclined to the view that Colleen would have a big appetite because of the extensive physiotherapy sessions she was undergoing. They did not see it as an issue. We did not want her to develop bad eating habits. In the years to come it turned out we were right to be concerned. Her weight became a real issue.

We were sympathetic when Colleen screamed in pain during her physiotherapy sessions, but we would not tolerate the loud even aggressive behaviour she was displaying. Shower time was obviously difficult for her and her aggression towards her nurses was unacceptable.

Also during the mixed group therapy sessions, she conducted herself inappropriately. We took her aside and tried to school her in the manner in which she should approach certain subjects.

'Colls, there are things you do not talk about with the other patients,' Christine said quietly. 'You embarrass them.'

'I only said I had women's trouble,' Colleen said petulantly.

'It's a secret time Colls, the whole world doesn't need to know,' I said.

'The men especially don't need to be told,' Christine added. 'You can talk to Mum, Suzanne or me about it, no one else, got it?'

It has always amazed me that with all her body was coping with, Colleen continued to menstruate regularly. It was always a trauma for her. Apart from the obvious distress this caused her, to this point of time in her recovery, the monthly curse was not a problem. Later on though, we did have to take decisive action.

The issue of Colleen's behaviour was discussed at length at the regular family meetings we had with the staff.

'She is so loud,' Christine commented at one of these meetings.

'She's always been loud,' Paul said laughing.

'She's excited to see us when we arrive, and it's certainly great to see her so happy. The other day when I arrived she was scooting up and down the corridor in her wheel chair yelling out at the top of her lungs and calling to the other patients "What would you know?"' Christine said, herself smiling.

The staff told us we would have a long road and have to go back to basics to teach Colleen manners. She had no social skills whatsoever. When we took her out, regardless of where we were, she would loudly declare that she wanted to go to the toilet.

'Just look at me and blink, if you need to go to the toilet Colls,' Christine had suggested to her. She thought she might be able to curb Colleen's natural exuberance by teaching her some signals which would make her behaviour socially acceptable.

'We have to realize that although she has come a long way, there is still a long way to go,' I said with a sigh. 'We must be patient with her.'

The family was marvellous about taking her on outings, despite the logistics of coping with her wheelchair and the hard work this entailed. Each expedition was an experience in itself, and a sharp learning curve for all of us.

'You won't believe what Colleen did today, Mum,' Christine said after one of these excursions with Colleen to Church Street, Richmond. She and Suzanne had called in to see me after delivering Colleen back to Royal Talbot.

'Here we were guiding her chair along past the shops and Colleen was calling out hello to people we passed,' said Suzanne.

'Then out of the blue she spies these two guys walking along holding hands and she laughs, points, and yells at the top of her lungs 'Poofters!'" Christine said. 'I said crossly to her, 'Colls, you can't say that!"

'We were mortified,' said Suzanne. 'Christine went up to these fellas and apologized, explaining that Colls has a brain injury and that she is just getting used to being back in the world, and that she did not mean any harm.'

'They were really good about it, but I felt just terrible,' said Christine.

I really admired my two eldest daughters and the way in which they coped with the problems they encountered.

We loved the weekends we spent at Broadford as a family. The girls' friends always included Colleen in social activities, and one weekend the three girls went to friend Megan's kitchen tea and stayed over night at Fleming Drive. It was just like old times. Suzanne and Christine had become experts at chauffeuring Colleen.

Christine was always strict with Colleen making her do for herself whenever she could.

'Gav's a real push over, Mum,' she was telling me one day.

'We were walking down Puckle Street, and the next thing I know Colleen has conned Gavan into pushing her chair instead of wheeling it herself. I took him aside and insisted that he encourage her independence,' Christine said. 'Then the next thing I know she is pleading again with Gav. to do it for her. Poor Gavan, he did not know which one of us to obey,' she said laughing.

Peter now seemed to be more at ease with his daughter's condition.

'I thought I might take Colleen to the footy at the M.C.G. (Melbourne Cricket Ground) on Saturday,' he suggested. Peter still took every advantage of living so close to the football ground, and now that Colleen's condition was improving was keen to take his turn at rehabilitating her.

'I think it may be stimulating for her, the atmosphere,' he said. 'It may awaken memories in her brain.'

I could think of all sorts of problems he might encounter, but bit my tongue.

'Colls would love that,' I'd said brightly.

So that next weekend, after collecting Colleen from Royal Talbot, Peter set off on this big adventure, pushing the wheelchair. I was so relieved to hear them at the front door back safe and sound several hours later and could not wait to hear how they had got on, and after we had returned Colls to Royal Talbot Peter filled me in.

'The only really anxious time was when she needed to go to the toilet,' he said. 'I stood outside, picked a likely candidate and asked if she would help Colleen. The willingness of total strangers to lend a hand never ceases to amaze me. Apart from the curious stares we attracted on the way to the ground, people were considerate of our situation. And this perfect stranger, gladly helped. How good is that?'

I saw this as being a milestone for Peter too. Now he could feel that he also was contributing to Colleen's recovery in a tangible way.

At the beginning of May Colleen walked with the aid of a walking frame to the entrance door of Royal Talbot to greet us when we visited. From then on when she saw visitors through the window, she would make her way to the door on her frame.

On the 5th May, 1999 we had to return with Colleen to the Alfred Hospital for a major check up with her surgeon, Dr. Laidlaw. We were looking forward to seeing him and showing him how well Colleen was progressing. We had so much to thank him for when we considered how he had brought her back from the brink of death. Unfortunately he was extremely busy, and we were told we would have to see another doctor. To my dismay it was the doctor who had told us we may as well pack our bags and go home, that Colleen wouldn't make it.

As we were shown in to his surgery I said, Off we go, Colls, stand up tall.' She was scared but I said, 'We'll show him a thing or two.'

He was amazed.

'Do you remember us? You were disgusting to us. You told me the pneumonia would kill Colleen. How could you say such a thing? Just look at her! I hope you never say that to anyone ever again. I told you then you didn't know who you were dealing with. This is who you are dealing with,' I said triumphantly.

He was speechless and had the grace to look sheepish. He mumbled something incoherent, and scooted off to get Dr. Laidlaw.

'When are you going to throw away that frame, Colleen,' Dr. Laidlaw said with a grin. It was obvious he was most impressed with her progress.

Belinda and Jackie, Colleen's staunch friends continued to give her, and us her family, enormous support. They too would regularly collect Colleen for an outing. One afternoon they took her to a club, treated her to a wonderful meal finishing off her treat with a huge chocolate sundae and then attempted to make their fortunes at the pokies.

'We only put five dollars in the machine,' Belinda said when they dropped Colleen back home. Then giggling she told me, out of Colleen's hearing, 'You should have heard her burping, we said to her it must be in appreciation of the food.'

'Did Colls tell you we are taking her to Queensland,' I asked.

'Boy, that was all she did talk about,' said Jackie. 'She is so excited.'

We were all excited. My sister Margaret had suggested we take advantage of the guest unit at the retirement village where she lives in Robina. So my sister Pat and I flew up with Colleen the first week in June. We were housed in a beautiful two bedroom unit with a fully equipped kitchen. On the Friday night we joined in village life and were treated to a three course meal and entertainment. Colleen just loved being away from Royal Talbot and was becoming less and less dependent on the wheelchair. We took her down to the beach and she managed with her three wheeled frame to walk on the sand, as beneficial as any physiotherapy session.

Christine joined us at the end of the week and stayed on with Colleen to give me a break when Pat and I flew home.

Although we had taken Colleen to Queensland in her wheelchair, Christine decided that now she was walking with a frame, she was not going to let her go back to relying on the wheelchair.

'I made her walk around Dream World on the stroller, Mum,' she told me on their return to Victoria. 'We had rests and stuff and I'd tell her it was good exercise. She wanted to do it anyway,'

'I don't know how she is going to settle into being back at Royal Talbot,' I said.

'She's OK about it,' Christine replied. 'She knows she has to do the physiotherapy and water and speech therapy, and it's the only way she will improve.'

Peter again decided to take Colleen to the football at the M.C.G., this time without the wheelchair.

'It took us forty-five minutes to get there instead of eight,' he told me. 'When she went to the toilet I had to get a woman to check on her, she was taking so long, but other than that we managed just fine.'

The improvement in Colleen's condition was remarkable. By the middle of July, just short of her twenty-third birthday she was walking around without the walking frame.

It was at this time that I took up employment.

'If ever you want a job I would be able to employ you,' my brother Terry had suggested.

So I took him up on his offer and commenced working two days a week at L. & R. in Brunswick. This business, Lifestyle and Rehabilitation, is a supplier of rehabilitation, respiratory and aged care equipment, selling and hiring, wheelchairs, walking frames and crutches, and a whole range of products to assist people with physical disabilities. With Colleen's condition improving all the time, I felt I needed to shift my focus. Besides we needed the money. Tucker Tub business was not increasing despite all our efforts. I suppose it was rather ironic given our situation with Colleen, that I should find myself working in this industry.

Unfortunately our euphoria with the progress Colleen was making was short lived. Over the coming couple of months there was a shift in her attitude to her rehabilitation. She did not appear to want to move forward. The programmes which had previously stimulated her were now not a challenge. There was neither improvement in stroke development or leg strength from her hydro therapy sessions. The gymnasium class did not increase her weight endurance or see her seeking new tasks. Occupational therapy classes, especially cooking, became difficult for her as she was unable to initiate the steps in the correct order. Also her safety with gas was of concern.

Most disturbing though was her lack of concern for her personal hygiene. She refused to wash her hair even with prompting. It was as though she was trying to communicate to us that she was sick of all this, that she needed a change, a challenge.

In an endeavour to break into the monotony of life at Royal Talbot, on occasion we would arrange for a taxi to bring Colls to Lifestyle and Rehabilitation for a few hours. I would get her to help me with the filing, but of course I would need to be checking constantly what she was doing, and really it was a bit scary. I hoped that this activity would stimulate her brain in some way. We only did this a few times as I did not want to impose on my brother's good nature in allowing me to bring Colleen into my place of employment. Besides it really did not seem to be of any great benefit to Colleen.

We expressed our concerns regarding Colls' progress at a family meeting with the staff at Royal Talbot and all came to the conclusion that perhaps it was time to look for a different environment to aid Colleen in moving forward. We consulted with the management team and the social workers at both Royal Talbot and Melbourne City Mission in the hope of being able to place her in a shared environment, dismissing the possibility of her being able to be housed in the independent living quarters at Royal Talbot. She would not be safe.

We were told that unfortunately there is no specific place for young people with acquired brain injury, the places that are available are for T.A.C. (Transport Accident Commission) or Work Cover patients. Our enquiries confirmed this.

It appeared that what we had been told was correct there were no facilities in the community to cater for medically acquired brain injury patients.

And so we were advised to contact the Supportive Housing Development Foundation Inc. and were in turn provided with a list of Support Residential Services. The agonizing search for a nursing home began.

Chapter 10

APPROPRIATE ACCOMMODATION

The next three months were hell.

Suzanne, Christine and I visited all of the nursing homes on the three page list. We each did a section and over the coming weeks at the end of the day conferred on our findings.

'There must be a better solution, Mum,' Christine said throwing her list onto the kitchen table.

'We have to start somewhere, Christine,' I said with a sigh. 'Some of the homes have young people.'

'And some of those young people are very disabled; the ones that aren't, are just sitting there. There is no stimulation for them,' Christine said. 'Colls would go backwards in an environment like that.'

'Mum, these places are terrible,' Suzanne said close to tears. 'We can't put Colleen with people of an average age of eighty.' She blew her nose and avoided looking at me. I moved my chair closer, put my arm around her and blew my nose too.

'Well, we have to start somewhere!' I repeated. I didn't mean to speak sharply but it was the only way I could keep myself in control. 'We need to check out all the places on the list. You girls can continue to do that, I will make other enquiries.'

So on the days when I visited Colleen, I spoke with the various staff members at Royal Talbot.

'Well you could try Headway, or Yooralla,' the staff suggested without much hope, and gave me other alternatives to explore.

So I would use the orange phone there in the Acquired Brain Injury (A.B.I.) Unit and make contact with the various organizations to see if they could help, and if not, see if they in turn could make a suggestion as to where I could try.

The answers were always the same. Yes, we cater for young patients as well as the elderly, but unfortunately there is no vacancy. No, we don't have any accommodation available with our service. No, we don't cater for A.B.I. patients, we only take intellectually disabled people. It was all very discouraging. In any event, were these facilities what we would choose for Colleen to aid in her recovery?

I contacted the Australian Brain Foundation, Arbias, Communitique, organizations I had never heard of. I contacted the Catholic Church, Community Services, and numerous occupational therapists and physiotherapists. We were referred among others to Borool Lodge East Kew, Listerdell House, Dorset Private Hospital, Balwyn Manor, Hawthorn Grange, and then Boroondara Community Rehabilitation Centre.

'Yes dear, we can help. You need a list of our Support Residential Services.' My heart jumped with hope. The list arrived. It was the same list of nursing homes supplied by Royal Talbot. Back to square one.

Then I made a further discovery, Araleuin in Lower Plenty; now are we getting somewhere? Twelve units all with en suites and kitchenettes in a perfect setting amongst the gum trees, space, tranquility and all empty, idle. No funding.

Is this the same reason for the empty buildings at Royal Talbot? I had noticed two buildings lying idle that could be set up so easily. I could see it. Fence it off, refurbish and refurnish. Create flower garden plots, vegetable garden plots, install a few small animals to make this a stimulating, independent and encouraging environment for patients. Tap into the community services available and help the patients on their way. If only I had the financial resources, surely something could be done to house acquired brain injury patients in a safe environment. But unfortunately I don't. And neither so it seems, does the Government.

At every turn we seemed to be hitting a brick wall.

With a glimmer of hope we visited Glenhaven in Preston, a T.A.C. (Transport Accident Commission) establishment which is part of Bethesda Hospital. To our amazement the cost of this facility was $1,400 per week and in any event is not available to non-compensable clients. Colleen is a non-compensable.

The other thing that became patently clear to me as we made our enquiries, was the disparity between the care for people who had suffered a stroke or been affected by some other medical condition leaving them impaired like Colleen, and accident and work place injured people.

We were told that unfortunately there is no specific place for people, young or old, with acquired brain injury, the places that are available are for T.A.C. or Work Cover patients. The only option was a nursing home; totally inappropriate for young people.

'How unjust is this?' I raged. 'My car registration is assisting car accident victims, some of whose injuries would be the result of irresponsible drink driving accidents, and we can't get assistance for our daughter!'

By this time I had made so many appointments and visited so many facilities that I was running out of patience and at the end of my tether.

We turned to family and friends to spread the word in the hope that they may know of appropriate accommodation. All we wanted was a place that would basically feed and sleep Colleen with us arranging for continuing therapy to enable her to be re-introduced back into community life. Did they have an aunt or cousin who may work in such a place?

We petitioned our State Government politicians pointing out the disparity between T.A.C. and Work Care patients and young innocent stroke victims with nowhere to go.

Looking back now it occurs to me that never once did we consider shifting Colleen home to Broadford. Would we have been able to cope? But more importantly there would not have been the support facilities to ensure she had adequate ongoing therapy. This really was not an option in a small country town.

Finally my persistence paid off. It was suggested by someone who worked at T.A.C. that Libby Calloway, an occupational therapist, may be able to help us.

'There's a place just out of Geelong. It's a T.A.C. facility but I believe they may be willing to cater for Colleen's needs,' Libby said. 'Give them a ring.'

Having been disappointed so many times, we travelled to Lara near Geelong without any great expectations, to inspect Pirra Lodge.

It was just what we had been looking for. It was a beautiful old home housing about a dozen young people, looked after by a resident nurse, and although a T.A.C. facility, they were willing to accommodate Colleen. But we were in for another disappointment. The cost was $1,100 per week.

'We can't afford to place Colleen here,' I whispered to Peter. We told them how impressed we were with the facility and how happy we thought Colleen would be in that environment, but after reluctantly telling them we were unable to meet the expense, we made our way home very disheartened once again.

A couple of weeks later we received a phone call. A private contributor was willing to meet half the cost of Colleen's accommodation if we were still interested in placing her at Pirra Lodge.

We contacted Colleen's case manager from the Slow to Recover Programme, Kerry Spiby, and together we again visited to see how the place was run.

It was a residential living facility for the disabled and would only cater for Colleen's accommodation needs. Ongoing therapy would need to be arranged by us at external facilities. The Slow to Recover Programme Committee would have to agree to continue to supply funding to enable us to put a schedule of activities in place for Colleen's continuing therapy. This funding was vital as without it we would not be able to afford the specialized care Colleen needed. Ultimately this was forthcoming.

We could not believe our good fortune at finding such a place and more importantly having the financial assistance to be able to take up the position available.

'God is looking after us again, Pete,' I said as we excitedly hugged each other. 'We've applied for her disability pension, that will go towards the other half of the cost. How good's that!'

And so it was on the 21st November, 1999 we transported Colleen to what was to be her home in Lara for the next eighteen months.

Chapter 11

PIRRA LODGE

On discharge from Royal Talbot, Colleen was assessed and reports submitted to the Slow to Recover Programme Committee.

'These reports don't hold anything back do they Mum?' Christine waved the sheaf of papers in the air. 'Colls has progressed enormously and they only point out the negative aspect of where she is now.' She threw the reports down in disgust.

'It's all to do with Colleen meeting the criteria for the funding,' I said. 'Jenny was more positive when I spoke to her after she had seen Colleen.' Jenny Todd was the neuropsychologist at Royal Talbot.

Peter and I had met with the kids to tell them about Pirra Lodge, and what was planned for this next phase of Colleen's road to recovery.

Pirra Lodge was run by Rex Keogh and his wife. He was on the board of the T.A.C. (Transport Accident Commission) and I think having been left a dowry from a wealthy family, decided he wanted to do something to help brain injured kids. So he purchased the substantial residence previously known as Pirra Homestead. In 1960 a female juvenile detention centre known as the Pirra Girls' Home operated in the building as part of the Australian Prisons Services. The facility run by the Family Welfare Division of the Social Welfare Department, and accommodating female wards of the State aged between ten and fourteen years, closed in 1983.

The lovely old two story building eventually came into Rex Keogh's ownership and he arranged for an extension to be built. Then with Transport Accident Commission (T.A.C.) funding and Rex's generosity, young people (mostly males) with brain injuries were given the opportunity to receive the very best of care. We were never told who the benefactor was who was willing to put up half the cost of Colleen's accommodation, but we have our suspicions.

Pirra Lodge was wonderful and Jenny Warwick the resident nurse, marvellous. Having experienced a broken marriage, she had picked herself up and thrown herself wholeheartedly into the care of the dozen or so young people, day in day out, seven days a week. She had a wonderful sense of humor and a great relationship with all the residents.

I told the kids of the conversation I had had with Jenny Todd, the neuropsychologist.

'I found Colleen pleasant and cooperative,' Jenny had said.

I could not stop myself from beaming.

'Do you think she has improved since the last assessment a couple of months ago, Jenny?' I had eagerly enquired.

She was somewhat guarded in her reply. 'Well, there is some improvement although her memory and organization skills are still compromised.' Then she laughed. 'She certainly wants to pay attention and perform. She asked for the computer screen to be turned off because the screen saver was distracting her.'

I gave a hoot of delight.

Then Jenny continued, 'You'll be given a copy of not only my report but the reports of the physiotherapist and occupational therapist. You might find them a bit confronting. They are being written to ensure Colleen's funding continues.'

Because of this conversation, I wasn't really surprised at the tone of the reports. They were very thorough in detailing Colleen's shortcomings.

'That's why they don't make a big deal about all her achievements,' I comforted Christine.

'Well, we'll make sure she continues to improve. She's come so far and when she leaves Pirra Lodge she will be even better,' Christine said with determination.

On the day we took Colleen to Pirra Lodge the family travelled down to Lara and we had a barbeque. She had her own room and we took down all her own things. A chest of drawers, doona cover, photos and all the little things she was familiar with so she would not feel alienated in her new environment. The kids had been anxious to see where their sister was going to live. Colleen herself was very excited. Christine confided in me when I saw her a couple of days later.

'I just have this overwhelming feeling of relief,' she said.

'Why's that?' I asked.

'Well it's been so full on the whole time Colls was at Royal Talbot, and now I feel the burden of responsibility has been shifted,' she replied. I think that was the initial reaction of us all.

When we were organizing Colleen's accommodation at Pirra, we looked upon this facility as being an interim measure until she could be relocated to a more independent living situation. In fact when prompted, Colleen herself expressed the hope that she would eventually be able to live independently. She was anxious to leave the Acquired Brain Injury Unit and her aim had been to live in one of the independent living flats at Royal Talbot. This was considered inappropriate mainly because of safety issues and her inability to regulate her thinking. An incident when a paper towel had caught fire while she was cooking highlighted her inadequacies. She did not know what to do, not even to drop the towel to prevent herself from being burnt. It was very obvious that she would continue to need supervision especially when faced with new problems she would encounter in every day life. Her skills though had increased far beyond what many had expected considering she had only been given a slim chance of survival. With an artificial foot orthotic in her right shoe she was walking unaided. She was now able to plan and organize her own showering, and independently brush her hair and teeth. And although unfortunately she was not able to regulate the amount of food she ate, she was eating without assistance, and most importantly, except for occasional incidents of vaginal thrush, was medically stable.

We had become accustomed to family meetings when Colleen was in Royal Talbot. I saw this as a very important aspect of her recovery. I thought we all needed to know how she was progressing, what she was achieving and the plans that were in place for her continuing therapies, if we were to give her constructive help. I think sometimes the kids inwardly groaned and thought "Oh no, not another meeting!" but they were still willing to support me on this issue. In fact I was very grateful that I could bounce ideas off them. It helped me tremendously not to lose heart and gave me the impetus to keep forging ahead in my endeavour to ensure Colleen was given every chance of recovery. I needed their input and support and these meeting were the way I could achieve this.

'So what do we need to do now Mum,' Suzanne asked.

'Well, Pirra Lodge is strictly accommodation only. There's no physiotherapy room or therapists or anything like that,' I said. 'They have staff who are carers, but that is all.'

'Will they supervise Colls at all?' asked Paul.

'Yes, they will set up a timetable to assist her with her showering and dressing, but we will have to arrange for her to attend facilities externally to continue her therapy,' I said.

'Will that be difficult?' Christine asked.

'The guy who runs Pirra Lodge, Rex Keogh, he with Kerry Spiby from the Slow to Recover Programme will help us track down resources to cater for Colleen's needs,' I replied.

'It sounds as though there's a lot of organizing yet to be done,' Paul commented.

'Yeah, but Mum's the one to do it,' Shaun said with a chuckle.

Paul was right. It did take quite a while to get things organized, but before too long we had programmes in place for Colleen's care at Pirra, and for her ongoing therapies.

Lara, situated about fifteen kilometres north-east of Geelong which is on Corio Bay, is infamously known for having suffered massive devastation in a horrific bush fire in January 1969. More than forty homes were destroyed and twenty-five lives were lost, seventeen of which were motorist on the Melbourne-Geelong Princes Freeway, trapped in a fast moving grassfire. This semi-rural town with less than 13,000 people, is home to St. Laurence Community Services, which is a quality aged care provider set on forty-two acres of parkland, and operates the Eric Hart Activity Centre, a day care facility. This Centre caters for people living independently in little units rather than in the nursing home section of the St. Laurence aged care resource. It operates as a community centre with the government providing craft activities, exercise programmes, and also a meal for the elderly folk if they require it. It also has a pool. It was here that we arranged for Colleen to attend weekly hydro therapy sessions. Katrina, the physiotherapist there, organized Colleen's visits for hydro therapy and arranged for a weekly session of physiotherapy exercises. As time went on and Colleen became a little stronger Katrina arranged for her to interact with the elderly residents. She would talk with the old folk and assist with serving them their morning or afternoon tea. This helped her communication skills and was invaluable by making her aware that there were other people out there who needed help, not just herself.

But as we became familiar with the running of Pirra, it became even more evident to us how important it was for us to initiate Colleen's activities.

'Wouldn't you think they would let the residents take some part in the daily chores?' I said to Peter.

'Well, you don't always get the perfect ten. We just have to be grateful for all the other benefits Pirra gives Colls,' Peter replied.

'But really! Just setting the table or peeling the vegetables or doing the dishes surely would be beneficial.' I said in frustration. 'They don't even make their own beds!'

Anyway we arranged for carers to come from Geelong to take Colleen to the Eric Hart Centre. Likewise we arranged for a speech therapist, Sophie from Geelong to visit Colls at Pirra Lodge and for an occupational therapist to call, both on a weekly basis.

The residents at Pirra were not asked to contribute to the running of the household at all. They were T.A.C.

patients, and therefore fully funded, for them the Lodge was just a wonderful place where they could be looked after with the very best of care with no expectation that they need to put in an effort other than what they chose to do. Some residents were in wheel chairs, but most of them were not severely disabled. Their brain injuries meant that they had diminished capacity to care for themselves. With a community network, some of the residents were able to obtain some form of employment and therefore take up an active role in the community. As long as they obeyed the house rules of Pirra Lodge, they were able to come and go as they pleased with a minimum amount of interference, but with every precaution being taken for their well being. The primary purpose of Pirra was to ensure that they had a safe, happy environment catering for their physical needs in which to exist. For Colleen we wanted it to be different. We had greater expectations of what we wanted her time there to achieve for her.

Colleen was the first non T.A.C. patient to be accommodated at Pirra Lodge and to our knowledge, the only one. Why aren't there more places like this to cater for young people like Colleen with brain injuries? Why should young people struck down by stroke or other illnesses leaving them with an acquired brain injury, be limited to the choice of being cared for in an aged care facility? Why should they not receive the same consideration as work place injured or car accident victims? If only I had an endless pot of money to be able to help them.

By Christmas we had programmes in place for Colleen's ongoing therapy and early in the New Year she was established in her new schedule.

The funding from the Slow to Recover Programme was invaluable by paying for carers to see Colleen safely to and from her therapy sessions as well as paying for the therapy.

For the first three months that Colls was at Lara, we paid out the five hundred dollars per week for her accommodation, then we commenced to use her disability pension to cover half of this amount. A couple of months later we had a windfall.

Peter came into the kitchen after breakfast one morning with a bundle of papers in his hand, and a strange look on his face.

'What ever's the matter?' I asked him, alarmed at his expression.

'I've just been going through Colls papers,' he replied. 'What do you think this Insurance Policy is about?'

We rang the Insurance Company and it turned out that Colleen had taken out an insurance policy with the Superannuation Child Care Industry. She had ticked the box for a benefit to be paid if she ever suffered a disability. We filled in the necessary forms and since that time she has received four small cheques each year, sufficient at that time to cover our share of her accommodation. What a God send that we did not have to pay the amount each week. Especially as Peter had finally sold Tucker Tub and was not working.

I was worried about my husband. He did not appear to be well. He was short of breath and seemed generally unfit. He had enrolled in a gym and visited three to four days a week working with a personal trainer in an endeavour to improve his fitness.

Like the rest of us he was struggling with the separation from Colleen. After our initial reaction of relief, we were now feeling bereft. It was a long way to Lara and whereas each of us was able to visit her several times a week when she was at Royal Talbot, we were now limited by the tyranny of distance. We still had the use of my brother's unit, but we were spending more time at Broadford now Colleen had shifted to Lara. Sometimes we would use the unit as a half way house when we visited Colleen at Pirra.

How grateful we were for Peter's sister Maureen's friends, Mary and Udo who live near Lara. They visited Colleen shortly before she was discharged from Royal Talbot, and when they heard she was going to be shifted to Lara, well, they sort of adopted her.

Nearly every week they would take her and Byron home for tea. Byron, about thirty, was also housed at Pirra. He had had a terrible car accident and although he could hold a really good conversation with you, brilliant really, he was prevented from returning to his profession of journalism by his brain injury. At one stage we thought he and Colleen may be able to share a flat or other accommodation. But it wasn't to be.

'She's far too noisy,' Byron announced when we mentioned this one day way down the track in the course of conversation with him. But in the meanwhile Mary and Udo gave these two young people a break from the routine Pirra offered.

Then Katrina from St. Laurence Services had an idea.

'I'd like to get Colleen into horse riding,' she said. 'I think she would do so well at it and it would be very beneficial.'

'How would we arrange that?' I asked, my mind racing ahead trying to work out how it would be able to be organized.

'Leave it to me,' Katrina replied.

So Katrina set about sourcing a riding school for the disabled.

'I've found just what I was looking for,' Katrina announced to me a short time later.

'Wonderful,' I said enthusiastically. 'Is it somewhere close by?'

'Well that's the problem, it's at Ocean Grove. How'll we get her there?' she queried.

'Oh, I'll take her,' I quickly announced without further thought, until later.

'Ocean Grove! You've got to be kidding,' Peter said.

'Oh jeepers, how stupid am I?' I replied. 'Well it's organized now, we'll just have to see how it goes.' I was still employed at Lifestyle and Rehabilitation but for only two days a week so could make my self available.

'Well, we can each take a turn,' said Peter, and initially that was what we did, but then Fridays became my day with Colls.

I would pack a picnic lunch and head off early from Broadford, travel two and a half hours to Lara via Melbourne, collect Colleen, and then on for the further half an hour drive to Ocean Grove via Geelong. We would attend the morning horse riding session and then return to Geelong, perhaps have a cup of coffee, go for a walk along the beach and there enjoy our sandwiches. It was a very special time for me to share with Colleen, apart from the benefits for her.

Horse riding was a very involved set up. There was the teacher, Penny Bailey, a beautiful lady, and each 'rider' would have two carers who walked along beside the horses. The riders would mount the horses from what was like a little train station platform. Penny spent ages telling the pupils how to get on the horses. She was so patient and very skilled in instructing the handicapped riders. She was not the only one with patience. The horses were amazing, just standing there until their charges were safely on board before slowly starting to walk. The assistants who led the horses and walked along beside them were all volunteers. Travelling this road of recovery with Colleen, I have been amazed at how many wonderful volunteer people there are in the community giving freely of their time to help the disabled, elderly and disadvantaged people who live among us. God bless them all.

It was twelve months before Colleen could actually mount the horse from the platform by herself. Meanwhile with a great deal of assistance, they got her astride and there she sat anxiously hanging on, peering out from under her helmet with a look of studied concentration on her face. I could see how determined she was not to fall off. Over the coming months it became apparent how beneficial these excursions were. Stomach, pelvic, hip and back muscles were all brought into play, to say nothing of the brain power it took to ensure she stayed astride. Her posture improved, and there was a marked improvement in her mental ability. It was absolutely brilliant. This was confirmed at the regular meetings we had with her carers every couple of months. More importantly at these meetings we discussed how her programmes were working and what further assistance Colleen might need with everyday living at Pirra.

All the family attended these meetings with Jenny Warwick and Rex Keogh, Kerry Spiby from the Slow to Recover Programme, Katrina the physiotherapist, Sophie the speech therapist, and Jan Lowry, a behavioural consultant. There was lots of inappropriate behaviour happening.

Colleen was looked upon as being very supported. If the T.A.C. residents' families were not pro active, then they were just left to their own resources, which of course were very limited. We had decided we would use our funding for the maximum benefit and consequently Colleen thought she was very special because of all the attention she received and all the activities in which she was involved. She was loud, bold and brash and this attitude had to be curbed. We would be told about her behaviour at these meetings.

'Oh, look at you! Posing again?' she apparently would yell out to Darren who was in his wheelchair doing some exercises with weights. 'I'm going swimming,' she would say importantly. Darren of course, we were told, would respond in kind. He did not have a programme in place to assist him.

Of a greater concern was that she insisted on complaining to all the male residents when she had her period, speaking in a very loud voice and telling them about her troubles.

'Colleen, you must stop. If you wish to tell someone, tell Christine,' I said to her. Everyone re-enforced this directive, but after a long time we despaired that we would ever be successful in curbing her natural exuberance on this issue.

In addition to our campaigning her we decided we would have to take the matter in hand. After discussions with her doctor we agreed to her receiving depo-provera injections. These injections, given three monthly, inhibit ovulation and after the second injection usually cause the cessation of periods. We thought these injections were desirable on two counts. Colleen's inappropriate revelations were not the only reason we took this course of action. She was residing in a house with virile young men, and even though Jenny was on duty twenty-four seven, she was not able to monitor all the residents movements at all times. These young men with brain injuries with little to occupy their minds, were not sexually impaired. Her taking the pill was another option, but we could not be sure she would remember to take it regularly and any way it would not solve the problem of her discussing her 'women's problems' with the male residents. As for keeping these young men at bay….well we just had to hope that Jenny was vigilant enough to prevent Colleen from being pestered. When it was all said and done, Colleen would probably be a willing participant in any overtures. At this stage though we did not think there was a problem in this regard. We had to hope that keeping her busy was enough. And she was busy.

Now for a couple of hours, four days each week, we had activities arranged for Colleen; hydro therapy, physiotherapy, speech therapy and horse riding. Then we found an activity for the fifth day.

We discovered Geof Dunblane living right next door to Pirra Lodge. He was a brilliant musician. Living a somewhat hermit existence, he agreed to tutor Colleen. Each week for a couple of hours he would play the piano and transport her into another world while she played the flute. Arriving one day at the end of one of their sessions, I was amazed to hear the music my daughter was making.

'Geof that was absolutely fantastic,' I said applauding. 'Well done Colleen!'

'I've worked her really hard today, Bernadette,' Geof said, 'a most enjoyable session.'

He really did seem to enjoy the time he spent with Colleen. I think he found her a challenge, more so than his other students.

'You have done wonders with her,' I said.

'It's great to know I am helping,' he said shyly.

As when Colleen was reading she would miss words, some of the notes of the music were missing. But she would just improvise and seemed able to catch up and continue on.

We were delighted with the progress she was making, not only with her music but we could see how beneficial her other therapies were being. Each time we visited we could see the improvement in her condition.

It wasn't all hard work for Colls. Pirra Lodge was a very social environment. In addition to the arts and craft activities which she loved doing, visits to the local bowling alley kept her amused. Although her participation was limited, she loved the outings. She also looked forward to the time the family spent with her at weekends when a picnic lunch or barbeque would entertain her and give her a break from the routine Pirra Lodge offered.

It was March. We had settled into a comfortable pattern. Colleen was fully occupied each day of the week. Before or after whatever therapy she attended she would happily spend her time at Pirra, one or other of the kids would visit her at the weekends, I would accompany Peter down to see her one day most weeks, and I would spend Fridays with her. Every thing in our world was going along like clockwork. That was until Peter was admitted to the Alfred Hospital.

As I said, I had been worried for some time about my husband. The gym programme was doing nothing to improve his fitness. He was still short of breath; in fact he was becoming breathless with very little exertion.

'It's time you visited the doctor,' I said, and was surprised when he did not put up any opposition.

Tests followed when it was discovered he had a heart murmur. The results also showed that he had several arteries that were almost totally blocked. He was admitted into the Alfred Hospital for immediate surgery.

'Mum, whatever is the matter,' Suzanne asked when she opened the door to me and saw the look on my face.

'Your father's been admitted to the Alfred hospital,' I told her.

'Not another thrombosis?' she asked.

'No. I can't believe it. He's to have heart surgery,' I replied. My hands were shaking and I dropped down into the nearest chair. I was trying very hard not to cry. I hated being the bearer of this news. The kids had enough to contend with, what with trying to fit visits to Lara into their very busy lives they had been organizing a Fun Run and it was proving to be a very stressful time for them.

I told her the little I knew about the problem Peter had with blocked arteries in his heart.

Suzanne sank down onto a chair too and I leaned across and clutched her hand.

'He'll be OK, I'm sure of it,' I said in a whisper.

'Of course he will!' she declared. 'People have heart surgery all the time.'

I looked sharply at her. This seemingly unsympathetic remark coming from my eldest daughter was out of character.

'What is it Suzanne,' I asked. I straightened up, and blew my nose.

'Sometimes I wish Christine had never thought of having a Fun Run. Now with Dad in hospital ….. he will be all right, won't he?' She stopped abruptly and looked anxiously at me.

'He's in the best of care,' I said. She came and knelt on the floor beside me and I tucked her long dark hair behind her ears and held her face between my hands. 'We all know that the staff at the Alfred is wonderful.'

'Yeah, but I did not plan on seeing them again,' she said and managed a small smile.

'And I'm sure the fun run will be a great success. It will be over in a couple of weeks and you will be pleased you did it,' I said. I was surprised that she seemed to be more preoccupied about the fun run than concerned about the surgery her Father was to undergo. What really was the problem with the fun run?

'We'll see.' she whispered.

Chapter 12

THE FUN RUN

'We'll have to call it off,' Suzanne said.

You've gotta be kidding!' Christine replied, 'what about all the advertising, what about the media coverage?' She flicked through the Kilmore Free Press, then finding the article she was looking for, 'Look, this is only one of many press items,' she said pointing to a four column article at the top of the page.

'Well, it's better than going to gaol!' Jim heatedly said putting his arm around Suzanne's shoulders in a show of support for his partner.

'You're dramatizing. There must be a way?' Christine said slamming the paper down on the kitchen table and turning her back on all of us.

We were at Suzanne and Jim's. I had been to see Peter who was recuperating at the Alfred following his heart surgery, and as requested by Suzanne, called in before returning to the unit. Paul and Christine had been called too. Shaun was in Broadford. The Fun Run was to be held on the 16th April, just over a week away. I could not believe what I was hearing. There had been a massive amount of work involved in getting the Fun Run organized from the time Christine had initiated the idea. Now it appeared all was in jeopardy.

Our children were passionate about helping not only Colleen, but other young people with a brain injury. This had come from their exasperation at the lack of support for people who suffered a brain injury caused by illness, in comparison to accident or work place injuries leading to a brain injury. They planned to lobby the Government and raise awareness of this disparity. With the vision of a ten year plan, they hoped sufficient funds would be raised in the first year to help Colleen, and then in successive years to help others. They had talked about where they could buy land and build a home for young people with brain injuries who do not receive funding. Shaun, who was planning to be a builder, would build it. They had investigated the legalities and were advised that their idea was fine.

Melbourne City Mission also supported the concept with the idea being that funds raised would help not only Colleen but others who would be eligible for funding through this organization.

The kids hoped to raise awareness of the plight of Acquired Brain Injury victims and also obtain funding for not only Melbourne City Mission but also Royal Talbot and have these two organizations recognized for the wonderful work that they do.

So "Breathe for Brain Injury" was born. With the support of over twenty sponsors, including Ansett Australia, Channel Nine, Smiths Snacks, Amway, Collingwood Football Club and the Footy Show, they proceeded with their plan and had this business name registered. The venue was sourced, the course the run would take plotted, and the necessary Council permits obtained.

Pamphlets promoting a "breath in, breath out" theme had been created, printed, and widely circulated, inviting people to register for twenty dollars as a participant in the run. Colleen's circumstances were briefly outlined in the pamphlet highlighting the importance of her receiving funding from Melbourne City Mission to enable her to receive the necessary treatment for her rehabilitation, and the lack of adequate funding for the more than 160,000

Australians affected by Acquired Brain Injury, most of whom do not receive Government funding or carer support.

Raffle books had been printed and widely distributed promoting wonderful prizes from the many sponsors. Herein apparently lay the problem.

'Whatever has happened?' I asked.

'We don't have a permit for the raffle,' said Suzanne.

'Well, we'll get one,' I said.

'It's not as easy as that,' Jim said. 'And anyway, we need the abbreviated word "inc." included on the tickets to make it legal. We have become incorporated since the tickets were printed. We didn't think to include this.'

'Wouldn't it have been smart to check all this out first?' I asked wearily. I raked my fingers through my hair, and then elbows on the table, put my head in my hands.

'I suppose we just have to put it down to our inexperience, and not knowing what questions to ask to get it right,' said Christine. 'Anyway, we had the very best of intentions planning to organize the event.'

'Well I think Mum's got enough on her plate, without this,' Paul said.

Frankly, I thought to myself, he's right. Although Peter's surgery had been successful and he was expected to be discharged from hospital in about a week, I was spending as much time at the hospital with him as I could in and around working two full days a week, and traveling to Lara at least twice a week to visit Colleen. I was emotionally drained and physically exhausted. I did not need this.

'But she had to know. We have to make a decision,' Suzanne said. She commenced crying softly.

Finally after a lot of discussion, it was decided that Suzanne and Jim would approach Melbourne City Mission and ask for their assistance. Suzanne told me later the result of their visit.

'We had to beg Mum. Really beg,' she said. She went on to say that Melbourne City Mission had said that they could not have their name associated with the "Breathe for Brain Injury" organization because the committee hadn't organized a permit for the raffle. But apart from that it seemed the biggest problem was that the kids had not included "incorporated" or "inc." on the raffle tickets.

'What have you decided to do?' I asked.

'When all the raffle tickets come in on the day we will have to include "inc." on them before the draw,' Suzanne replied. 'Other than that we'll just have to keep our heads down and hope for the best.'

It had been decided that with all the advertising that had been done and sponsorship that had been obtained, the backlash of not proceeding was greater than the problems associated with continuing to hold the event.

So at 6.00 a.m. on Sunday 16th April, 2000 on the banks of the Maribyrnong River, preparations for the first Fun Run organized by the Breathe for Brain Injury committee got underway.

Marquees were erected. One was for late registrations, another for drinks and serving food, and a third set up for massages. The kids had also hired a small truck which was decked out like an office. It was in here that Peter (who had been discharged from hospital a couple of days before) and I sat and laboriously included "inc." on the raffle tickets as they were delivered before they went in the barrel for the draw.

The support received from volunteer helpers made the day run like clockwork. People came from all over Melbourne and of course from our home town of

Broadford to participate. But the star of the day was Colleen herself who participated. We thought she may not make the distance but she amazed us all by walking the six kilometre course albeit slowly. I had brought her home from Lara on Friday following her horse riding lesson. She was so excited and greeted people, some she had not seen since before her hospitalization, by name with a minimum of prompting.

Everyone agreed that the day was great fun apart from the success of raising $5,000. At a family meeting after it was held it was conceded that the trauma leading up to the run was worth it.

'Did you know that the couple who won the year's supply of M & M's had to give them away?' Paul asked us. 'They were going back to Sydney and they could not take the three huge boxes.'

'Talking of giving away, we gave far too many things away,' Jim, ever the analyst, commented. 'We could've made more money.'

Everyone agreed. After all the hours of organization, the committee was too generous. A barrel girl dressed up for the occasion, kept on drawing ticket after ticket out of the raffle barrel and wonderful prizes were distributed. For the value and number of prizes, the tickets could have been sold for much more. The massages were free. Masseurs that Christine had organized to attend had generously donated their time and tirelessly attended to the sore muscles of the participants as they completed the course.

'Even though the hot dogs were donated, we shouldn't have given them away free of charge,' Jim said.

I think perhaps the kids were so anxious for the day to be a success and as a forerunner of Fun Runs to follow, they wanted to ensure that everyone of the five hundred or so people who participated would tell their friends about the event and be keen themselves to come back the next year.

My knowledge of the problems associated with that first Fun Run I believe was nominal. Looking back I think there was a lot that the kids chose not to divulge to me, and I myself chose not to enquire about. The monetary success of the day outweighed the negative aspect of holding the event and gave the Committee the impetus to want to make plans for a run the following year. With the money raised placed in a Trust Fund, they could see this as a basis for the realization of their dream of helping young people affected by medically acquired brain injury. There was no doubt that they would work towards an event the following year.

Colleen talked about the event for weeks. Her therapists were encouraged when they heard how well she had coped with the day and anxious to set new goals for her recovery programme. Now was the time to push just a little bit harder, building on the confidence she was gaining. She needed the exercise and to be as active as possible. I was becoming increasingly concerned about the amount of weight she was gaining. She was not burning sufficient calories for her food intake. Some of the food was inappropriate. Fish and chips were served once a week, which in itself was not an unreasonable routine, but at meal times she always had second helpings. Jenny was aware of this and worked hard to try and address the problem. Because Colleen was doing lots of things, she was always hungry but not capable of regulating the amount she ate or the appropriateness of what she ate. Apart from this, I was pleased with her progress.

My other patient was not faring quite so well. It was about this time that we finally gave my brother back his apartment in East Melbourne and shifted home to

Broadford on a permanent basis. Peter, recovering from heart surgery found the next couple of months a very difficult time. Footy season had commenced and he no longer had the M.C.G. (Melbourne Cricket Ground) at his back door. I think I had underestimated the importance of this distraction to his overall well being. Emotionally he was still struggling to come to terms with Colleen's illness and now the problems he had experienced with his heart compounded his difficulties. My time was taken up with work and my trips to Lara, and a good deal of the time I was away during the day. Peter hated not being employed, and although I kept on telling him his health was more important at the moment, he became more and more morose, especially when I was not at home.

Then the recollection of a chance encounter turned the tide for him.

Peter relayed to me a conversation he remembered having with an orderly who pushed him in a wheelchair to the front doors of the Alfred Hospital when he was being discharged after the heart surgery in April.

'Yours is a decent sort of job,' Peter had commented to the orderly. 'How do you go about securing something like this?' he had asked.

'Well, you just tell them you are interested and put your name down,' replied the orderly.

It turned out to be just that easy and in July 2000, Peter commenced employment as an orderly at the Alfred Hospital, traveling up and down between Broadford and Melbourne. What a difference this made to his outlook on life and to his well-being in general. He now had a reason for getting out of bed each day and could spend a fulfilling shift working with the staff, and in the hospital we had come to admire so much during the time Colleen was hospitalized.

We settled into this new routine and thought we were coping quite well, until early in September, when both Peter and I on separate occasions nearly fell asleep at the wheel of the car on the way home from Lara.

'It's just ridiculous, Mum,' Christine said heatedly when I told her. 'You'll just have to find somewhere to rent in Melbourne before you kill yourselves.'

Within two weeks we had shifted to Bunbury Street, Newport, leaving Shaun to look after our Broadford property. Over the coming year Shaun came to see Broadford as his and took great pride in looking after it.

For Peter and I our changed living arrangements were much more satisfactory. The trip to Lara was halved, and we were both now within commuting distance of our jobs, although I was becoming restless and thought that working for my brother at Lifestyle and Rehabilitation was not where I wanted to be. So I commenced looking for something more fulfilling but which would still fit in with the time I wanted to devote to Colleen. It was only a couple of months until Christmas and I thought the New Year was as good a time as any to move on.

We were to see Colleen's condition continue to improve in the coming year, but the first few months were very emotional and family relationships were to be put under enormous tension.

Chapter 13

EMOTIONAL TIMES

I decided I should know more about people like Colleen affected by acquired brain injury in order to better cater for her needs. I applied for and was accepted into a twelve month course on Disability Studies at Royal Melbourne Institute of Technology to obtain a Certificate in Community Studies. This was to be a stepping stone to further studies in this field. Why did I take a year off work and not earn an income I ask myself now? At the time it seemed like a good idea, and besides Peter was working.

Five days a week from nine until three, I would join my fellow class mates, three other mature age students, the rest younger though not necessarily straight out of school, in the class room.

Two of the lecturers were excellent but I found the others rather ordinary. There seemed to be a lot of time wasted. I think I could have covered the course in six months. A large part of the course was essay writing. In addition to attending lectures, the other part of the course was excursions to various aged care homes, and facilities for the severely disabled. We also had regular trips to the autism ward at the Royal Children's Hospital. You realize your lot in life is not that difficult when you see what the parents of an autistic child have to cope with.

Another afternoon was spent in Footscray at a facility catering for people with multiple sclerosis. A lovely group of people, but it was disturbing seeing how debilitating the condition is, especially when a couple of the patients were young women in their thirties. These visits gave us a view of hands on expertise in managing patients, although some of the students were aware of this already as they were working in the industry outside of course hours.

The main benefit for me in doing the course was being able to tap into the system, seeing how things ran and sorting out the good from the bad. One thing was strikingly obvious. It was going to be a long, hard, solitary crusade to tap into resources that may be available to assist with rehabilitating Colleen. Another thing I learnt was that acquired brain injury people cannot be mixed with people with intellectual disabilities although they can participate together in some activities.

Because my Fridays were now occupied, I was no longer able to attend horse riding with Colls. She had advanced wonderfully in the twelve months she had been attending riding classes. At this stage, having mastered mounting and dismounting and staying astride the horse, she was attempting to hold the reigns as well as a plastic champagne glass full of water in each hand, trying not to spill a drop. The look of concentration on her face was priceless. We thought it was important to continue this activity because now without hydro therapy, this was the most physical exercise she had. Over the last four years we had not taken up the one hundred kilometers travel funding per fortnight which was available to us, once again from Melbourne Central Mission, so we decided now was the time to do so. We employed a qualified local girl to collect Colls from Pirra Lodge and transport her by car to and from Ocean Grove so she could continue with her lessons.

Still attending her gymnasium programme and continuing with her speech and music therapies, Colleen now started another activity. As well as taking Colls to their home for a meal each week, Udo and Mary suggested she attend a computer course with Mary. It was an adult community and further education course, just a basic course that Mary had enrolled in and she thought Colls would cope with it, which she did, attending one morning a week. It only ran for two months, but it was a wonderful brain exercise for her. At the end of the course, recognized by Barwon South Western Regional Council of Adult, Community and Further Education, she was presented with a Certificate of Acknowledgement for having successfully completed units of study in windows, word processing, file management, internet and email. During this time our daughter's first paid employment commenced.

Through SupportWorks, an enterprise of Karingal, which is a not-for-profit, community based organization established to improve the lives and options of people with a disability, Colleen was given a job at the Safeway Supermarket in Lara three times a week from ten until one.

A SupportWorks trainer was assigned to Colleen and worked with her as she packed the supermarket shelves and did other menial work like cleaning out the freezers. Initially Colleen had a very short attention span, but within a short while she had a good grasp of where things in the store were and knew all the other staff members by name.

How grateful we were to the manager and staff at Safeway for the opportunity given to Colleen to integrate into the community in this way. It was wonderful for her self esteem and certainly gave her much needed stimulation.

This work became her therapy to a certain extent because on the days she worked, the walk to and from her job became her much needed exercise. We would then alternate her other therapies on the one other day she had free other than her horse riding day. If we thought it was becoming too much for her we would have her driven to

Safeway, but we encouraged her walking, accompanied by her trainer, to try and help keep her weight down.

Colleen was still behaving badly, especially when she did not get her own way. She would get angry and scream at people. Jenny, the manager, handled her beautifully.

'Colleen, go for your walk. You know what has to be done. Off you go,' she would say. Colleen would then set off on a one kilometre walk, and by the time she returned she would be contrite.

'I'm sorry Jenny, I'm sorry,' she would apologize. She was always apologizing for her inappropriate behaviour.

Her music therapy took on new meaning when Paul and Rachael asked her to play the flute at their wedding which was scheduled for the 31st March, 2001. She was absolutely thrilled and with Geof Dunblane helping her to prepare, diligently practiced Greensleeves over and over again. I too was delighted that Paul and Rachael wanted Colleen to be a participant in this very special day.

Suzanne and I found some beautiful material, a gorgeous cherry red cum orange fabric and had a dressmaker sew a lovely creation for Colleen.

The wedding day dawned picture perfect. The groom, his best-man and three groomsmen (one of whom was Shaun) arrived at nine o'clock as arranged for breakfast at our Bunbury Street house.

'I'm just popping out to Coles, be back in a minute,' I said brightly as I bustled out the door as the boys filed in. As I looked back I saw Paul standing in the doorway scratching his head.

I stood in the checkout queue at the supermarket and felt angry tears sting my eyes. What am I doing here? This is my son's wedding day. I should've been organized and sitting at home relaxed and waiting instead of stocking up on supplies. I had always thought I was a very organized person. I've really stuffed up here, I thought. This set the tone for the whole day and I was glad the tension was broken when the boys finally got in the car to go to the church and I had five seconds to myself. No-one had commented on my outfit.

I sat looking proudly at my handsome sons standing at the front of the church waiting for the bride to arrive. I squared my shoulders and determined I was not going to let a bad start to the day spoil the occasion.

The bridesmaids preceded Rachael down the aisle and I bit my trembling lip. The bride joined Paul in front of Father Conroy (my sister Pat's brother-in-law) and I felt the tension slipping away as the priest commenced the familiar words of the marriage ceremony.

Ten minutes later the lights in the church went out.

'This parish must not pay their bills,' joked Father Conroy and continued on with the service.

'There's a fire!' Rachael's mother who was sitting across the aisle from us called out pointing to the ceiling. 'Father, there's a fire,' she repeated a little louder. Sure enough there were flames around one of the globes in the ceiling. The phrase, there's a fire, was repeated creating a buzz as it was passed on down through the congregation.

'Will someone do something, there is a fire,' called Father Conroy.

That galvanized action and Rachael's father along with another guest raced and got a fire extinguisher.

'Wait, it's the wrong one,' cried Rachael's father and another guest raced to get the extinguisher for electrical fires. There was no immediate danger and a rumble of laughter went through the congregation. But the church started filling with smoke and it became very unpleasant causing people to cough.

'I think we'd better move outside,' Father Conroy suggested.

The one hundred guests vacated the church and as instructed by the priest, assembled in a circle on the grass where the ceremony proceeded. I could see the women struggling to prevent the heels of their shoes sinking into the soft grass, a very different surface from what they'd expected to be standing on. Peter's Mum sat proud in her wheelchair, not fussed with this change of venue. It was so wonderful to have her there with us.

Then it was time for Colleen to perform. I held my breath. Would she pull it off? She did, note perfect. The atmosphere was electric. As the last note faded, the congregation loudly and enthusiastically applauded. I felt frozen in time. All I wanted to do was to sit down and sob. I was filled with pride. I glanced across at Peter and saw him wiping his face with his handkerchief. I did the only thing I knew to break the tension. I laughed, and quickly brushing an errant tear from my cheek, joined in the applause. Even today I cannot talk about the moment without crying. It was magic.

Someone must have rung the fire brigade because as the ceremony concluded a couple of trucks sped into the churchyard. But the fire had been extinguished and there was nothing left for them to do but to check the building.

Not wanting to let a good opportunity pass, the photographers took photos using the fire trucks as a back drop.

I went and offered Paul my congratulations. He put his arm across my shoulders, pulled me to him, and laughing said, 'Well I did try very hard to have a church wedding,

Mum.' I put my arms around his waist and clung wordlessly to him. I knew I was forgiven for my earlier blunder.

I happily went off to ask my sister Maree to secure some video footage for me. I had borrowed a video camera for the occasion but the one tape I had brought with me was soon full. I told Maree not to worry, I would buy another one.

'You're going where?' Peter asked.

'I'll catch up. You go on,' I replied as I walked off heading down the road to Coles for the second time that day. Peter never gets cross, but I could see he was wondering why on earth I was choosing to do this. Looking back now I wonder myself. Why would I put myself through so much trauma? I ended up missing all the pre dinner drinks and nibbles and arrived at the reception just as everyone was being seated.

Then to cap it off, the second tape ran out just as Rachael was about to give her speech. I'm sure she was annoyed. To this day I have never asked if she has forgiven me. I have often queried how it was that I came to be responsible for the videoing at my own son's wedding. I just seem to get myself into these situations with the very best of intentions and cause myself a whole lot of grief.

One would think that Paul and Rachael would be honeymooning for the next couple of weeks, and I think they probably did go away for several days. But they were certainly around for the next Saturday which was the weekend of the second Fun Run.

The organization of this Fun Run took on a more professional approach than the first. I think Suzanne and Jim decided after the problems that had been encountered with the first it was important to get it right the second time around. A lot more of the promotional work was handled by them and they invited friends to join the committee and contribute their expertise to the organizing of the event.

Unfortunately conflict arose because everyone seemed to have different goals and expectations, and Suzanne found this especially stressful. She and Jim were looking at the bigger picture. They had visions of lobbying the government and creating awareness of the plight of acquired brain injury victims, especially through advertising and media coverage. Their idea was that it was all about raising awareness not actually getting people to participate in the run. Suzanne was employed in the television industry and Jim was in production so they had the contacts for getting exposure through the media. They arranged a segment on 'Good Morning Australia' and had advertisements run on all three television networks, all through the advocacy of colleagues. The whole thing just snowballed and as it grew it just seemed to leave the rest of the family behind.

Arrangements became more and more complicated and the workload became greater and greater. Jim prepared a forty-two page presentation to put before the committee outlining how he and Suzanne envisaged the whole thing would happen and detailing strengths and weaknesses in the plans. Their friends also had a really big vision for the production. The rest of the family found this rather intimidating and were on a completely different level, just wanting to have things done as they had in the previous year, just better, and keeping it simple.

We were still having family meetings on a regular basis, and the conflict within the family was very apparent.

'I'm over bloody family meetings,' Christine announced on one occasion. 'I just want to move on and get on with my life.'

Family meetings had become a part of our lives. All through the time Colleen was at Royal Talbot and continuing on now she was at Lara, they were held regularly.

I had sensed that all was not right with my family, and Christine's comment confirmed my view. It was not so much what she said, it was the underlying emotion that was expressed in her harsh words. Over the course of Colleen's illness, we had all been offered counseling and had as a group attended the Bouverie Centre which provides among other things, therapy services for families dealing with and helping them to cope with the impact acquired brain injury has on the families of those affected by this illness.

We were not very good at opening up. Everyone was trying to be strong. The barriers each had built up were not easily broken down and therefore were inhibiting us from being able to express what we were really feeling. Each was trying to be brave and not feel sorry for themselves while perhaps thinking, I hate the world, and why did this happen.

I found the counseling very beneficial. I think Paul and Rachael went once together, I don't know about the girls. I don't approach it, it's a very personal thing. I think at the time of the second Fun Run all the little issues my family had had during the initial period of Colleen's illness were surfacing and the different approach to the Run highlighted the diverse personalities and the individual's way of handling situations. Whereas my children had always been good friends, they now rather than enjoying each others company seemed only too anxious to have nothing to do with each other.

I was in no condition emotionally to help them through this crisis. I was a bit like an ostrich in my approach channeling my energies towards Colleen's ultimate rehabilitation, and not wanting to know about the complexities of my other children's relationships.

'Jim and I are putting all this together. I don't think you realize how big an event it is going to be. The least you can do is be supportive,' Suzanne replied to Christine's outburst.

The second Fun Run was more successful than the first, that is if you gauge it on the $15,000 raised. But one thing all the kids agreed on was that they had more fun at the first run.

Once again Colleen participated and we could see the improvement in her condition since the time before. She of course was unaware of the conflict between her siblings and started talking about next year's run straight away.

I was not surprised when Suzanne came to me and advised of the decision not to organize a run for the following year. The committee had had a debriefing meeting and then floated the plans for the following year's run. She told me she and Jim were walking along St. Kilda Road following the meeting when she dropped the bomb shell.

'There is no way I'm doing it again. It is destroying our family. There's too much at stake,' she had said to Jim.

She went on to tell me how it was not only conflict with her family, she and Jim had experienced difficult times during the organization of the Fun Run. She said Jim was trying to help her family, but there were arguments about how the event was to be run and that then caused trouble between her and Jim. She told me how upset she was with the division in the family too.

'Paul and I used to socialize together all the time, now we have not been together socially for over twelve months,' she said starting to cry softly. 'We don't go out together as a family anymore. What's happened to all the happy family times we had? It's just too stressful. It's not worth it.'

Yet another family meeting was held at which Suzanne told of the decision not to continue with planning next year's event.

'Well I didn't intend to be there anyway,' said Christine bluntly.

'What's to happen with the money we have raised?' asked Paul.

It was decided that for the moment the money would be held in the trust account and we would obtain advice on how it could be used. It was obvious that the vision of building a facility for acquired brain injury victims would have to be shelved, if only for the time being.

I just hoped that my family could resume the happy relationships they had had with each other. Then an incident involving Colleen highlighted the solidarity of their bond. Just when we thought things were settling down to a comfortable routine, Colleen's environment was disrupted and we had to make alternative arrangements for her.

Chapter 14

KIDNAP FROM PIRRA LODGE

Colleen's recovery had been remarkable. It had been nearly three years since she had the stroke and been brought back from death's door. We were still seeing an improvement in her condition. Would she ever fully regain her pre stroke faculties? Would she be left with physical, cognitive, psychological and social impairments? We could only continue with the therapies we had been employing and hope that given every opportunity she would one day be completely well.

Acquired brain injury is complex and individual. No two persons can expect the same outcome or resulting difficulties. Appropriate treatment plays a vital role in determining the level of recovery. Would Colleen have an understanding of the person she was before the stroke? If so, and she knows that she will never be that person again, would the knowledge haunt her for the rest of her life? Not to be confused with intellectual disability, people with an acquired brain injury usually retain their intellectual abilities but have difficulty controlling, coordinating and communicating their thoughts and actions. We had seen this in the inappropriate behaviour that Colleen had been displaying. We had worked hard to try and curb her discussions on inappropriate topics and to improve her social skills. The trouble was she was living with people who also had diminished responsibility, most of them males. Therein lay the problem we next encountered.

It appears that one of Colleen's housemates had a bit of a crush on her that extended to nocturnal visits.

'Chris is a nice lad,' Rex Keogh, the owner of the Transport Accident Commission facility had said to me when I mentioned our concerns to him. 'Why not let the relationship develop?'

'But we don't think either of them has the capability of knowing what a relationship is,' I'd replied, 'and besides whose going to monitor this liaison between these two young people with diminished capacity. It's not appropriate.'

We could not expect Jenny the carer to be made responsible, besides what control could she exert over hormones running rampant. Thank goodness Colleen was still receiving the depo-provera injections. A pregnancy would be disastrous.

Some young people are sexually uninhibited in an inappropriate way following brain injury. Because Colleen had poor awareness and impaired social skills we could see that this situation which had arisen was going to cause us a great deal of anxiety. We had already had problems regarding her inappropriate discussions on menstruation, now it appeared we were facing another dilemma.

I could sort of see where Rex was coming from but in my heart I knew that it was wrong and not what I wanted for my daughter. Colleen would not have any control over how much of a liberty this young man would take, and if she was not in control, if she was unwilling, would it not then be rape? Apart from anything else, I could envisage the psychological damage that this may cause Colleen. Where would you draw the line? Would she not be seen as a willing participant? There were no locks on the doors, and even if there had been, would Colleen have been able to deny her hormones?

It was not until some time later that I found out that she had confided in Christine who in turn told Suzanne. Both the girls were horrified with Colleen's revelations. Apparently Chris was not the only male resident Colleen was "having a relationship with". My children chose to protect Peter and I from knowing the magnitude of the predicament, although they knew we were aware that there was trouble.

'It was dreadful Mum,' Suzanne told me later. 'Jim and I went to see Colleen and after guarded questioning the full extent of the problem became apparent.' She went on to say that back at home she was distraught. Both she and Jim decided that the situation could not be allowed to continue. Suzanne had said to Jim she could not leave Colleen there knowing that she was being taken advantage of. They had come to the conclusion by what Colleen had said that she was not a willing participant and that she was being forced into situations which were unpleasant for her.

'I can't be there for her, Jim,' Suzanne had said sobbing. 'It's terrible, we must do something.'

The next day after a sleepless night, Suzanne contacted Melbourne City Mission and demanded to know what they were going to do to protect Colleen, after all they were providing the funding for her accommodation, surely they would expect quality care. She was told they were unable to help and that unfortunately it happens in institutions.

'Would you leave your daughter there knowing what's going on?' Suzanne shouted into the phone.

'Well, um, no,' came the unequivocal reply.

'Right. Because let me tell you. We're going to take her out.' Suzanne had slammed down the phone.

The following Thursday evening two of our other children had decided to take some decisive action. At 10.00 p.m. there was a knock at our door. There stood Christine and Shaun.

'What on earth are you doing out at this time of night?' I asked. One look at their faces told me it was not good news.

'We've just driven back from Lara. We wanted to see Colls,' Shaun said glancing anxiously at Christine. On the drive home they had decided that Peter and I needed to know the truth. They felt they could not protect us any longer.

'You'd better come in and tell us about it,' I said ushering them into the family room where Peter sat reading the paper. Parking themselves side by side on the lounge Christine took the role of spokesperson.

She said they had decided that Colleen was not going to spend even one more night in vulnerable circumstances. Then on the way to Pirra Lodge they decided perhaps they could not just snatch her away and thought if they could get Colleen to handle the situation it might be defused. They worked out a role play scenario with Shaun as the perpetrator.

'It was amazing to see Shaun play acting,' Christine said looking fondly at her little brother.

She went on to say that firstly they took Colleen back to basics to try and teach her what was right and wrong and what was acceptable behaviour. They told her she did not have to give in to these boys' demands. They schooled her on what to say if someone came to her room in the middle of the night and how resolute she would have to be in getting them to leave.

'Shaun was quite rough with her. Pushing her around a bit and getting her to respond and shout no, no, get out.' There was a glimmer of a smile that passed between Christine and Shaun.

But I wasn't smiling. By the time the two of them had finished telling Peter and I all the details of what they knew had been happening at Pirra Lodge, I was sobbing.

'I can't believe you kids kept this from us. You can't take on everything the way you do,' I said. Peter had come to sit on the arm of my chair, and when he put his arm around my shoulder I turned and clung to him. He rested his head on mine. He was crying too.

It was 1.00 a.m. before Christine and Shaun left.

That weekend, (it was the end of May), as we had been doing for a couple months, Colleen was put on the train at Lara and we met her at our end. Usually she would spend the weekend with us and then we would put her back on the train and she would be met by one of the staff from Pirra. But by Sunday night we had made a decision.

'You're not going back to Pirra Lodge, Colls. You don't need to go back,' I said to her, and then went to the phone.

'I've kidnapped my daughter,' I told Jenny. 'We're going to trial it for a fortnight. I can't see why it won't work. I think it is time for us to move on.'

Three days later a letter came to ask whether they were to keep the room for Colleen. I was horrified. Then I thought, no they have a business to run. So we made the decision. We were out of there! It had only been a week. Colleen was home.

Chapter 15

BACK INTO SOCIETY

Looking back we thought that probably Colleen had outgrown Pirra Lodge. She needed a structured environment and Pirra was more social. It was wonderful for her to have had the social contact with people, but if her condition was to continue to improve, each day needed to be planned for her. We had done as much as we could for her, from a distance, but we could see that her management was stalling.

When she came home the funding from Melbourne City Mission continued, but was reduced. Without the accommodation costs, this was not really an issue. We still received sufficient to maintain Colleen's therapies and to ensure we could pay carers when they were required.

After Colleen had been home for a few weeks, I sat her down and had a chat with her.

'Look Colls, about these injections you have been having, how about we discontinue them?' I suggested. I thought that with all else her body had had to cope with, it would be better to at least let this one bodily function happen normally.

'You're not in a relationship. It takes a long while for a relationship to develop. If in the future you do meet someone, well we will talk about what we will do then,' I said. I was concerned about the side effects of the injection, and now that she had left Pirra Lodge and was back in a safe family environment, it seemed pointless to subject her body to unnecessary change. She agreed.

Our contact with Pirra Lodge did not cease completely. There was the job at Safeway to maintain. She had a twenty-six week contract to fulfill. So having experienced train travel when she had visited us at weekends when she was at Pirra, Colleen now travelled to and from Lara by train, was met by Jenny or one of the other staff from Pirra, and taken to Pirra Lodge. From there the Supports Work trainer would collect Colleen from Pirra and take her to Safeway, staying with her for the three hours work time. This routine was also used to enable her to continue her horse riding and visits to the Eric Hart Centre.

When I took Colleen to Newport Station for her first train trip after she shifted home, I met this pretty blonde lady. We chatted and she said she caught the train every day.

'Oh that's great, this young lady is going to be on it every day too,' I said introducing her to Colleen. I think I may have suggested perhaps she would be willing to assist by making sure Colleen got out at Lara. I thought to myself, given the same situation, I would have been only too willing to do so. She seemed quite agreeable to the idea.

That was the first and last time we ever saw her.

'She must've thought we weren't worth knowing,' I said laughingly to Peter.

As his shifts as an orderly at the Alfred were less rigid than my routine, on subsequent journeys, initially Peter would take Colleen to the station and then escort her to a seat on the train. He wanted to make sure she was seated before the train moved off. She did not have very good balance. Because she was slow, he found on occasion that the train was going to leave with him on it. So he devised a method of ensuring this did not happen.

'I stood in the doorway, one foot on the train the other on the platform until she was in her seat,' he told me.

'Get away from the train, we're running late,' the train conductor ordered him.

'I'm not going to move for anyone, pal,' Peter told me he had retorted. He was really upset that they had this attitude.

As time went on Colleen would walk to the station by herself, purchase her ticket and make her own way to Lara. Apart from losing her ticket on two occasions, she managed the money and brought home the correct change.

On one journey though, Colleen went through to Geelong. I received a phone call from an elderly lady advising me Colleen had just missed getting off the train at Lara. Colleen had given her my telephone number.

'Don't worry dear,' this dear soul said to me. 'My friend and I will look after her and make sure she gets off at Geelong and back on the right train.'

'You're wonderful. Thank you ever so much,' I replied.

I rang Jenny who had been left standing at Lara, and asked her to wait on the other side of the platform until Colleen returned.

'Boy Mum,' Colleen said to me that night, 'I thought, oh oh, I'm in trouble here!'

'How clever of you Colls, to give those ladies my telephone number,' I praised her. It was indeed an indication of the progress she was making. How grateful we were for this act of kindness by two ladies.

Amazingly as time went on, by prearrangement with her, Colleen comprehended that on the return journey, she was to alight at either Footscray or Newport to be met by Peter or I to fit in with our schedules.

At the beginning of August, 2001 the Government funded job at Safeway ended. For a while the only activity we continued was the horse riding at Ocean Grove. But because we did not have Pirra Lodge as 'home base', once again we had to make the commitment to transport Colleen on a Friday. This was almost impossible to achieve. We then found an alternative closer to home and our trips to Ocean Grove ceased. Through the network of connections we had sourced, we were able to have Colleen enrolled in a riding for the disabled programme at the Police Barracks in St. Kilda Road which she attended every second Thursday night.

We had actively started to look for alternative employment for her. Following appointments at two job placement agencies, Colleen was put on their books awaiting something suitable and meanwhile we explored activities for the disabled. We had eighteen hours funding and so we arranged for private therapy sessions at our rented home in Bunbury Streeet so she could continue speech and music therapy. We had English (reading) and mathematics programmes set up for her and one morning a week she would attend the gymnasium in Mason Street, Newport.

While we were awaiting suitable paid employment, Colleen was offered a voluntary position at St. Albans North Primary School. Peter's brother Jim was principal there and he suggested that Colleen might like to help the teacher in the art room. So her carer, Sarah, would drive her there on a Thursday and Colleen would mix up the paints and get out all the brushes ready for the classes. This was where the funding under the Slow to Recover Programme was invaluable. We could create whatever activity we thought appropriate and employ a carer to implement it.

Peter and I had joined the Mass Reader's group at the St. Mary's Parish Williamstown. We thought it important to connect to a community. After being so actively involved in Broadford we had this desire to feel we belonged in the area we had chosen to live. It was obvious it was going to take a long time to be integrated into the community. There we met a couple of lovely ladies and a man who ran the Williamstown opportunity shop. They very kindly said Colleen could attend the shop one morning a week, so either Peter or I would drop her off.

'Guess what they have her doing?' I with a chuckle, said to Peter at the end of her first day.

'Well, stop laughing and tell me,' he said grinning too.

'Folding clothes! What a joke!' I said. Colleen's room was always untidy with clothes strewn everywhere. I fought a losing battle to have her put her things away tidily. This activity together with other mundane jobs at the op. shop worked for a while but it was only a temporary arrangement.

I had had to put the practical part of my course on hold for a while in order to focus on setting up activities and organizing pursuits for Colleen. It would have been impossible to arrange these activities had we still been living in Broadford. There were so many resources we could tap into here in Melbourne, and I left no stone unturned.

I investigated voluntary organizations such as Red Cross, Bear in Mind, Volunteers Victoria, and finally the organizastion we settled on, the Footscray Community Art Centre. I sourced therapy programmes; water therapy, dance movement, stretch theatre, netball for the disabled and organized a physiotherapy programme with a fellow called Geoff Bell so that Colleen could do exercises at home to help maintain movement in her joints. In the end, Colleen did not have a spare minute. It was certainly a challenge to have her up in the mornings in time to shower, dress, have her breakfast and generally be organized in time for Peter and I to be able to attend to our occupations. A timetable was in place for her that was structured and therapeutic.

Colleen was still limping, so her physiotherapist, in association with Royal Talbot, had her assessed and a new orthotic (a special brace fitted into her right shoe, which provides support) helped to minimize this. Other than this we could not have been more pleased with her progress. With the oversight and prompting of her carers, simple every day tasks such as, choosing appropriate clothing, dressing, assisting with dinner preparation, doing her own washing including correctly measuring the detergent, and making her own lunch were all now achievable for her.

The Footscray Community Art Centre runs a programme called ArtLife, specifically structured for people with disabilities. We enrolled Colleen and she participated in the art activities aimed at developing life skills.

Having crammed as much activity as we could into the five day work week, we also looked for leisure interests at the weekends. We tried water exercise and had Colleen attend the SWEAT programme designed for people with special needs managed by the Y.M.C.A. and run at the Werribee Sports and Fitness Centre. This was excellent, but as we found it difficult rushing to get there on a Sunday morning, in the end we finally ran out of steam and discontinued this activity. She was doing water therapy with a carer at Altona Swimming Pool during the week anyway. We had already found another occupation which Colleen found totally absorbing for four hours on a Saturday morning.

Towards the end of the year, she commenced playing her flute with the Western Region Concert Band. This band, formed in 1977, gives students in western metropolitan Melbourne the opportunity to play more sophisticated music than what they would be exposed to in their own school bands. Community performances during the year are highlighted by an annual 'Last Night of The Proms Concert' held in August. Practicing on a Saturday and eventually playing with the band at events held Colleen's attention for years. Without an argument she would be up, dressed and out of the house by 8.30 a.m. each Saturday. She absolutely loved it but would come home exhausted.

'Colls, you must have a rest,' I would instruct her. Off she would go only to wander out a few minutes later saying she was thirsty or needed to go to the toilet.

'You won't be able to stay up tonight when Christine and Gavan come for dinner if you don't rest now,' I would suggest. I did not like having to resort to bribery, but knew she would be impossible if she did not have some down time.

In the evenings we encouraged her to do jigsaw puzzles, and the degree of difficulty was increasing. She attended a library and would choose books to read. We saw great improvement in her ability. She would have homework from the Footscray Community learning programme which she was always keen to do, although she said she was bored with the programme generally.

It was at this point that I decided that I could not continue with my studies. I was just overwhelmed. Here I was learning about people with disabilities during the day and then coming home and coping with it at night. I had completed the first year which gave me a sort of support worker's certificate, sufficient to make application for employment in the industry, and so I set about finding a job.

'How did it go?' Peter would ask me after I had returned from an interview.

'I reckon, I'll get that one,' I so often confidently replied. But I didn't. It appeared that I was not sufficiently qualified in comparison to the other applicants.

Finally I lowered my aspirations and contacted Australian Home Care and took on casual work assisting people in their homes. This was very convenient as I could choose my shifts and still be available when needed for Colleen.

On my way to and from my various placements, I would pass the Southern Cross Home for the Aged. One day I plucked up courage and went in to see if they might have a position for me. They welcomed me with open arms.

I had the opportunity to apply for a position as a personal carer. But there was a problem. I had a qualification as a disabilities studies worker, but I wasn't qualified as a personal carer. I contacted my Royal Melbourne Institute of Technology (R.M.I.T.) co-ordinator.

'I don't want to do another course, but I don't have the necessary qualification. What would you suggest?' I asked.

'You'd bolt it in,' my co-ordinator replied. 'Because you are working in the industry and have completed your course, you'll have no trouble getting the necessary certificate. I'll contact your employer.'

So it was arranged, Virginia came out from R.M.I.T. and met with Helen and I at Southern Cross. I had to answer all these questions, and then lo and behold, I had my personal carer's certificate. I started work at Southern Cross Homes for the Aged straight away.

I commenced the morning shower shift from seven till eleven. It was brilliant. I loved the people. There was one particular lady I got on with like a house on fire. She reminded me so much of my own mother. We would laugh together all the time. Why wasn't I doing this while I was doing my course? Surely I could have fitted in the evening tea shift? Now all I had to do was walk around the corner from home for the morning shift after I had organized my own household. In the afternoon I had two clients in Newport whom I visited for Australian Home Care.

I was once again earning an income which was certainly a help. The best thing though was that I was now qualified to 'care' for Colleen. If one of her carers were unable to meet their commitment, I could fill in and be paid for it. It was just fantastic.

Then Australian Home Care began ringing me. Outside of the time I was at Southern Cross I would attend the homes of elderly or disabled people and just "care" for them. Things like making sure they had eaten the meal which Meals on Wheels had delivered, do a little bit of washing or take the washing off the line (perhaps only three garments) that the morning carer had hung out, or sometimes just sit and chat. As a carer, I was not expected to do any cleaning, although sometimes it would get the better of me and I would be compelled to clean up a little. Some of the houses were very unhygienic. These people were so appreciative of my presence, it was very humbling. I would go home to Colleen and be grateful that she was not like the people I had seen or the people I visited. She was not sitting in a corner being drip fed, she could talk, she could fend for herself. This helped me keep my sanity.

At Christmas time that year, we went to see Colleen perform with the band for the first time among the hustle and bustle at the Footscray Shopping Mall. As far as we could tell Colleen was hitting the right notes of the Christmas carols she had been practicing. In between carols, she would look across to where we were standing and wave to us before busily finding the music for the next carol, aided if necessary by the player sitting next to her. The band master was beaming as he conducted, but the shoppers were rather apathetic regarding the whole performance. No doubt they had more important things on their minds! For us it was so wonderful to see Colleen taking an active roll in the community.

With the year drawing to a close it was time to set goals for 2002, the most important of which was trying to secure employment for Colls.

Chapter 16

BUSY TIMES

The job advertisement would read: Young person with a bright and cheerful manner who relates well with people, required for repetitious work, three to four hours, two to three days a week, while being supervised as part of a small group.

What a tall order and narrow field of options for us to explore. When the twenty-six week placement with Safeway at Lara was completed, the SupportWorks trainer advised us Colleen had initially been keenly stacking the supermarket shelves, but she quickly became bored and disinterested. While the trainer worked with her and kept her interested Colleen's memory certainly improved, but without that stimulus, she would lose interest and her work degenerated. She needed supervision. Her pleasant demeanor though meant that we could look perhaps at something with a degree of customer service. But however approached, it was going to be difficult for us to find a job advertised which would fit her limited expertise and endurance.

Before we could settle to fine tuning Colleen's therapies and occupations for the coming year, our lease being up, we needed to find alternative rental accommodation in which to live. We were amazed when we found the house next to the Southern Cross Homes for the Aged was available for rent. We did not have to move out of the area as we had feared, which meant that the arrangements we had in place for Colleen could continue until we chose to alter them, and I was right next door to my work.

If we were going to be successful in finding employment for Colleen, we decided we needed to explore pursuits for her which would unlock her potential, and really we did not know what her potential was. Having advanced this far in her recovery, how much more could we hope for? I was still confident that given the opportunity, Colleen still had a way to go, and I refused to give up and accept the stage she had arrived at as being as good as she would become.

'I think the Footscray Community Art Centre programme is no longer stimulating Colleen sufficiently,' I said to Peter.

'Yeah, its boring,' chimed in Colleen.

'But you've brought home some great work Colleen, look at this painting,' said Peter holding up one of Colleen's masterpieces. Colleen grinned at his praise.

Her time at Footscray Art Centre had certainly been beneficial for Colleen. She had taken on a voluntary work experience placement and had received training in customer service, filing, faxing and photocopying, but having received a glowing reference referring to her great communication skills, enthusiasm for learning new things and positive interaction with others, she now needed to move on.

'What do you think Colls, will we see if we can find you something else to do, something which will help you get a job, eh?' I'd asked.

'Yeah, great Mum,' Colleen readily agreed. She was always enthusiastic when I made suggestions.

My investigations led us to the Kumon Method of learning.

'It sounds like this is just what we have been looking for,' I excitedly reported to Peter. 'The programme helps children master fundamental skills in English and mathematics. It says here that the Kumon Method was developed to unlock the potential in every child. Isn't that just what we are looking to do, to tap into Colleen's untapped abilities?'

'Is the programme designed for students like Colleen who have special needs?' Peter asked. 'I think we had better find out more. Get additional information. See if in fact they would be willing to enroll Colleen in the programme before we get too excited.'

'That's what I intend to do,' I replied.

What I found out was fascinating. The Kumon learning method commenced in Japan some fifty years ago. Mr. Toru Kumon wanted to help his son do better in school and so he created a unique instructional method focusing on his son's actual ability. The method was so successful that his son was able to do calculus by the time he was in the sixth grade. The after school programme of learning with centres in forty-four countries has helped students succeed worldwide. All the instruction comes from worksheets which are matched to each child's need. They are designed so the students move up in small increments once what they have been working on has been mastered. The student does not progress until each level has been mastered, repetition of some sets of work being done, three, four, five or as many times as is needed until he gets it right. The steps of difficulty are always very small. Some of the work is done at the Kumon centre, some at home.

'We would not be allowed to help Colleen,' I explained to Peter. 'There's a quote on the wall at the Centre that says 'be prepared to let children make mistakes, let your child develop self learning'. They correct each student's work and need to see the mistakes so the student can benefit by the correction and learn by their errors. Can you believe the Centre supervisor has to send the results of every student's worksheets into Kumon Australia's head office in Sydney where they are assessed to ensure there's smooth progress and the students feel comfortable with the material they're doing at all times. How good is that!'

'So will they take her on?' he asked.

'Yes. She is to take an initial diagnostic test which will determine a comfortable starting point with work she can complete easily. They then build gradually on her ability and the learning becomes more enjoyable and less pressured. Oh Pete, I am so excited, it all sound wonderful,' I said.

'How long will Colls attend, and how much is all this going to cost?' Peter asked.

'Because of Colleen's special learning needs, we will just have to take it month by month and see how she goes. Usually the kids attend for at least eighteen months. It costs $60.00 per month.' I told him.

'Thank goodness for the funding we receive,' Peter muttered.

'I'm sure it will be worth every dollar,' I replied.

So this new learning programme, replacing the Arts Centre programme, was added to Colleen's very busy weekly schedule. She settled into a routine which kept her fully occupied throughout the coming year.

Starting on a Monday morning, she would call in at the Southern Cross Homes for the Aged at 9.30 a.m. so I could see her safely across busy Melbourne Road on her way to the Williamstown Learning Centre. Here she was instructed in the three R's for the morning session and then had craft activities until 3.00 p.m. Her carer would see her safely home and make sure she completed her Kumon lessons in time for the evening class in which she was enrolled.

Tuesdays were a whole new experience in travel for her. Needing a slow start to the day following her Kumon class the night before, Colleen would excitedly await the arrival of her therapist who attended at the house for a fun filled hour of music. Angela would bring along all sorts of instruments, the bongos, tambourines, castanets, and a keyboard and they would sing and have a fantastic time. As I walked up the path at the end of my nursing home shift, it was wonderful to hear their laughter as Colleen attempted to play the various instruments, and sang off key. Then just before midday, we would enjoy a healthy snack before Colleen embarked on her journey to Love's Cake Kitchen. Paul had purchased this business in February.

'Do you think you'd like to come and work for me, Colls?' Paul enquired after he had settled into his new venture. He had already floated the idea before me and we had discussed how Colleen would get there. I accompanied her on a few trips to accustom her with the routine, and then left it up to her to cope with her weekly journey. She would catch a train from Newport to Flinders Street Station, Melbourne's busy central terminal, and then change platforms to catch the train out to Caulfield Station from where she would catch a taxi to Love's in East Malvern. I could not believe that she was able to successfully, and more importantly safely navigate this journey, but she actually enjoyed this expedition. I think her attitude to the work at the shop was another matter.

'It's boring, Mum. All I do is dry the dishes and stuff,' she said to me after she had been attending the shop for several weeks.

Paul laughed when I told him.

'I'm sure it's because I'm her brother. She thinks she can get away with complaining about everything,' he said.

He went on to tell me he would get her to make up the boxes for the cakes to be packaged in, or have her bag some biscuits ready for sale. She would also make breadcrumbs using a kitchen appliance designed for the purpose. He said she had to be supervised at all times, was very slow and was able to concentrate only for short periods of time.

'I'm always pleased when Auntie Pat comes to collect her,' he said chuckling. 'She sure is hard work.'

This conversation I had with Paul reinforced our concern about how difficult it would be to find employment for Colleen. Still, just the exercise of having to negotiate her way to the shop was a learning experience, and we were very grateful that Paul was giving her the chance to be in the work force. My sister Pat would take Colleen home for afternoon tea, a sleep and a walk before returning her to us in Newport.

On Wednesdays Colleen would attend Stonnington Children's Centre working on a voluntary basis from 9.00 a.m. to 12 noon before returning home with her carer Margaret Wilson, who would assist her prepare a healthy lunch. I would then have a range of activities organized for her to do for the rest of the day. We felt it was very important that the tasks we set were enjoyable and therefore aided her progression. In addition to her Kumon homework lessons, she would job search thereby brushing up on her computer skills, do reading or any one of the many other tasks I had put in place for her. Margaret would have Colleen read articles out of the newspaper and would then discuss them with her. She helped her tremendously with her social skills. It wasn't all work though. Often they would play UNO together. I would listen with delight as she and Margaret sat at the kitchen table laughing as they played. Margaret had a hard job to beat Colleen. They got on so well.

Sarah Olsen the Thursday carer would take her the next day to St. Albans Primary School where she continued to help in the art room from 9.00 a.m. until noon. Sarah and Colleen would then do some cooking, go swimming, exercise or power walk, read the paper and search the local job market. Then at 6.00 p.m. either Peter or I would take her to her second Kumon lesson for the week. Following this, fortnightly, we would go on to the Police Barracks at South Melbourne for her Riding for the Disabled session at 7.00 p.m. Lessons ceased in June and we arranged hydro therapy to replace this activity. On the alternate Thursdays, Colleen would attend Rotoract (a junior Rotary group) at Williamstown. This was marvellous as Colleen was able to socialize with a mixed group of young people, average age thirty, and was always invited to attend their social nights out. In the second half of the year she attended an International Dinner with the group.

Because her week was so jam packed with activities, Fridays were paced slower. Colleen had a well earned sleep in, then attended leisurely to some of her lessons before being taken either by a carer or Peter or I for a private swimming lesson at Laverton in the afternoon. In October another Friday activity was added for a month. Libby Calloway who had been instrumental in finding Pirra Lodge for us, suggested that her trainee occupational therapist could assist Colleen with cooking, including the purchase of the ingredients at the supermarket. We continued to be concerned about Colleen's weight. No matter how diligent we were about her food intake, her weight was still increasing. We hoped that this assignment would help

Colleen to make the right choices not only about the food she chose to eat but the quantity she had.

Then enthusiastically on a Saturday morning Colleen would head off for band practice. The music was of such a high standard, I could not believe how she managed it.

Peter turned sixty in April. He insisted that he did not want any fuss but I thought we could not let it pass without some sort of celebration. He had belonged to a Y.C.W. (Young Christian Workers) group, formed through the church when the young men left school and commenced work so that the Christian group would stay together. Now aged sixty and over they still meet socially each year, have a gospel reading and plan social outings, and sometimes celebrate birthdays together. Paul organized the food and the group came and joined the family for a surprise afternoon tea. Peter was very touched and to top if off the kids gave us tickets to Sydney. We added a couple of extra nights and leaving Colleen in their care had a lovely break.

The second half of 2002 was particularly busy, and not only through having to keep up with Colleen's activities. I travelled to Queensland in August for the celebration of my sister Maree's sixtieth birthday. A surprise party had been organized for the occasion, and I decided Peter and the family could cope with Colleen for the short time that I would be away.

My focus on Colleen was taking its toll. I needed time out. Peter and I were not seeing eye to eye. Indeed we were having trouble communicating. Was it because my quest for Colleen's recovery was all consuming? Looking back now all I know is that I was trying to do my very best. Sometimes that seemed not to be enough. Perhaps I spread myself too thin as far as the rest of the family was concerned. But wasn't Colleen's need greater than theirs? I was aware that Peter was still experiencing difficulty in coming to terms with Colleen's illness, in fact at times it seemed he could not rise above the bouts of depression which gripped him. I suppose I thought I had enough to deal with organizing Colleen without having to prop him up too. I felt totally overwhelmed.

Suzanne was rightly expecting me to show a keen interest in her wedding which was scheduled for the end of October, but as she and Jim were making all the arrangements, I could only listen as she excitedly told me about their plans for the service at Geelong Grammar, and the reception to follow at the Barwon Head's Golf Club. I think she sensed my reticence because she seemed to withdraw from not only Peter and I, but the rest of the family too. It was as though she did not want our preoccupation with Colleen to encroach on what was her special time. We walked on egg shells in our conversations with Suzanne regarding the wedding.

I had come to terms with the wedding not taking place in a Catholic church. The important thing was that it was to be a faith based ceremony, and after all it was their choice. Suzanne would have known the significance I placed on a church wedding, and one night when she and Jim were on the way back from Geelong she rang me.

'Mum, we thought we would drop in and see you and Dad. We've just been to see the minister. The service is just going to be fantastic. We want to tell you all about it,' she said excitedly.

Unfortunately it was an occasion when Peter and I had been at variance and I just felt I could not cope. We were at breaking point. The constancy of catering for Colleen's needs and trying to accept her disabilities was taking its toll.

'No Sooz,' I said as gently as I could. 'You can't come over. Not tonight' I thought I heard a catch in her voice as she said goodbye and hung up. It was a very emotional time for us all.

The night before the wedding I cooked a roast dinner at the house we had hired at Barwon Heads and transported it to the house a couple of blocks away where Suzanne and her bridesmaids were staying. We had a family dinner together and the tension that had been building in the lead up to the wedding dissipated as we chatted animatedly enjoying each other's company.

All went exceptionally well on the day. Shaun drove Suzanne with Peter to the church, and Paul and Rachael took Colleen and I. Colleen, in an outfit created by my Broadford dressmaker Lena, handed out the orders of service to the guests as they arrived.

The next day we all relaxed in a warm and friendly atmosphere at the post wedding barbeque. We were all pleased that everything had gone like clockwork for Suzanne and Jim.

Christmas was not far away. We were no closer to finding Colleen employment. Every three weeks during the year she had attended an employment agency at Footscray, but to no avail. Still we refused to give up. I made contact with D.E.A.C. (Disability Employment Action Centre) to see if they could offer Colleen skill based training that would lead to employment. This agency provides legal services for people with a disability and assists in accessing employment through a variety of social services. Also with the year drawing to a close I had investigated T.A.F.E. (Technical and Further Education) courses for her for the coming year. She was doing well with her Kumon lessons and had received Achievement Certificates. I was always on the lookout for ways to further stimulate her brain and perhaps capture some of the person she once had been.

Colleen had been assigned a new Case Manager with Care Connect, a not for profit organization which works for people with complex care needs to improve their quality of life and ability to remain living in the community. This joint State and Federal Government programme took over Colleen's management and funding from Melbourne City Mission and assigned a new Case Manager. Towards the end of the year they offered Colleen a week's holiday at Yarra Trails for which they would pay $2,200. This seemed exorbitant and I suggested as an alternative an upgrade of Coll's flute. A lifetime of pleasure to be gained from her music seemed to me to be far more beneficial than a week's holiday, especially as she seemed to be doing so well with her music.

'Is she doing OK?' I asked the band leader. I was curious to know if she was really contributing or if they were having difficulties with her. But I was assured she was doing fine, and there were no problems. I decided they either didn't want to know or her playing must've been reasonable. This was confirmed some time later.

'Mum, guess what?' I'm going to be in a concert!' Colleen excitedly announced when she arrived home from band practice one Saturday afternoon.

'Really Colleen? That's great,' I replied.

Sure enough a few weeks later there was Colleen with an intense look of concentration on her face, sitting up in the front row of the Band as they performed for their annual "Last Night at the Proms" concert.

I leaned across to Peter and whispered with a chuckle, 'Is she bluffing do you think? Is she only pretending to blow the notes?'

But there were no wrong notes that I could hear and I could only assume she was contributing.

'Well done Colleen,' Peter said giving her a big bear hug after the performance.

'Yeah, it was grouse!' Colls replied. 'It was really hard though,' she confessed, and my eyes pricked with tears as I thought just how far she had come.

In November we sold Broadford. Shaun was devastated. He had come to regard this home as his own. He had spent a lot of his time there alone since Colleen had taken ill. His childhood sweetheart Laura had been tremendously supportive during this time. Now as a final farewell he wanted to have his twenty-first birthday celebrated there. Before we sold we had made a concerted effort and the garden looked beautiful. By December we had moved most of our things to Melbourne and the house was virtually empty. The garden was a dust bowl.

'The place looks terrible, Shaun,' I said.

'I don't care. I want the party in my backyard,' Shaun insisted.

So everything had to be transported from Melbourne back to Broadford; crockery, cutlery, tables and chairs. For some reason the girls were out of it, over it, switched off. Peter was absolutely out of it. So on my own I catered for one hundred people. I took everything to Broadford for this crappy party. Shaun thought it was the best party ever. He had a wonderful time.

It would seem that 2002 would pass without finding employment for Colleen. But then a couple of weeks before Christmas, success came from an unexpected quarter.

Chapter 17

BACK TO THE ALFRED

'I reckon Colls could help Kelly,' Peter said to me one night when he returned from his shift at the Alfred Hospital.

Kelly was a young woman, mid twenties, who worked in the mail room at the hospital. She was a bright, bubbly girl who had special needs. Peter had become friendly with her, probably took an interest in her because of Colleen.

'I'll make some enquiries,' he had said.

He did. He asked the management if they thought it would be possible for Colleen to perhaps accompany Kelly to learn the ropes. He told them that if they were to take Colleen on she would need some assistance initially and perhaps some ongoing guidance. He kept on about it. Anyway eventually he must've convinced them it was a good idea because finally they said yes.

'That's fantastic, Pete,' I said, and was delighted to see him more animated than I had in a long while. I think he felt at last he was contributing to Colleen's progress in a tangible way.

It took about a month to set up. Firstly we had to obtain approval from the Slow to Recover Programme and Colleen's case manager in due course gave us the go ahead. Peter and I worked in conjunction with Libby Calloway (Colleen's occupational therapist), a representative of the Alfred Hospital, and the case manager. After several meetings we finally had a programme in place. Colleen was to work two thirteen week blocks. Work structures were put in place so that she was not held responsible for the complete task. Someone would always oversee her work. After clocking on in the morning, she was to work for three hours delivering the mail to certain areas of the hospital. As long as someone kept an eye on her it was thought she would cope. The other thing she had to contend with was the travel.

At that time Peter's shifts were mostly in the mornings. Walking together to Newport train station, they would catch firstly the train to the city and then a tram up St. Kilda Road to the Alfred. Colleen would do her three hour shift commencing at 8.30 a.m. and then, initially helped by Libby Calloway with Slow to Recover funding, travel home. After several trips with Libby she had mastered the routine and managed on her own.

We now entered a new practice with Colleen being responsible for getting up bright and early and being ready in time to leave, on most days with Peter, four days a week. It was very wonderful seeing them head off together. For so long this is what we had hoped would be achieved, Colleen taking up a useful role in society. She was being paid the princely sum of $10.17 per hour, a combined payment made by the Alfred and the Government. Here was an organization willing to give her a go. She was on her way. We thought it was fantastic. Colleen hated it.

'What did you think you were doing Colleen?' Peter asked her one night after she had been at the job for several weeks.

'I was hungry,' she answered petulantly.

Peter had walked passed the canteen and there was Colleen sitting back and taking her time over a cup of coffee and a muffin.

'You can't take time out on the boss's time,' he said. 'You have a job to do and he's not paying you to drink coffee.'

I supposed she was expending a lot of energy, walking to the station and then around the hospital, but part of the effect of her brain injury was that she ate indiscriminately anyway. We were now faced with the unfortunate combination of her not liking the job, together with the compulsion to eat, influencing her behaviour. We had always let her have a little bit of money in her purse but now found we had to discontinue this as she could never help herself where food was concerned.

'Colls, you're only there for three hours. You should be able to wait until you arrive home to eat,' I suggested. She certainly had a reserve of padding to see her through the morning.

I so much wanted this job to be successful for Colleen. If she could be disciplined sufficiently to carry out her tasks responsibly it would perhaps lead the way to further employment. Not only was this wonderful for Colleen, but I could see how beneficial this period of employment for Colleen was for Peter. He had told me of Colleen's first day on the job.

'I couldn't believe it. When I walked into the temporary staff office with Colleen she was greeted enthusiastically by the folk there,' he said. 'It was as though she was normal and didn't have special needs.'

As she settled into the job, the people at the Alfred came to know Colleen as "Peter's daughter". For him this was very special as during the time of Colleen's illness he had thought people saw her as "Bernadette's daughter". Now he was contributing and had a role to play in her recovery.

Not all of his experiences were positive like this and some were even charged with emotion.

'I feel people are staring at me all the time,' he told me. He was constantly whispering to Colleen to hurry up. Sometimes she seemed totally unaware of time constraints.

One morning there were no seats available on the train and a young woman immediately offered Colleen her seat.

'I had trouble controlling my emotions,' Peter told me. 'Then the person next to her offered me a seat. I had to dig around for my handkerchief and covered my tears by blowing my nose,' he said. 'I was really touched that these people were so kind and considerate.'

As time went on and Peter's shifts did not coincide with Colleen's work time, she would make the journey both ways on her own. On these occasions when Peter arrived for his shift, he would wander around to the office to check that she had arrived safely.

One Thursday her sleep had been disturbed by emergency vehicles in Melbourne Road during the night and consequently she was not properly rested by morning.

'What say I drive you into work today, Colls?' Peter told me he had suggested. He was not due at the hospital himself until later that day. Great idea, except that day the traffic over West Gate Bridge was chaotic.

'I'm going to be late, Dad. Just take me to Footscray Station. I'll catch the train,' Peter told me Colleen, with rising panic, had said.

Rather than get her more agitated, he agreed and headed back home after leaving her at the station.

At 11.00 a.m. the phone rang. Colleen was in the emergency department at the Alfred.

'I freaked out walking into Emergency,' Peter told me. 'All I could think of was that dreadful day when Colls was first taken to hospital. It all came flooding back.'

This time Colleen required a couple of stitches to a gash in her leg. Being fretful that she was going to be late for work, in her distress she had got her leg caught in the door of the train.

The first thirteen week block ended and Colleen with perhaps a little more enthusiasm launched into the second term. It was during this time that Peter and I were thrilled to put a deposit on our house in Ashburton. It would be wonderful to shift out of rental accommodation into a home of our own again. The timing was perfect. Colleen would have completed her time at the Alfred when we shifted in, and we would then be able to explore fresh avenues for her in the new suburb. Because Ashburton was the other side of Melbourne from Williamstown, we would need to reorganize her therapies, but we thought this might be a good thing and give her other experiences.

Also we had plans for organizing more independent living quarters for her. The new house had a garage in the back yard which we thought might be able to be converted into a little flat. A more ambitious idea was to install a granny flat in the back yard. Both ventures would need a good deal of capital. But I wasn't going to let a little thing like lack of finances hold us back. There just had to be a way.

A change in her living environment together with a new routine would be good for her too. We had had to put up with yelling and screaming matches. She did not like the situation we were in.

'Why are you working?' she'd shout at me. 'Why can't you stay home and be with me?'

'Because we are renting Colleen, because we want to get out of here,' I would reply quietly. Most times she would see sense and calm down.

I sometimes found our situation a little bit depressing too. Our twenty-six year old daughter should've been out having fun, or working as a normal woman her age does. Instead we had to cope with where she was.

I came home one night to find she had made a batch of drop scones and eaten the lot. Another day she made a cake and then ate more than half of it, leaving only a couple of pieces for Peter and I. It was as if she was only ten or eleven. But you have to move on. Build on the positives. The band was going on a camp, and Colleen was to accompany them. She was so excited. Arrangements had to be fine tuned, but we were as thrilled as our daughter. Each experience like this was a step forward. Unfortunately fate took a hand.

During the time Colleen had been at the Alfred, we had rearranged her other activities to take place in the afternoons. Margaret Wilson was still her main carer but we had to arrange for a further carer to fill in for the times that Margaret was not available. We had met this lovely couple at church. Katherine O'Keefe, was one of their eight children. She was an occupational therapist and when I said we were looking for another carer we arranged for her to join the Australian Home Care organization so she could look after Colleen. The girls got on famously. They did the gym programme and other activities. Everything was going along so well. Then towards the end of the second thirteen week block at the Alfred, Colleen broke her ankle. It was beyond me why the girls would set off on their expedition with Colleen not wearing her leg support, wearing only loose canvas shoes. Katherine's family was very embarrassed. We were very annoyed. It was a terrible situation.

We weren't the only ones who were angry. While waiting to have the ankle pinned, Colleen expressed her frustration.

'I hate this plaster. I hate this wheelchair,' she said angrily.

'Listen here Colleen,' I said, 'you made the choice to go for a walk without the proper shoes and without your leg support. You're not to use that word hate ever again. We're in this mess and half of it's your fault and the other half is Katherine's. It's certainly not mine. You've stuffed everything up, Colleen. The shift to our new home, and the job interview you had next Wednesday. So listen here honey, get hate out of your vocabulary because we're not going there. We have to deal with this and it's a bloody nuisance, Colleen.'

'Yeah, all right Mum. I'm sorry, I'm sorry,' she kept on saying repeatedly.

'Please don't keep saying sorry,' I said softening. 'It's OK, I didn't mean to be angry but all this is really unnecessary.'

So there we were with Colleen back in hospital the day before her twenty-seventh birthday. She looked as white as white. She was so confused with the transfers and had found it all very traumatic. I could see it had been terribly draining for her. But the reception she received on being admitted to the Alfred was just electric.

'Oh, Colleen, you've come back to us. We all loved you. Haven't you done well.' I could not believe the staff remembered her and was delighted with their reception. Then a new male nurse came in.

'I've read just one-tenth of your history Colleen. You've had a very interesting five years. Wow, what a success story,' he said.

That night I visited again and found Suzanne and Christine in the ward with her. Over the past couple of days Christine had again taken up the role of carer. I was concerned because she had taken two days off work to be with Colleen.

'How can you do that, Christine?' I had asked her the day before.

'I'm old enough to deal with my issues Mum, just back off,' she retorted.

I always seemed to be putting my foot in it with Christine. When she had been sorting Colleen's clothes to take to hospital I commented on her efforts.

'Oh, beautifully folded,' I said sarcastically.

'Trust you to find fault,' she said stuffing yet another garment roughly into the carry bag.

I knew I should not have said it but it was out before I could help myself. We seemed destined to clash. I backed off.

Now here she and Suzanne were in the hospital, playing charades with Colleen in her wheelchair, having the best fun. Although it was classic watching them, it was eerie too. I got this impression that Colleen was quite normal. She seemed so sharp, so switched on. She spoke so naturally. Was it just because she was being led by Suzanne and Christine? Was I a drawback? Had I just been feeding the problem by the way I had been handling Colleen's rehabilitation?

I left them to it. Traveling home in the car the tears ran unchecked down my face.

'Whatever is the matter?' Peter asked when I arrived home and threw myself down onto the couch covering my face with my hands.

'What have I been doing?' I said through my tears. 'I feel so inadequate.'

I told him about my impressions of Colleen that night.

'No, Bern. Colleen wouldn't be where she is today it if wasn't for your efforts,' Peter said gently.

I managed a tremulous smile.

'Perhaps I could get her into a theatre or drama group?' I said blowing my nose. 'You should've seen her Pete. The girls were so funny. Colls was so entertaining.' I stopped. 'What are you laughing at?' I said.

'You. See, you're always thinking of ways to take Colleen forward,' Peter said still grinning. 'Don't ever think you're inadequate.'

'Perhaps it won't be so bad having Colleen out of the house,' I suggested giving my nose another hearty blow. 'We'll get shifted and settled into our new home. We know she will have the very best of care at Royal Talbot while she is in rehabilitation, and meanwhile we'll have a break.'

'Will we be able to keep up her activities while she's in care?' Peter asked.

This was something that I had been very concerned about. It was essential that she be stimulated. At that time she was allocated twenty hours care a week and we knew we would have to ensure that her activities continued during her time in rehabilitation.

'Perhaps I'll see if she can do some tapestry, discover some new skills.' My mind was racing again, thinking of the possibilities. 'We just have to think out of the square and hopefully there'll be some great positives to come out of all this. The first thing, Pete, is to get her settled at Royal Talbot and see if we can organize for her carers to attend there.'

The other thing we wanted to explore was the preferred option of building Colleen a granny flat to further her independence.

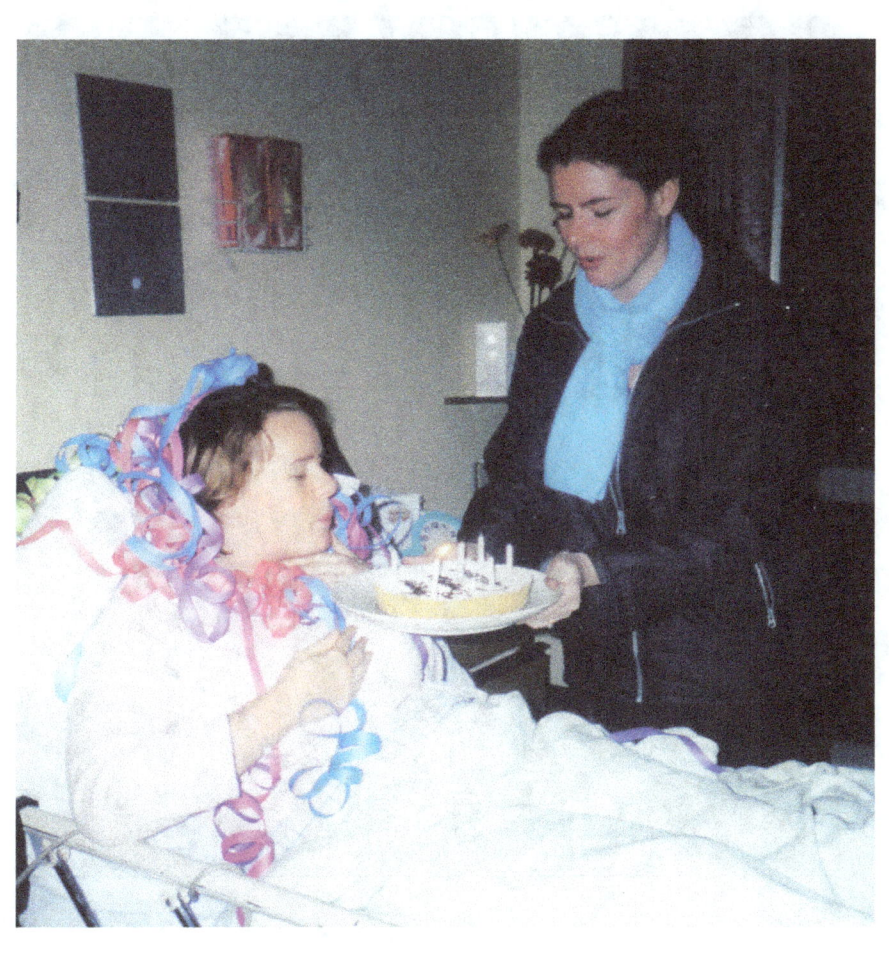

Colleen celebrating her 27th birthday in the Alfred Hospital with Suzanne

Colleen with Christine

At home in Newport the wheelchair helps with broken ankle

Chapter 18

THE GRANNY FLAT

The reception Colleen received at the Alfred was special. The welcome she received at Royal Talbot was amazing. She was placed in a different unit from her first time there, but was able to travel in her wheelchair to visit the Acquired Brain Injury (A.B.I.) Unit. She remembered the names of all the medical staff and the women in the kiosk, and when she visited the gymnasium and physiotherapy rooms she chatted animatedly with the therapists who had been so important in her recovery.

After being confined in the Alfred for eight days, she now had relative freedom in Royal Talbot. The transition was quite easy for her because of her familiarity with the staff. She was housed with other wheelchair patients, of lot of them male amputees. Despite her exuberance, zipping here and there in her chair, she found that the other patients did not really respond all that readily.

'Nobody talks much, Mum,' she said to me when Paul and I visited one day.

Paul found the visit quite depressing.

'Well Paul, this is where we have to be. We just have to get on with it and get Colleen out of here,' I said to him.

After the initial excitement of the first few days, Colleen was bored out of her brain and very frustrated with inactivity.

My attempt to interest her in knitting had failed. I thought perhaps I could introduce her to tapestry or craft, something to keep her hands occupied. She was similarly disinterested. I was delighted that limited funding was to continue whilst she was hospitalized and Margaret was able to attend twice a week to supervise her Kumon lessons. Colleen had not responded to my overtures of encouragement for her to do her work. Margaret also went with Colleen to the computer room and they would send emails. This was a wonderful way to improve on her word skills. Sometimes there would be words missing, or perhaps the sentence would not quite make sense, and a couple of spelling mistakes wasn't the end of the world, but at least it was some communication. It was exciting for her too when Suzanne, Christine, or her friends Nardia, Jackie, Sarah or Belinda replied to her letters.

These activities helped with her language and speech skills. She was speaking very fast, we believed because she was in an agitated state.

'Slow down, I didn't understand what you said. It's no good Colleen, I'm just going to shake my head. That means I don't have a clue what you are saying. It will show you that you will have to slow your speech down,' I said to her in desperation one day.

Because of her environment, we believed she'd had a bit of a set back. Her self confidence had suffered a blow and she was worried about her weight.

As time had gone on some of her restlessness gave way to resignation, but she had turned to the comfort of food. In no time at all her seventy kilogram weight had increased to eighty-six. The girl who weighed her was singularly unhelpful when I suggested the kitchen be advised that Colleen was to have a high fibre low fat diet.

'Well, she just has to make the right choices,' she said.

'I am fully aware of that, but are you not aware that she has an acquired brain injury?' I asked

She shrugged her shoulders and replied, 'We all have to make choices in life.'

'Excuse me, I live with this day in and day out and I know damn well what Colleen is capable of and I know she won't make the right choices. If she has the choice of a chocolate or dry biscuit, I know what she will choose,' I said and stormed off to ring the occupational therapist with my complaint about this attitude.

After I had calmed down a bit the occupational therapist persuaded me to leave it for a short while. Colleen knew putting on weight was the wrong thing. She could never commit a crime without confessing. So I was heartened when she advised me a couple of days later that she had her main meal for lunch and salad for tea.

'If I'm allowed a sweet I have a low fat jelly or a yoghurt,' she told me.

'Just as well for you!' I admonished her. No way was I going to say, oh well done. 'Unless you continue to be careful about what you eat not only will your knee collapse, but you will have trouble with your hip. It's up to you Colleen.'

Art and drama classes helped to keep her occupied.

'It was a scream, Mum,' she told me one day. 'At drama, three of us pretended we were in a night club. We had so much fun,' she said, her eyes shinning with delight.

That is the other avenue I must explore for her when she comes home I thought remembering the incident in hospital with Christine and Suzanne.

After four weeks Colleen returned to the Alfred for the plaster to be removed and her foot was placed in a moon boot. At first she was not able to weight bear on the injured ankle but eventually when physiotherapy commenced this gave her much more mobility. The nursing staff was very particular about supervising how much weight she put on her leg and made sure that she did not overdo it. One day she told me she had been naughty.

'I was ringing and ringing, Mum, and no one came,' she said. 'I just had to go!' Because of this excursion to the toilet by herself, she was not allowed to do physiotherapy that day.

By now we were comfortably settled into our new home in Ashburton. With Colleen more mobile, we thought it would be wonderful if she could come and visit. We have a family day in late July and as it was a special occasion, we were given permission to take Colleen out for it. Christine and Gavan collected her and were impressed with how she managed to transfer herself from the wheelchair into the car. It was brilliant to watch as she excitedly wheeled herself through the rooms of our new house.

My brother Peter always manages to put on a spectacular do. Three generations, about sixty-five of us meet at his home for a catered meal. Over the years we have been gathering material for our family tree, and this was an opportunity to do some more work on it. Suzanne and Jim decided to run a quiz with multiple choice answers. We had a family crest made which would become a perpetual trophy. One of the questions was: why did Colleen fall over and break her ankle? The answers to choose from were; one, to get away from Mum and Dad; two, to go back to Royal Talbot, aren't 391 days enough for her; and three, to get seven screws. It was fantastic to hear the hilarity this question caused and to see the joy on Colleen's face at being back in the family fold and a part of this gathering.

Reluctantly she had returned to Royal Talbot and we were pleased when in the coming days she made friends with a girl, Kathleen who at thirty-five had also suffered an aneurism. This might be a really good buddy situation we thought, but unfortunately the friendship did not develop.

'She cries a lot, Mum,' Colleen told me. 'I just tell her I'll come back when she is not crying.'

Once again the tragedy of acquired brain injury was brought home to us. No brain injury is the same. What was the future to hold for this young woman? Was a nursing home going to be the only option?

Friends Mary and Udo who were so good to Colleen when she was at Pirra Lodge, came to visit her.

'You'll never guess what,' Mary said. 'Pirra Lodge has closed.

'No!' Why?' I asked in amazement.

'I don't think they were making any money out of it, or the Government dropped the subsidy or something,' Mary said.

'Also I think the building had to be upgraded, fire safety issues or some such thing. Perhaps it just became unviable,' said Udo.

'How terrible! What about the patients who lived there?' I queried.

'Well I guess they had to be shifted to somewhere else,' said Mary shrugging her shoulders.

I was stunned. There were so few places catering for acquired brain injury patients, and now there was one less. Twelve young people would have lost their accommodation and may have had to go into a nursing home. Although Pirra Lodge was a Transport Accident Commission (T.A.C.) facility, they did have the flexibility to cater for people like Colleen. Now even this was not available.

'There should be more places like Pirra Lodge instead of young people being placed in nursing homes.

Why can't anyone see this?' I said angrily. And not for the first time, and no doubt not for the last, I wished I had a pot of gold to turn into appropriate accommodation for these young people.

It had been hoped that the money which was raised progressively through the years by successive Fun Runs would eventually, when sufficient had accumulated, be used to provide accommodation for young people with acquired brain injury. When the project became too much for the family to handle we approached Melbourne City Mission in the hope that they would be able to take over the project. We presented them with all the marketing means we had employed, the videos that had been made of the two Fun Runs, all our bookwork and brochures, and suggested it was a project begging for some organization to co-ordinate. When we initially approached them they advised they were committed for that year, but said they may think about it the next year. Unfortunately they never took it up. So the money the kids had raised just sat in the ANZ Fun Run bank account.

Over the years we had attended many workshops and acquired brain injury forums. Different community groups and government departments campaigned for appropriate accommodation for young people instead of them having to be provided for in nursing homes. All the pleas for assistance for people having to care at home for loved ones with an acquired brain injury, and accounts of how stressful this burden can be fell on deaf ears. It would appear the Government had still not been convinced that accommodation is required nor turned its mind to addressing the problem.

'If these pro-active groups have failed to even raise awareness of, let alone find a solution to the problem, how the hell are we going to do it?' I raged to Peter.

'What if we use the money raised by the Fun Runs to help us provide accommodate for Colleen?' Peter asked.

'Do you think we could?' I queried.

After much deliberation and consultation we decided to apply the money to help install a granny flat in the backyard at Ashburton. Because it was to be a free standing structure, in the future in the event that Colleen no longer needed to be catered for, it could be shifted and used to help someone else with an acquired brain injury. Peter and I used our own resources and the funds raised by the Fun Runs contributed to about a quarter of the cost of the granny flat, and we thought well, we will sort that out down the track if and when we need to.

'I can't help feeling a little bit guilty about using the money just for Colleen,' I said to Peter. 'That wasn't what we had planned.'

'Ninety per cent of the people who participated in the Fun Runs were our friends, family and their connections. I'm sure these people would prefer the money to be used. After all it has just sat in the bank account for five years, surely it's preferable that it not sit there for another five years or indefinitely,' Peter replied.

'I won't give up. My dream is still to get on a committee and fight for the cause of accommodation for acquired brain injury victims,' I said with resolve. I sighed. The enormity of the task was not lost on me. I found that my time was swallowed up with looking after Colleen, coordinating her therapies, looking for employment for her, getting her involved in special needs groups, connecting into the community, and visiting this or that specialist or trying to find a doctor who may be able to help with her excessive weight gain. At times I felt completely overwhelmed.

The necessary approvals were granted, and work on the granny flat commenced in October. Shaun had been working with a builder for some time and was well on the way to achieving his ambition of becoming a qualified builder. At the end of an eight hour day on the job, he would rush into the drive, unload his tools and throw himself wholeheartedly into construction. The project became a huge family effort. I became very efficient at sourcing materials, and even the girls chipped in, with Colleen anxiously looking on as the work progressed. Paul would call in too to help. He was not very good with tools (Peter even less proficient) but Shaun would patiently teach him how to put things together. Colleen (who had recently been discharged from Royal Talbot) would fuss over Shaun every time he came. It was a big project but as the weeks went by I was delighted to see the flat taking shape.

About this time Colleen had an unfortunate incident which left her quite shaken. It was the end of the day and I was helping her get ready for bed. I had ducked out of the bathroom leaving her having a shower which was situated over our very old deep bath with a curved base.

'Mum!' I heard her scream preceded by a crash and dull thud.

I rushed to the bathroom fearing what I would find.

'I slipped over Mum,' she said tearfully. She sat in the bath holding the soap holder tile up to me. 'I broke this off the wall.'

'Never mind about that, are you all right?' I asked anxiously. I could see a little bit of blood staining the bath, but thought, oh you'll be all right. But I could not get her out of the bath by myself. Peter had gone to visit Paul so I summonsed them. When Colls was upright we found she had a gaping hole in her buttock where she had collided with the broken tile. So at 9.00 p.m. we were off to the Alfred again. At 2.00 a.m. we arrived home with a very distressed Colleen sporting twelve stitches to repair the damage. How lucky we were that she had not suffered some other more serious injury. She could have broken her hip.

A few months after we had shifted to Ashburton I had ceased my employment with the Southern Cross Homes for the Aged in Williamstown. It had become tiresome travelling from Ashburton to the other side of Melbourne for my employment and I was pleased when I secured four shifts at Highwood Court Aged Care Facility in Ashwood, only a short drive from our home. It was much more convenient being available to cater for Colleen's needs when she had returned home from Royal Talbot by being employed part time. Now with the granny flat construction well under way, and planning for Christine and Gavan's wedding on New Year's Eve I had plenty to think about.

In September I had completed a four months floral arts course and Christine had suggested I do the flowers for the wedding. Paul and Rachael had purchased a home in East Malvern, and the reception was to be there after the wedding service which took place in an old bluestone church in Port Melbourne. Christine decided not to have any attendants, just a little flower girl. She had something special in mind for Colleen.

'How would you like to walk down the aisle with me Colls?' she asked.

'Yeah! Really?' Colleen replied, and she turn to me and asked, 'Can I, Mum?'

'Christine that is a lovely idea, of course you can Colls,' I said.

'And can I have another new dress?' Colleen asked excitedly. It had only been a little over twelve months since Suzanne and Jim's wedding.

I laughed. 'Why not,' I said. I planned to make my own outfit from a style I had seen in a dress shop and thought I could stretch the budget to get Colleen something new too.

The 31st December, 2003 was a very hot day. The challenge was to keep the forty cream rosebuds to go with Christine's coffee coloured lace dress, from opening up too much. I made up the bridal bouquet and the posy for the flower girl as well as the buttonholes for the men. I put them in a box in the boot to transport them to Moonee Ponds where we had photos taken while sipping champagne in the gardens with eight of Christine's girlfriends before the wedding. We then drove to the church in Port Melbourne.

No mater how emotional I knew I would feel when I saw Christine and Peter coming down the aisle with Colleen beside them, I determined I would not cry. After all it was a happy occasion. I firmly planted a grin on my face and as I turned to watch them approach I realized that I had left the men's buttonhole flowers in the boot of the car. Oh, Bern you are so silly, I thought. I am sure no-one noticed and I pinned them on before the photos were taken.

In the lead up to the wedding Christine, Peter and I had spent hours helping Paul and Rachael prepare their house for the occasion and had festooned the garden with hundreds of fairy lights. Christine being a home body, did not want a reception place, but all the eighty or so guests were catered for in great style with finger food being served throughout the night up to and after the stroke of midnight and the guests continued partying on into the New Year until five a.m.

I wondered as I crawled into bed what the New Year would bring. It would be exciting, knowing it was nearing completion, establishing Colleen in the granny flat. Would I be able to find employment for her? In addition to my four shifts at the Aged Care Facility, I had just taken up employment again with my brother Terry at Lifestyle and Rehabilitation in Brunswick and needed to ensure that Colleen was occupied when I was not at home.

I had a good feeling about 2004 and hoped my expectations would be realized.

Shaun commences work on the granny flat

The completed granny flat

Chapter 19

AFL SPORTSREADY

'Pete, what do you think about this?' I asked.

It was late one Sunday afternoon in early January. We were sitting outside with Colleen in the shade on the deck at the back of our home. Earlier I had encouraged her to make an attempt to tidy her room. It was always a mess with her clothes left where she climbed out of them. Left to her own devices she could live in total, amazing chaos. The sultry heat of the day didn't encourage activity and she'd soon lost interest in the task. I'd kept on saying to myself, this can't continue, I'm not going to tolerate her untidiness any longer, but I'd said it so many times without resolution that I'd decided I would have to change tack, work out another mechanism. But it was too hot for it to be this day. Perhaps when she was in the granny flat it would be different.

I had been languidly turning the pages of the local paper as I sipped an icy glass of wine and tried to work up enthusiasm to prepare our evening meal. Since Colleen had returned home from Royal Talbot in August, each week, I avidly scanned the papers in the hope that I would find some meaningful occupation for her. I had spied an advertisement.

'An organization called AFL Sportsready are offering traineeships, I wonder what that's all about?' I said.

'Only one way to find out,' Peter replied.

So the next day I rang them. My enquiry started Colleen on what was to be a rewarding four year association with this establishment.

AFL Sportsready is a not-for-profit employment and training organization with high profile Essendon football legend Kevin Sheedy as Patron, and Bill Kelty, a key figure in the Australian Trade Union movement as Chairman. Initially conceived by Kevin Sheedy to provide football players with an entry into the work force, subsequently Sportsready traineeships became available to all young male and female school leavers in not only sport related employment but in any industry. By providing trainees with direction and support, the programme helps them to achieve long-term vocational goals and obtain lasting employment. With the important values of honesty, mutual respect and co-operation being promoted as the key to the success of the trainees, Sportsready aims to foster an environment that empowers the individual. Its goal, by providing relevant education and on-the-job training, is to sustain a high quality service to meet the needs of the trainees and host employers.

I was so excited when I got off the phone having found out all this from my initial contact.

'I told them briefly about Colleen, and asked would there be any hope of them considering her for a traineeship. Guess what they said.? Apply for it!' I said breathlessly. 'We are to fill in the application and send it in. They said let them worry about any problems that might be encountered. I have a really good feeling about this, Pete. Their attitude was fantastic.'

So I had knuckled down to complete the application form. I wrote all the things Colleen could do rather than list what she was unable to do. Ultimately we were called in for an interview with John Keogh and his boss Philip Warbridge, the Chief Executive Officer, who before taking this position with Sportsready had been principal of Xavier

College after leaving the priesthood. He conducted the interview and directed all his questions to Colleen. I sat anxiously listening to Colleen's replies and thought she had not done too badly. After some considerable time Philip Warbridge turned to me.

'Well, I think Colleen would go really well here, don't you John?' he said with a sidelong glance at his companion.

'How would a traineeship work,' I asked beaming.

'Oh, don't worry about a traineeship. We just want to give her a job,' he replied exchanging smiles with John Keogh.

I was gob smacked!.

'Wh....what sort of a job?' I stammered.

'I think Colleen would work wonderfully well in office administration,' John replied.

I looked across to Colleen and saw her face light up.

'Does that mean, I'll work here?' she turned to me and asked excitedly.

'It certainly does, Colls,' I replied grinning at her. 'How do you feel about that?'

'Grouse,' she had said, and we all laughed at her expression of enthusiasm.

It all sounded so very up-market, could it really work? We then went on to discuss the terms of employment. Initially Colleen would start on four hours for four days a week. This ultimately proved to be too much for her to cope with so when I rang to discuss this with them, they obligingly reduced it to three days a week for four hours.

One of her tasks was to make up the 'show bags' for the trainees. These kits contain all the information required to help the students understand all that is entailed in taking on a traineeship.

'Don't you think Colls should cut back on some of her other activities, Mum?' Christine asked. She and Suzanne had delivered Colleen home after they had been shopping together one hot Saturday afternoon.

'Oh no. It's important that she keeps on with them. She still needs to do her Kumon lessons, physiotherapy, speech and music therapy,' I replied.

'But Mum, she has an additional activity with special needs people swimming,' Suzanne said. 'Don't you think she is doing too much?'

We had commenced travelling out to Carey Grammar pool for training on a Tuesday night.

'If I am good enough, I will go in the Olympic,' Colleen told her sisters excitedly.

'She's managing fine,' I said, smiling at my youngest daughter. 'Besides, her activities keep her occupied while I am at work.' My brother Terry's business, Lifestyle And Rehabilitation had moved from Brunswick to Mitcham and I had increased the time I was working to three days a week. I had decided to cut back on the clients I attended for Australian Home Care.

'Well I think you should cut her some slack, Mum,' Christine said bluntly, and I was puzzled by the look which passed between her and Suzanne. I was doing the right thing by ensuring that Colleen was being stimulated to the maximum, wasn't I? How else was she going to progress? I decided not to pursue this topic of conversation and moved on to less contentious ground.

'Anyway, how are you going, Suzanne? You look great,' I said. There was great excitement in the family. Peter and I were to be grandparents and were looking forward to the end of July when Suzanne was due to give birth.

But before this event, at Easter time, Colls moved into her granny flat. Everything in our lives seemed to be going along smoothly.

Then in May, Peter was retrenched. He had been at the Alfred for four years and had really enjoyed his job as an orderly. The ensuing laborious search for alternative employment was interrupted when he had to be hospitalized for an operation on his knee. What was quite a routine procedure was complicated when he contracted golden staph (staphylococcus aureus), an infection which can make patients seriously ill, especially if the infection resists treatment by antibiotics. Staphylococcus aureus is carried on the skin or in the nose of healthy people. Two to three out of every ten people carry the bacterium in their noses. The infection can be spread by skin-on-skin contact or by touching contaminated surfaces and poor personal hygiene, and not covering open wounds can also lead to infection. Before antibiotics, a severe staph infection was fatal for many people. Penicillin was initially effective, but strains of the bacteria evolved which were resistant to treatment. Hospital patients are more likely to be infected because of surgical or other wounds. We were seriously worried about Peter. After spending two weeks in the Alfred Hospital, he was transferred to Caulfield Hospital where he was treated for the infection and eventually after another three weeks was given the all clear and was discharged.

During the last week that he was in hospital, at the end of July, we were very excited when Suzanne and Jim's twin girls, were born.

It was a wonderful homecoming gift for Peter, and while he was recuperating, a great interlude and distraction before he launched again into the search for employment.

He hoped to pick up some work in a newsagency but in the meanwhile he did some work for Australian Home Care.

'Just pick and choose your clients,' I suggested to him. 'Start with about three and see how you get on.'

It was terrible. The placements did not suit him at all.

'All she did the whole time I was there was to criticize my efforts,' Peter said despondently when he returned home one afternoon. He had been doing the cleaning for a particularly fussy client. 'How can you go wrong pushing a vacuum cleaner around?'

I could see it was soul destroying for him. After all vacuuming was pretty basic, and his efforts surely not deserving of this client's disparagement.

'You don't have to do this work, Pete. It doesn't suit you. Something will come along,' I reassured him. Shortly thereafter he commenced work at a newsagency at Camberwell. Unfortunately it was only a fill in position, but it gave him the step into the next job at one of two newsagencies at Glen Iris. He loved being back behind the counter and having the contact with customers.

'I'm learning new things all the time,' he said animatedly. Computers had been introduced into shops since we'd sold Broadford, and this was a challenge for him. Unfortunately Glen Iris could not support two shops and the one at which Peter was employed closed down.

A position became available at Hawthorn, but after five weeks he was dismissed.

'My little Asian employer, Sammy, told me I was not fast enough on the computer,' Peter said disgustedly. 'I suggested that there was heaps of other stuff I could do instead of computer work, but it wasn't good enough for him.'

Poor Peter. He was so anxious to work. He needed to be employed. I was so disappointed for him. I just hoped it would not be too long before he was gainfully employed again.

My sister Pat continued to take an active interest in Colleen. Each week she had been meeting Colls for a cup of coffee, and then when we had shifted to Ashburton, she'd decided perhaps she could do something more constructive.

'How about we go to Hip Hop, Colls,' Pat said, giving me a wink.

'What's that?' Colls asked, a puzzled expression on her face.

A learn to dance programme was starting up at a local church hall. They enrolled and had marvellous fun. On one occasion Pat was unable to attend so I decided I would take Colls. Well my goodness; the teacher was amazingly agile and fantastically spritely. This is a bit tricky, I thought. How does this work for Colleen? But although she did the moves slowly, she did seem to get it together. I did wonder to myself how Pat coped because she is very uncoordinated. Anyway, that did not matter. This one hour one night a week was wonderful entertainment, and I was ever so grateful to my sister for spending the time with our daughter.

The year sped past. Christmas 2004 came and went.

Colleen had settled into her three days employment with Sportsready, coping with the travel to and from the Melbourne Cricket Ground (M.C.G.) and managing not to file too many things in the wrong place. All the young people who were doing traineeships had paperwork which needed to be filed alphabetically. This was one of Colleen's tasks. She was able to cope with this quite well but she would conk out before she reached the end of the alphabet. Broderick the second in charge who supervised her work would despair.

'He said to me, Colleen, you have to finish, you can't quit now,' Colleen told us he said to her one day.

'And what did you say to him?' I asked.

'Oh, I said I would finish it tomorrow,' she said nonchalantly.

'Colls, you can't do that,' Peter said. 'You have to finish, it doesn't matter if you have to stay there a little longer. If that's the task, you have to finish it.'

'Oh, I just can't,' she replied shrugging her shoulders.

Unfortunately the pressure she felt she was under at work started to have an effect on her behaviour. She would become more difficult at home. It became necessary for us to let them know at Sportsready when she was not coping. I rang Broderick.

'We can tell when Colleen is under stress, she gets more aggressive and more verbal here at home,' I told him. 'She is even suggesting she does not want to go to work.'

Fortunately they were able to adjust her work load so she could manage. It was certainly a steep learning curve for us all trying to ascertain how much she could cope with.

Out of work time she had been enthusiastically practising for the swimming for the disabled Olympics.

'Colls is doing really well, Mum,' Christine reported when she delivered her home after the swimming trials. Colleen had gone out to her unit to change and get things ready for work the next day.

'You know, she is a completely different person when she's in that environment,' Christine continued.

'What do you mean?' I asked.

Christine had gone on to say that perhaps it was more difficult for Colleen now than previously.

'We are bringing her out of her world and are trying to assimilate her into ours which is causing conflict. She just doesn't cope with the normal everyday stuff, therefore she becomes anxious and angry. I think she is more comfortable when she is mixing with people who are also impaired. Surrounded by other people with disabilities, she is so peaceful, so calm and so in control. I was very impressed, apart from how well she is doing with her swimming,' she said. Then she laughed. 'I did rather think though that she looked like a beached whale as she was helped out of the pool.'

I'd laughed and said, 'She's managing a little better now and being more dignified in her efforts, although she still needs two people to assist her.' The pool didn't have easy access, even at the shallow end. Colleen had to be bodily lifted out. Her backside was plonked on the edge and her legs lifted up, splayed out in a most indecorous manner, her movements being impaired by her crook leg.

Christine cupped her hands around the small mound of her own stomach. We were to be grandparents again later in the year. 'We're not winning the battle with her weight, are we,' she stated rather than questioned.

I sighed and said. 'No, you'd think with all the activity, especially the swimming, the weight would fall off her. I think she just eats more to keep up her strength.'

When I was watching at training sessions, I was amazed at how hard the swimming coach drilled his charges.

'Come on! Get going! Do it this way,' he would shout instructions and give directions from the sidelines.

I had decided that rather than just cheering Colleen on, I would attend the meetings of the swimming organization. Come election night and everyone is cringing when nominations are called for a minute's secretary. As I sat there I was thinking, well it's only doing the minutes and then posting or emailing them out. Surely that's not a great deal of work. So up went my hand. Well, the meeting was thrilled. Here was their newest member, willing to take on an active roll. Each person in the room had an adult dependent with disabilities and I knew only too well the burden which this occasioned. I was pleased to be able to do my bit. I collected all the books from the previous secretary who had done the job for twenty years, my notes from the meeting, and prepared to give the job my best.

And then my computer died. The computer man kept on promising and promising to call, but never came. Eventually I had to go to the library just before the next meeting to do the minutes. I was feeling quite pleased with myself to think that I had overcome my difficulties to deliver on time. The meeting was not quite so pleased. I had failed to include any surnames and this caused great offence. On reflection, no-one suggested that they could do better and relieve me of the job. So I battled on. I was now very anxious about the whole secretary thing. I had to get back into the practice of writing notes not just listening at the meetings. The next meeting loomed and my computer remained out of action. We had also put in a call to the phone company, we only needed a new extension, but we were still waiting. I had thought I might find an hour at work sometime to do the minutes, but there were too many phones ringing and lots of customers to attend to. Looking back, I'm not sure how I managed to survive those first few meetings, but I soon settled down to a routine which seemed to suffice.

With her swimming, Colleen never got back to butterfly. She was either lacking in co-ordination or the strength in her arms. We told her not to worry and to put her energy into freestyle and backstroke. In March she competed in the "Special Olympic Games". This wonderfully organized event took place one Saturday and attracted participants from southern, northern and inner regions of Melbourne as well as country areas including Bendigo and Ballarat. At the opening ceremony, the athletes marched around the oval before being marshalled to the individual events in which they were competing. These included swimming, basketball, tennis and athletics. It was wonderful to see the enthusiasm of the competitors, and I was especially touched as I watched those with Down Syndrome, going around excitedly hugging everyone. Over the day the scores were tallied up for each region and at the end of the day presentations were made to the successful competitors at a barbecue.

Colleen did very well and brought home two silver and a bronze medal. How proud we were of her achievement. How happy she was and thereafter excitedly brought them out to show visitors and boast of her success.

'Colls always did like to be the centre of attention,' Christine said.

All the family was visiting for Sunday tea. I had persuaded Colleen to rest before the occasion and she had not yet surfaced from her unit.

'Whatever do you mean?' I asked.

'She's a middle child. When we were growing up she was always competing, trying to be noticed,' Christine replied.

'Yeah, remember she was always loud,' Paul said with a chuckle. 'She still is.'

'It's wonderful to see her so happy,' Suzanne said. 'You know, it's amazing how her childhood personality traits still show through. You see that in her drive to succeed with her swimming and the confidence with which she plays her flute.'

Suzanne was right. It was amazing. Sometimes I had an uncanny glimpse of what Colleen had been and would never be again. I sighed and tuned back into the conversation.

'I swear she can talk underwater,' Rachael said laughing. 'When I went swimming with her the other day she was chatting all the time. At one stage she stopped a couple of metres from the end of the pool, gasped and just started talking. I told her she should have completed the lap, but she insisted she had to stop and tell me something.'

How lucky Peter and I were with our wonderful family. Each in their own way had contributed to Colleen's rehabilitation. Each had been profoundly affected by Colleen's illness. Peter and I would not have survived the pain and anguish without their support.

'I wonder if these surgeons know the physical, emotional, financial and social effect their "life saving surgery" has on the family of their patients?' Paul mused. A silence descended on our gathering. There were tears in his eyes as he continued.

'Let's face it, it has taken a massive toll on you two,' he said looking from Peter to me. 'Here you were thirty years in business, looking forward perhaps to travelling and being able to enjoy each other's company in the "golden years". Instead…..' His voice trailed away. 'It hurts me,' he said in a whisper. I was quick to take up his point.

'It's only what any parent would do,' I said in a choked voice.

Rachael had gone to sit on the arm of Paul's chair and she took his hand in hers. He looked up at her and continued.

'I'm so lucky. I have a loving wife and with the baby coming ….. ,' he smiled and then went on, 'it's hard to get past all the things Colleen may never have. I hope one day she might. I often wonder.'

I could understand the way he felt. Once before he had said to me that everyone has battles in life and most people put their heads down and get on with it. We were probably no different. He also said how tough it is on relationships and how lucky it was that our family had survived and were richer for it.

Georgia and Olivia, Suzanne and Jim's twin girls chose this time to have a dispute over the building blocks and we all welcomed the distraction. Suzanne had returned to work and Peter who had been looking after the girls one day a week for her, quickly intervened in the argument.

Paul's concern for Peter and I was touching. But I'd never stopped to consider what might have been for Peter and I. Colleen needed us and that was all there was to it.

Recently we had been persuaded to have a week away at Coffs Harbour. It was so easy to get bogged down in daily routine and be totally absorbed with catering for Colleen's needs. Suzanne too could see this was taking its toll.

'It's not all about Colleen, Mum. You do have a choice. Set yourself some goals. You and Dad head off for the day. Go to the movies. You need some time to reconnect with each other,' she observed.

So Coffs Harbour was a welcome break. But why was it that it did not live up to expectations? Had we both been wanting so much more than what was delivered? Or did we just feel guilty about being away from Colleen? I could tell that Suzanne was disappointed with our attitude when she picked us up from the airport. Colleen having been looked after by one or other of her siblings, had survived without my supervision. Perhaps I should relinquish my hold a little more often. Was I wrong in wanting Colleen to reach a stage where she could be independent? After all Peter and I would not be around forever.

I knew Colleen often turned to Christine for help, sometimes in the most mundane matters. Christine told me Colleen had rung her one day quite distressed. She had told Christine she had run out of sanitary napkins.

'Well what do you think you should do, Colls,' Christine had asked her.

'Um, walk up to the supermarket and buy some?' Colleen queried.

So after Christine confirmed for her that was the right course of action the problem was sorted. Likewise Christine had told me of an incident when Colleen had visited her for an overnight stay.

'It was only an upset stomach, Mum, but she was so anxious. She was ready to sit up all night waiting for the next trip to the toilet. After I had showered and changed her I persuaded her to go back to bed.' Christine told me. She went on to say that the situation needed to be simplified for Colleen, so she pointed out that it was a simple thing to go from the bed to the toilet and back to bed again. This seemed to work by taking the anxiety away from Colleen. 'She then slept through the night,' Christine finished.

I myself had been anxious when Sportsready gave Colleen a month's holiday. How was I going to keep her occupied during this time?

'It's OK Mum. Dad can see she attends her activities. Other times she can come and visit. It will be good to have some 'Suzanne and Colleen time'. No problem,' Suzanne had said when I expressed my concern to her. I think it was a steep learning curve for Suzanne. Colleen had spent a few days with her.

'It was really great having her Mum,' Suzanne had said to me. 'Colls was relaxed and happy to be with us. There was just one little incident though.' And she went on to tell me. Suzanne was desperate to do some shopping. Colleen was nursing Olivia, and Georgia was asleep. She told Colleen she was just going to run across to the supermarket and would be back very soon. When she returned a short while later Olivia was alone on the couch and there was no sign of Colleen. She was in the toilet.

'I didn't realize Mum. You have to spell everything out for her. Now Colleen if you need to go to the toilet this is what you must do. If the doorbell rings, this is what happens. She just doesn't know how to manage the whole thinking process,' Suzanne said.

'I know. It amazes me that Sportsready cope as well as they seem to with her. How wonderful it is that they have taken her on and given her employment,' I said.

Then half way through 2005, Sportsready offered Colleen a traineeship.

Chapter 20

A TRAINEESHIP

It wasn't all plain sailing in the early days of the Traineeship. Because she was comfortably familiar with her surroundings, Colleen was inclined to be loud and disruptive at work, especially if she found the task allotted her beyond her endurance. Not only that, she would down tools, walk off the job, and go for a cup of coffee.

'You can't do that Colleen,' I'd said when she told me what she had done. 'Surely you don't need a cup of coffee when you're only there for four hours.'

'Oh, yes I do,' she said defiantly.

That wasn't the only issue, apparently she lost some documents. Well, I thought to myself, that's out of my control. They'll just have to set up a structure so that that doesn't happen. I can't do it. All the same I would ring every couple of months to ask how things were going.

Traineeships were originally offered to students in country areas who, being unsure of the direction or career they wished to pursue, were given the opportunity to experience first hand what it is like to be in the workforce. It was not necessary for the students to be good at or even play sport, but just have some sporting knowledge. They would then choose an area of the workforce in which they were interested, say turf management or information and technology, and Sportsready would find a place for them in a company offering experience in this area, such as Telstra or a private company. Funding is provided by the State government for a twelve month period during which time the trainee attends the workplace for say three days a week and the other two days are spent at Sportsready. At the end of the traineeship the trainee is then equipped to decide the direction they wish their life to take, be it to do a tertiary course, or seek employment in the workforce. Sportsready now offers traineeships to students from a broader community base, not necessarily taking on only those interested in sport.

Colleen's traineeship was conducted at Sportready rather than her being placed in a position out in the wider community. She was assigned a mentor by the employment agency Disability Employment Action Centre (D.E.A.C.). Sally would oversee her progress and help with Colleen's special needs. During the course of the Traineeship, Colleen was required to complete two text books. Sally would visit weekly and give Colleen guidance with the work she was doing, tick off the book to confirm Colleen had successfully attained a certain level, and generally "look over her shoulder" to ensure she was progressing.

D.E.A.C. works with Sportsready and other training and pre-employment programmes to assist people with a disability, or from a disadvantaged background, to access employment. It is a Melbourne based, not-for-profit organization founded on the principles of human rights, equality, equity and social justice. It believes every human being has a right to participate, and be valued in our society, and to be treated fairly, humanely and with respect, because they believe people with a disability are social citizens with the same rights as everybody else. They engage people with disabilities and other significant disadvantages on a journey of empowerment and self determination, with the goal of improving their skills and ultimately allowing them to make decisions that hopefully may enhance their quality of life.

Sportsready work in with D.E.A.C., by employing a few people with special needs. At the time Colleen was doing her Traineeship, there was also a guy in a wheelchair and a young woman with a debilitating illness which affected her physical capabilities, to whom Sportready had given employment. Colleen though was by far the more disabled, and over and over again we realized just how fortunate we were that she had been offered this opportunity.

At home we were still having issues with Colleen's weight. She was now thirteen stone (eighty-three kilograms) and indiscriminate in her choice of diet. Our home being in close proximity to the shops had its draw backs. We had found it necessary to ensure she only had sufficient money for the train ticket.

'Colls, if you go up the street, that's fine. Take your magazine. Sit down, have a cappuccino or a bowl of soup or sandwich, but not fish and chips,' I would say to her.

The problem was, instead of making these excursions into a meal break, for her they would be a snack and she would then come home and eat a hearty meal. I was still encouraging her to prepare her own meals. But it didn't happen all that often.

'Why don't you go and cook yourself an omelet, Colls?' I would suggest. 'I'll come and help you get started and Dad and I will come to visit you for tea tonight.' But I think it was just downright convenient for Colls to think, well Mum's there cooking a meal, why should I put my stove on? We would laugh to ourselves at the meals she would concoct. An egg, baked beans and mushrooms was a beautiful meal for her.

I was still working at Lifestyle and Rehabilitation at Mitcham for my brother Terry, but hated it. I was totally intimidated by the woman in charge; a super sales woman who was intolerant of what she saw as the staff's inadequacies, an attitude which consequently saw a regular turnover of employees. I thought I could not be a wimp and would hang in there, but was always on the lookout for an alternative. A neighbour Michelle, and I, through many conversations found we had a common interest in gardening and tossed around the idea of starting up a gardening service. So at my suggestion, "The Garden Tarts" was born. The idea was not to embark on heavy stuff, but to "tart up" peoples' gardens, say when they were selling, just general maintenance, pruning roses and neatening things up. Full of enthusiasm we had vests made and approached estate agents who thought it was a great idea. We had flyers printed and walked the streets delivering them. We never had any feed back. Oh, we got a couple of jobs, but I thought, well this isn't going to pay the bills but it might grow into something. We persisted. Then after one particular job, for which our endeavours were criticized, we sat down and worked out how many hours we had worked, how hard it had been, and how little we had been paid for our efforts, and our enthusiasm sort of fizzled. I could not give up my work to do it. Anyway Michelle went on and did a horticultural course, had cards made, and ran with the idea. She seems to be quite busy, and I'm sure she is happy with my input into the venture.

Colleen commenced spending more and more time in our place rather than in the granny flat. She was fortunate that there were excursions which gave her a change of scene.

She was invited to visit her friend Danni at Mulwala on the Victorian/New South Wales border. This three and a half hour trip entailed a journey by train and bus.

'How are you going Colls?' I'd said when I rang her early on in the trip.

'Only three hours to go' she replied with a groan.

I chuckled to myself. I had suggested she take a puzzle book with her or something else to help pass the time but she had been adamant that she would not need anything to entertain her. Peter had seen her onto the train and spoke to the train conductor, requesting he check that Colleen got off the train at Benalla and asked him to direct her to the correct bus for the journey to Mulwala. We were confident she was capable of finding her way, but could not help being concerned that she might find herself on a bus back to Melbourne. But all went well.

We were now well into the second half of 2005 and she had become proficient in navigating the train system in Melbourne. In addition to travelling to work, for twelve months she had been visiting a naturopath in the central business district, and managed to check the timetable with only a little assistance from me to sort out the 'to' and 'from' pages for her, and was able to get herself to the appointments at the designated times.

On some occasions following these appointments, Colleen would meet Christine for coffee in the city before catching the train home, and then if the appointment coincided with a weekend and there was a social event on, Paul would meet the train, take Colleen home for tea, and she would join Paul and Rachael at whatever event they were frequenting with their friends. I have never ceased to be amazed by the amount of support Colleen has been given by her siblings. Sometimes at family dinners though, I have thought that they seemed to forget to include her in their conversation, so I would intervene and make sure she contributed.

In addition to treatment from the naturopath, Christine had also suggested that kinesiology may be of assistance to Colleen, and this therapist encouraged us not to interfere with Colleen's attempts to do things for herself, like reading a timetable.

Kinesiology, originating in the 1960's, combines Western techniques and Eastern wisdoms to promote physical, emotional and spiritual health. It identifies factors which block the body's natural healing processes. These dysfunctions are then rectified by attention to reflex and acupressure points, helping to relieve pain, stress and muscular and nervous disorders. We were advised that it can also assist with psychological and learning problems, and it was in these areas we hoped that Colleen could be helped. Kinesiology looks beyond symptoms and does not diagnose, treat or prescribe named diseases. Rather through manual muscle testing, the exact nature of blockages in energy flow can identify stressors to the body or mind through accessing the body's wisdom with a kind of body biofeedback. Once imbalances are identified, then a variety of techniques can be used to release energy blockages and allow the body's innate healing process to heal itself.

This was all difficult to take in, but coming away from my first of several appointments with the kinesiologist, I thought to myself that we at least should give it a go. We had been told mental performance can be dramatically improved as techniques used enhance neurological functioning. The idea was to tap into Colleen's brain and teach it to travel on new paths, and have Colleen make the right decisions with situations which are presented to her. For example, if she has to choose whether to walk on the road or on the footpath provided, her brain has to have her choose the safest option.

As time progressed, issues which had never crossed my mind were brought to the surface. Colleen brought home a drawing of her and Suzanne's twins with a heavy black line on the page separating her from them. I had not thought anything of it, but for Colleen it was of great concern that she was not physically able to pick up the twins. From then on, without drawing attention to it, I would suggest Colleen sit down and I would pass her the babies. Another time she brought home a drawing of herself, Peter and me, and the iron and vacuum cleaner. At the top were the words "why do I always get angry with Mum and not Dad". When I enquired about this drawing she told me she wanted to do her own ironing and vacuuming.

'Wow,' I said. 'This will be good.'

Colleen laughed. She absolutely hates these chores and carries on such a treat when these jobs and others like cleaning the toilet are to be done.

'But Colleen, I don't do your vacuuming. Occasionally I do your ironing, but your carer does that for you.'

'Well, I want to be able to do it,' she'd replied.

The kinesiologist said to me that everyone was telling her what to do. Have you set your alarm, are you organized for work, do you have your money, have you got your lunch, pick your clothes up off the floor.

'You must hold back and don't organize anything,' the therapist said. 'I know it will be hard, but especially with the things which do not matter, leave her to her own devices. If she cannot get into her bedroom because of all the things on the floor she will have to pick them up. That is where the brain is being trained to take a different path. Then it will be her brain telling her to go a different way, not you.'

Colleen began to display a determination to do things her own way. I watched her putting chunks of carrot into her avocado sandwich. I'm glad I'm not eating it, I thought.

'Would you like me to grate that carrot for you, Colls?' I'd asked.

'No! It will be fine. Thank you,' she said emphatically.

The kinesiologist also said she would appreciate it if all the family would not mention Colleen's weight. Throw the word out of our vocabulary. She said that Colleen knows she should not eat the wrong foods because we are always on about her weight. On the other hand her brain is saying, they don't know what they are on about. So she thinks she will do what her brain is telling her, and that is to eat. She said if we stopped the pressure, then Colleen would stop putting pressure on herself.

I'd thought to myself, well at least this therapy is providing her with opportunities to make some choices. We will just have to see if it is ultimately beneficial.

August presented a dilemma. The people at Sportsready travelled to Sydney for a conference and there was no work for Colleen. I did a slow panic. I didn't like her being on her own. How could I organize the week so that she would be occupied? My first thought was for her to catch up with a few of her friends.

'What do you think, Colls? You could ring Nards and Angela and see if they can meet you in town for lunch?' I'd suggested brightly.

'I've rung them and left messages,' Colleen replied sullenly. 'They got back to me but they're busy.'

'That was a while ago. Ring again,' I persisted. Angela was pregnant and it would be a great opportunity for Colleen to see how she was going.

'Yeah. Whatever,' Colleen replied.

I sighed. What a shame. We must not give up on her friends I thought to myself. But you can only go so far. Colleen was obviously not happy. I didn't know what else to do so I left it.

Recently, Colleen had not been happy about a lot of things. Her speech had deteriorated to the point where I was again unable to understand what she was saying. I was trying not to say "slow down", because I would end up saying it time and time again. So I just didn't answer her. I would just give her the hand signal to indicate that I hadn't heard. Finally, after about the sixth time I would finally have to say, 'Colleen, I can't understand a word you are saying'. It was so frustrating. I didn't know whether we should get help for it, or just monitor it. Was the kinesiology just stirring up Colleen? The really sad thing was that I hadn't seen any improvement in her condition of late which was so disappointing. This just proved to me how difficult a brain injury is; the patient's not in control and you can't control it.

Anyway, finally we organized the week so that Colleen was occupied. My sister Pat took her shopping, the next day Colls met her ex-carer from Newport in town for lunch, she helped Peter look after the twins the day after, then she went to her art group at the local community centre, and the last day she attended her computer lessons. I really had had no reason to panic. I suppose my concern was that I was worried about how upsetting Colleen's routine would affect her. She was easily thrown. Just having her period was enough to upset her equilibrium. Fortunately she was back on the depo-provera injections because even the slight discomfort she experienced at these times upset her. We had investigated the contraceptive pill as an alternative, but she would not cope with the added discomfort of a heavier period. Besides we could not take the risk that she may forget to take the pill. We again considered she was very vulnerable, especially catching public transport. It would be dreadful if someone took advantage of her. We did not want to consider having her tubes tied. Not yet. But how dreadful would it be, irresponsible in fact, if she became pregnant. We could not allow that to happen. So again the depo-provera remained the obvious choice.

In an endeavour to keep her on an even keel, I would try to ensure she got her proper rest, which was easier said than done. One late night and she would become obnoxious.

'Colleen…..time out….you can be angry, but can you be angry in your own room and in your own space?' I would say to her.

'Fine. I'm going to go where somebody loves me. I hate Mum and Dad,' she would yell, storming out the door to her unit. We would know it was the opposite of what she really meant but she would be full on abusive. Being overtired she would just not cope. I would give her time to cool down and then go out to her unit and give her a big hug, ignoring the chaotic mess which greeted me.

'Come on, I'll put your wheat bag in the microwave. You get into your pajamas, brush your teeth, and I'll help you get your clothes ready for tomorrow, and you can cuddle up in bed.' I would say to her. The kinesiologist had suggested that Colleen should be responsible for her own actions, but I tried to explain that this does not happen with brain injury people. Unless I took control and made sure she received adequate sleep, she would become obnoxious at work. So really it was a vicious circle. I kept on reminding myself that it was amazing that she was out there working and leading a very full and active life.

Another time I tried taking a different tack, and threaten not to take her to swimming because of her bad behaviour. This did not work as she went off on another tangent of yelling and then became rude and abusive.

"Colleen, just remove yourself. You're not allowed to be in this room if that's your behaviour.

'Well, I'm going out to my flat and I'm going to leave,' she shouted before stomping out and slamming the door behind her. After a while she'd cool down and come meekly back in.

'I'm sorry. I shouldn't have said that,' she said.

'No! You shouldn't have. It's really hurtful and doesn't do you any good Colls. You expend all that energy on being angry,' I said to her. I'd thought to myself, she tries to understand it, but she cannot control it. That mechanism isn't there.

We looked upon every distraction as a welcome change. Colleen's dear friend Belinda invited her to accompany her and her mother and cousins on a girls' day out. Soon to be married, Belinda wanted to show Colls the wedding dress she had chosen to see if she liked it. I will be eternally grateful for friends like Belinda who still make the time to include Colleen in their lives.

I was always looking for something new to occupy Colleen in an endeavour to stimulate her and improve her condition. Left to her own devices she would sit on the couch watching the same DVD day in and day out, or she would play the same CD a million times. We saw a local production of the show 'Chicago' and she played the score over and over. Another favourite 'Grease' would go on the player day after day, and she would even leave it on when she went to work, put it on again when she came home, and it would still be going when she went to bed. She just seemed to be in a different world.

Other times she would make you wonder. She'd say some funny things, especially when we didn't give her our full attention.

'Oh it's all right. I know you're not listening to me. That's OK. I'll just go and talk to myself,' she'd say in this funny different tone of voice, laughing.

How does this work? It's bizarre. She seemed so normal, and I'd think to myself, we're doing all right.

In an endeavour to seek help in modifying Colleen's eating habits, I rang Brain Injury Australia, a brain foundation, and asked for a list of doctors who helped with weight management for patients with acquired brain injury. After many phone calls I finally attended at a doctor's in Kew.

'You are doing a wonderful job,' she said to me. 'Really there is nothing more I can tell you to do.'

And stupidly I paid the bill! I should have written a letter to ask what I was paying for. Hello! I despaired at this attitude. It was disgraceful. Some people just lack in common sense.

Apart from the odd negative experience, we had some wonderfully positive moments in our lives.

In October the Craig Family Centre here in Ashburton holds its annual Art Show. Since our shift in 2003 Colleen had been attending the 'Ace Space' Group at the Centre. With a strong community development focus, this organization provides services to support individuals and families within the local community, and on Thursday afternoons caters for young people who have an intellectual disability. Colleen would look forward to these relaxed social sessions, where she would do craft or cooking, play games, go to the movies or take a trip into the City, go to the museum or visit other places of interest. A strong component of their activities is art. In September a specialist teacher helps with the creations in preparation for the Art Show and the best of the collages, sculptures, and photography and paintings which have been expertly framed, go on display for sale. The second year we attended we arrived late.

'Why Colls, we can't buy your work, it has all been sold!' I'd exclaimed.

Most of the exhibits sell for about fifty dollars and in addition that year I had volunteered to organize the raffle which raised further funds for the Centre.

In the weeks leading up to the show, the exhibitors make beautiful finger food, sausage rolls, pin wheels and the like and store them in the freezer in preparation for the event. On the evening, they serve the food with champagne, wine, orange juice and punch. The families are sent a special invitation.

The first year I sent out personal invitations to all the people I knew and they all turned up and created a real buzz. It was wonderful to see Colleen proudly showing her work to them and talking animatedly.

The year was drawing to a close and we were looking forward to Christmas with Suzanne and Jim's twins. This year there would be another two presents under our Christmas tree. Christine, and Paul's Rachael had increased the count to four grand-daughters.

Chapter 21

NEW EXPERIENCES

In January 2006 Colleen fell in love. But it was short lived.

I had decided that Colls needed to go away with young people of her own age. Usually I would only let her embark on an activity like this after a great deal of research, but having sourced this holiday at short notice, I relied on the organization being highly recommended and instead of meeting with the group first, we ended up taking Colleen to the airport to meet them for the first time. It was nerve wracking for me, but Colls was very excited. The group of about a dozen special needs people, all with a similar level of disability to Colleen, were to be supervised by four carers.

'Oh dear, Pete, Colls looks a lot brighter than some of them. Do you think she will get on OK?' I'd whispered

'You're being a bit judgmental aren't you? You know she's pretty good at relating to people,' he said.

I could see he was right as she turned and gave a quick final wave while talking animatedly with one of the group before boarding the plane on the way to the Tamworth Music Festival.

Brian was one of the group. He lived at Yarram, in Gippsland, Victoria. He had an acquired brain injury resulting from a motor bike accident a few years earlier, had recovered sufficiently to do gardening work for a landscape gardener two days a week, but needed help to organize his home facility. He and another disabled fellow lived together and were looked after by a carer who was allocated fifteen hours a week for their supervision. Colleen thought he was wonderful. He was all she talked about for days after her holiday. He was besotted with her and on their return from Tamworth he commenced a barrage of phone calls and emails. Beautiful romantic love song tapes would arrive in the mail. She was overwhelmed by all the attention. Perhaps it is just as well he lives so far away I thought, this could be a bit tricky. I was concerned she was not keeping up with the pace of his advances, and although I encouraged her to reply to his emails, was surprised to find she became reluctant to do so.

Meanwhile she was distracted from Brian's attentions by rehearsals for the Amuseability Theatre performance which was to take place mid March. Two very clever girls put on a show organizing the participants who all had a disability. It was a very colourful scene on stage with the performers wearing beautiful scarves. There was wheel chair dancing and lovely singing. Colleen felt the whole focus was on her as she was to play her flute, but really speaking she was a team player. She was very stressed being up on stage and as the time drew near we could see that she was daunted by the thought of performing in front of a large audience. In fact the local St. Michael's church hall was a packed house for the three performances, and for all Colleen's anxiety, she executed her part beautifully.

Then on April Fool's Day Colleen's very dear friend Belinda was married. Before the wedding I had attended the hen's night with Colls, and for the wedding, Maree, Belinda's mother, had asked me to help with the table decorations so we felt really involved in the event. I had always marvelled at the girls' friendship, even before Colleen's incident. Belinda has always been extremely organized and pays a great deal of attention to detail. She does amazing scrap booking. Colleen has always been the opposite. This family's continued friendship with Colls is fantastic. Perhaps their sympathy to her plight comes from their own background. Although Maree battles with incredibly bad arthritis of the feet, she works four days a week as parish secretary, organizing funerals and coping with the emotional turmoil of this job. At home she helps her son James (mid thirties) deal with the bipolar disorder with which he has been diagnosed. This disorder is not fully understood, but it seems very likely that there is a genetic component, and the fact that James' father also had bipolar would seem to support this theory. Like other depression related illnesses, the burden of bipolar disorder can be very disruptive to quality of life. James and his brother Mark always speak beautifully to and about Colleen. They just seem to connect. James once even took her out to dinner. She was so excited and got dressed up for the occasion. Not too many boys would be bothered. Not unexpectedly, she adores him.

 Thinking to advance the relationship between Colleen and Brian, we invited him to stay with us one weekend, and to accompany us to Christine and Gavan's place in Kensington after we all had attended their daughter Charlotte's christening. We thought how wonderful for Colleen to have a friend, even if it was not to be a romantic attachment, and therefore did everything we could to encourage the friendship. He was such a lovely young guy, just a little older than Colls, and obviously as keen as mustard. One thing we have found is that a lot of people who have a disability like Colleen's, do not connect. They will not initiate contact and need to have arrangements made for them, so we thought we would try and make her understand that he could be a friend, they could go to the football or pictures together without necessarily taking the relationship to another level. The encounter would do wonders for her confidence. On the morning of the christening, he appeared for breakfast resplendent in collar and tie, shoes buffed to a brilliant shine.

'It's cold Brian, do you have a jacket?' I'd asked him. He replied in the negative and so I said I had a lovely black one of Peter's that I thought would do the job. It fitted him perfectly and so I gave it to him when he returned home to Yarram at the end of the weekend. He had arrived with a little present for Colleen but she was reluctant to have anything to do with him, not even wanting to sit next to him in the church and was hostile toward his attentions to her. The visit was not a resounding success, but Brian was not deterred and the emails and letters kept on coming.

'How about I sit down with you and you can reply to Brian's letter Colls?' I asked. He had written a very touching, albeit fragmented note telling her she was his sweetheart.

'No way!' she said emphatically and snatched up the offending letter and consigned it to her drawer along with his other communications. I sighed. This was indeed turning out to be very tricky.

Not to be put off we invited him to stay the weekend of Colleen's thirtieth birthday party. Wrong move. It did not work. The party was quite a production. We hired a white marquee and it looked beautiful decorated with balloons and streamers. In addition to all Colleen's uncles and aunts and other relatives who attended the party, my sister Marg travelled down from Queensland and we had invited all the friends who had played a part in Colleen's rehabilitation. Jim and Suzanne prepared a slide presentation of her life and I was very emotional as I watched the journey of her recovery over the last ten years unfold in the pictures. Peter and I were so proud of what had been achieved, to see the advancements which had been made, and hopeful of the prospects for the future. Jackie and Belinda made a beautiful speech and amidst the laughter, there wasn't a dry eye in the house. The biggest disappointment of the evening was that the hired juke box didn't work. That and Colleen's attitude to Brian were the only things to mar what was a wonderful celebration.

We had picked Brian up from Melbourne's Southern Cross Railway Station. He was a seasoned traveller and would make the journey by himself from Yarram to Melbourne, usually by bus for the football. He was a mad North Melbourne supporter and Peter being like minded thought he might be able to develop Colleen's recent interest in the game and use this as a connecting point between her and Brian. On the way home Colleen sat in the back seat of the car gazing out at the passing scenery, not paying any attention to Brian and responding to all my attempts to draw her into conversation with monosyllabic replies. By the end of the weekend we saw that the chemistry just wasn't happening for Colls. We could tell he was hurt by her attitude to him. He wanted a girl friend. He was shattered. We could never fathom it out. Christine who can usually work out what was going on was at a loss.

'It appears she just does not feel for him, Mum,' she said. 'It just isn't right for her. Perhaps he wanted to hold her hand and she was repelled by his advances. Whatever it is she does not want to share it with me or anyone else.'

So as best we could we made sure he had a lovely weekend, even though the pressure was on having two special needs people in the house.

The tapes, letters and emails kept coming after the party.

'I don't want his stuff, Mum, ' Colleen said angrily. 'I don't want anything to do with him.' She was becoming quite distressed.

In the end it was really me chatting to his carer, not Colls communicating with Brian so I rang and told his carer not to let Brian think there was any hope because she was not interested. So the relationship, such as it was, died a natural death.

This contact with Brian though gave me hope that one day Colleen could be living in a similar situation to him. Not necessarily with another special needs person and a carer coming in, but perhaps living with a student who would be willing to keep on eye on her, see that she has a healthy breakfast and is groomed to go off to whatever activity is planned for her and to have a meal cooked for her in the evening. Instead of me telling her what to do, being encouraged by her helpmate to do those things she is capable of doing. That's what we were looking for.

We could see how Colleen being supervised could work when she accompanied her friend's basketball team to Queensland. She was invited by her ever attentive wonderful friend Jackie to be the "team manager". So off they flew for a week in July. Colleen made sure the score books were there and the oranges cut up ready for the team and generally "organized" the players. She took the job very seriously but it was a really fun time for her.

Colleen's disposition improved when the communications from Brian ceased. The family noticed a difference in her and Rachael told me about a time she spent with Colleen.

'We had a lovely day, Bern.' Rachael said. 'I thought we would laminate a growth chart for Isobella, but it wasn't working and Colleen soon lost interest in the project so we went for a walk.' They had stopped at a café for a coffee.

'This is the worst coffee I've ever had,' Colleen had said talking secretively from behind her coffee cup. It was difficult for Rachael to keep a straight face. She moved the conversation to football.

'I hate Wayne Carey,' Colleen declared.

'What do you mean you hate him?' Rachael asked. 'He came and visited you when you were in hospital. That was pretty amazing.'

'Oh yeah, but since then I don't like him because of what he's done.'

Rachael had been astounded at Colleen's comprehension of the scandal surrounding her football hero.

'She blows you away sometimes, Bern, you would almost think she's normal,' Rachael said. She'd continued with her account of her outing with Colleen.

'Let's go to Paul's shop,' Colleen had suggested.

'It's a long way, probably twenty-five minutes, we're only about half way there, are you sure Colls?' Rachael asked.

'Let's go, I'll push the pram,' she had replied eagerly.

So Rachael said off they went with Colleen chatting animatedly all the way. She was asking questions about how Paul and Rachael had met, all about their wedding and details of when Paul had got the shop. What amazed Rachael was Colleen's recall of pre-incident memories, the times she had visited Paul and Rachael when they were living in Deniliquin, and the recollection of being kissed by a boy.

'She could remember the names of all my family and all the people she had met. My legs were aching by the time we arrived home and Colleen must've been very tired. She said she was just going home to relax,' said Rachael laughing.

Even though Colleen's mood had improved after Brian's attentions ceased, we were still experiencing difficulties with her behaviour. We heard about Dr. Francis McNab through the Booroondara Stroke Support Group. This amazing man is one of Australia's best known psychotherapists and minister of religion and offers his services to stroke survivors like Colleen free of charge. He may not necessarily see people himself, but has a team of people who work for him through the Cairnmillar Institute. Offering assistance not only to stroke victims but to people with a wide range of problems, these counsellors have received specialized training to assist people. We first saw Dr. McNab in September and put before him all the issues which were affecting Colleen's behavior. Apart from the situation of Brian's attentions upsetting her, she was binge eating, experiencing frustrations at work having lost some time sheets and generally misbehaving. We found her session with him was very beneficial and this visit was to be the first of several over the coming years.

It was around about this time that Peter had commenced assisting a woman by transporting her to Cabrini Hospital for dialysis treatment. I was so pleased that he took on this job, and even though it did not occupy a great deal of his time, at least he was doing something.

In September the family got together to explore where Colleen could be a little further down the track, what her interests might be and how she could be motivated. This was initiated by Uniting Care Community Options which is a support service working in the eastern metropolitan region of Melbourne. Initially set up to help older people with dementia, in more recent times the organization works with people of all ages and abilities to help them enjoy normal, valued lives at home and as part of the community. It believes the best way to realize its goal to achieve a good life for all is to work with people facing these challenges. So Heather Burns guided us through the process of exploring the options for Colleen. Some wonderful ideas were discussed but the thing that kept on coming up over and over again was Colleen's desire to live on her own and not always be with Peter and I. This was certainly a goal which I aspired to reach.

Meanwhile I had an objective of my own. I had a dream of going to New Zealand. I started planning but as the year was drawing to a close put these plans on hold deciding that my sixtieth birthday was one worth celebrating. I had a bit of trouble whipping up enthusiasm within the family. I know it was my idea but surely they could be a bit more excited about my suggestions. Not to be put off in my endeavours, I rang around to different venues to see if they would be appropriate and was pleased when Suzanne drew up a menu which might be suitable. December is always a busy month and to find a weekend which was free was proving difficult. Then my sisters suggested that we go away, just the three of us to a bed and breakfast at Daylesford. I was running out of steam and a weekend escape sounded like a wonderful idea. So I abandoned my plans for a party and looked forward to a relaxing weekend and being pampered.

It was fantastic and I was sorry when we had to check out late on Sunday morning. My sisters were in no hurry to head home so we lingered over lunch and took in some sights on the way home.

'Surprise!'

When I entered my family room it was filled with grinning faces. I could not believe it. I didn't deserve this! Here were all these people, family and friends gathered to celebrate my birthday. It was wonderful.

'You made it difficult for us, Mum,' Christine had said laughing. 'We thought we would have to ring the venues you were contacting and tell them to ignore your attempts to make your own arrangements.'

'So you were just humoring, me,' I said also laughing. 'I thought you were being a bit lukewarm towards my suggestions.

Shaun gave a heartfelt speech.

'Everyone knows that when Bernadette is not organizing her family she is out organizing something else,' he said grinning cheekily. 'But seriously, we all know that Mum is the pivot around which the family revolves. We love you Mum. Happy birthday.'

Surveying the sea of faces as I responded, I'd thought how fortunate I was to have all these wonderful people in my life. Without the support, especially of my family I would not have coped over the past years. I looked at Colleen standing in line with her siblings, grinning at me, and thought how lucky she was to have such fantastic brothers and sisters. At that moment I felt truly blessed. I did not know what God had in store for me in the future, but I knew I would not have to travel the journey alone. Although I was astounded that I was moving into another decade, sixty did not seem so bad after all. I could not have wished for a better celebration.

I watched as Colleen limped away to the nearest chair and lowered herself onto it. I had a niggling feeling that trouble was looming with her leg and that once again I would have to take some action to ensure her continued mobility. But now was not the time to be anticipating. Next year would be soon enough to face any potential problems.

Chapter 22

TROUBLE ON THE HORIZON

Colleen had celebrated the coming of the New Year 2007 with Paul and Rachael at Deniliquin.

'It was grouse, Mum. Paul helped me into this old car tyre tube and towed me along behind the boat,' Colleen said excitedly. She had travelled by train to spend five days with them in their on site caravan. She had not been able to go swimming as she was too unstable to cope with the undertow. In fact as time went on I became seriously worried about her deteriorating foot function.

'I'm going to investigate private health insurance for Colls,' I said to Peter. 'I think it would be wise as her foot may require prolonged medical treatment.'

Shopping around I made dozens of phone calls. I was up front with Colleen's situation. I told them she was a stroke survivor, wore an ankle/foot orthotic and needed ancillary cover for podiatry and possibly acupuncture and physiotherapy. I told them everything. They didn't ask any questions. I don't know what they wrote down. Ultimately I decided on Medibank Private, not only for Colleen but for Peter and I also. We had dropped out of private health insurance back when Peter was having heart surgery. We'd been told that unless we had the top cover we were wasting our money, so all Peter's treatment was through the public system which we could not fault.

Colleen's funding through the Slow to Recover programme had finished and she was now on a system called Support and Choice which is provided through Human Services. It gave her ten hours a week attendant care and mileage to attend activities to a maximum of twelve kilometres per week. Her pension and quarterly insurance payments subsidized other expenses, but ancillary medical treatments were expensive and we needed to ensure that all avenues of care were available to her to guarantee she was given the maximum help for her well being.

At this time Peter and I were both struggling with our own health. My employment was taking its toll on my knee. I did home care for Tania every second Sunday. A young woman in her early thirties, she has a rare inherited disorder called Friedreich ataxia which affects the nervous system, mainly involves the spinal cord and has made her, like other sufferers, wheelchair bound. Victims inherit two abnormal genes, one from each of their parents, and any couple that has a child with this disorder have a one in four chance of having another affected child with any future pregnancy. Having to attend to Tania's needs in addition to my own household's requirements and being on my legs all day the days I worked at Lifestyle and Rehabilitation was causing me a great deal of pain. I'd commenced physiotherapy and found this gave me some relief, but reconstruction surgery would probably be the only permanent solution. But I couldn't be out of action. Perhaps when I retired.....

Peter was diagnosed with macular degeneration, a condition which reduces vision. The macula, a small but very important area in the back of the eye provides the sharp central vision needed for reading, driving and seeing fine detail. With age this can breakdown and cause sudden and severe loss of vision in the central part of the retina, but not necessarily affecting peripheral vision. Fortunately for Peter, many laser treatments later the condition was arrested. Apart from needing glasses for driving from that time on and having regular check ups he is no longer bother by it.

Although Peter had been unsuccessful in finding employment, he had commenced a bread run on Friday nights. He was now a contributor (like his father before him) to one of St. Vincent de Paul's very worthwhile causes. He would collect that day's left over bread products from a local bakery, bring them home, parcel them up and distribute them to needy families in the area.

Having found out about Dr. McNab from the Booroondara Stroke Support Group, we'd decided that it would be beneficial for Colleen to join and attend this group's activities. Jenny Chang, a highly motivated stroke victim herself organizes the group of about fifteen which meets fortnightly at the Hawthorn Leisure Centre. In addition to going to the Hawthorn gymnasium where they do an exercise programme, they also have access to a little community hall where they do art, wood work and singing. Colleen initially found these gatherings beneficial, but unfortunately the members were all quite a lot older than her and when she stopped attending, I thought to myself I must investigate other younger stroke victims that would benefit from this sort of contact with each other.

Family activities were the best form of stimulation we could give her though. Paul and Shaun were winning bidders at a football fundraiser auction and we all had a weekend away at Sorrento. The weather was perfect and the house was large enough to accommodate the whole family, including our four little granddaughters. Colleen loved the company of her siblings and their families, and it was a joy for us to have all our family together under the one roof for this weekend.

We were delighted when Angela, Colleen's cousin, invited her to her home at Frankston for the weekend. Angela and her two sisters and brother had had difficulty coming to terms with Colleen's illness. Their father (my brother John) having ultimately died from a stroke, had left its scar. Although over the years the cousins had kept up a regular flow of cards, letters and presents as a way of supporting Colleen, they found it very difficult to meet Colleen face to face, so this visit was a milestone.

I needed social contact too so I joined a women's church group which meet once a month on a Monday night. St. Michael's parish has a lovely lot of people and I usually managed to go to church once a week. If I was not able to attend I would think, oh well, Colls is my Mass or, chuckling to myself, Peter my double Mass. Often I would pray, Lord help me through this mess.

The Amusability Theatre group was once again practicing for a show which was to be held in September and held a fund raising trivia night in May. Colleen was going to participate in the performance which was to be held at the City of Whitehorse complex. As well as this social contact, she was still attending the Craig Family Centre on Thursday afternoons and Saturdays. We had stopped the Kumon lessons after she had broken her ankle, and subsequently we thought the traineeship at AFL Sportsready gave her sufficient stimulation. We also enrolled her in an Auslan Community Course which she attended at the local community centre. This course teaches sign language for communicating with deaf people and we thought perhaps this could open up a volunteer position for her. She enjoyed it but never really reached a level of proficiency. Perhaps if she worked with the hearing impaired her signing skills would improve. Hydro sessions which she attended three times a week were still possible with her deteriorating foot function, but we had discontinued physiotherapy.

We were again experiencing problems with her behaviour and so on the 14th June, took her back to see Dr. McNab. The AFL traineeship should have finished in June, but they were saying it would take Colls another six months to complete. Things at work were not going well. She had been warned that her loud behaviour would not be tolerated and if it continued her job would be in jeopardy. She was being obnoxious at home too. It was a battle to get her out of the house on time in the mornings.

'Here, let me help you with your hair,' I suggested.

'Why bother to do my hair?' Colleen had shouted at me. 'They don't look at me, they're not nice to me, why bother!'

'Colleen, that's enough,' I'd said sharply. 'You've just got to get in there and sock it to 'em. Say to yourself I can do this. Rise above it.'

'Well, I may just as well wear my pajamas for all they care,' she'd said sullenly but in a less strident voice.

'Colleen you'll lose your job if you're not careful,' I said sharply.

'I don't care. What do they know? They don't know what they are talking about,' she declared.

'But Colls, you must do as you are told.' I insisted. It seemed as though there were problems which, at least in her eyes, were insurmountable.

'I don't care,' she repeated. 'The others have gone. I hate it!'

The problem was revealed. The two girls who worked in the office with her had been shifted from the Melbourne Cricket Ground (MCG) to Telstra dome.

'I've got no one to help me, no one to ask if something goes wrong. I hate it,' she said with tears in her eyes.

Not wanting to interfere but thinking that I must take decisive action I'd rung through to management. I explained to them the reason for Colleen's bad behaviour. I told them they had pulled the rug out from under her.

'You can't do that to people like Colleen. She needs to have the support structure,' I said. 'If she is having a problem she needs to have at least one person available to her to ask for help.'

They were very understanding and things did improve. We did not expect Sportsready to keep her on indefinitely, but we were anxious that she finish the traineeship because she would be given a certificate to say she had completed to a certain level in office administration. Hopefully this would lead the way to further employment. The visit to Dr. McNab seemed prudent at that time. We had to do our bit to ensure her equilibrium was kept on an even keel. I'd accompanied her with a screed of what was worrying her. Sometimes when questioned she would be inclined to say yes when she really meant no, which would give a completely wrong impression of the problem, and I thought my input would be beneficial to the assistance she was given.

Theatre rehearsals were a wonderful distraction for her during this turbulent time at work. They were a lovely group of people and although with varying disabilities, very talented. The two women who wrote the play being performed arranged along with other cast members, for Ernie Sigley's daughter, Emma to star in the show, and the other disabled performers, some who had beautiful singing voices, did a marvellous job. But even the diversion of rehearsals eventually had problems of their own for Colleen. She began to feel out of her depth. She felt inadequate and became stressed and would yell at us. I thought to myself we would never do this again. The time for the performance came. The City of Whitehorse auditorium was a much larger venue than St. Michael's church hall where the previous show had been performed before a packed crowd. Unfortunately there were very few in the audience for this performance and the whole show lost a bit of atmosphere.

'Look Bern,' Peter had whispered. 'Colls is taking off her shoe and support.'

Sure enough, there she was up on stage during the performance, removing the offending articles.

'Oh dear Pete, that foot must really be worrying her,' I said stifling a laugh. 'I wish we could've got an earlier appointment with Doctor Cunningham, I will ring and see if I can get it brought forward.'

Well I tried. It was no good. I was told she was not the first in the queue and she would just have to wait her turn.

As if one crock in the house was not enough, in the surging football crowd Peter had walked into a concrete pylon on the way home from the grand final. In a dazed state he managed to struggle home by which time his thigh was rock hard. We called an ambulance and pain killers were administered, but ultimately though he didn't go to hospital. In the days that followed he became black and blue from the waist to his knee, and with the associated swelling was in excruciating pain, to say nothing of the damage he'd caused to his already bad knee. He was so stiff and sore he was virtually bed ridden for about two weeks. Fortunately he was soon able to get about again as it became necessary for him to drive Colleen to and from work. It was too difficult for her to manage the walk at both ends of her journey. Her toes were starting to turn under and she was having leg spasms more frequently.

She had been fitted with a new ankle/foot orthotic because calluses were forming on her foot and she was limping more than necessary. We hoped this would assist with her walking and reduce the pain, but she was not finding it as comfortable as her old one. Orthotics are made from a variety of plastics or fiberglass and can be of varying thickness depending on the extent of rigidity required. They are used quite extensively for improving posture, pain reduction and for sports injuries. Colleen needed to use an orthotic because of her gait post stroke. The right side of her body had been affected following the damage caused to the left hemisphere of her brain. The damage to her brain was permanent, and consequently the functions affected by those brain cells stopped. She had lost control of some of the functions of the right side of her body and her right leg, in particular her ankle and foot had been affected. This disability was of a permanent nature, but with appropriate therapies we hoped to minimize the effect it had on her mobility. Her orthotic was strapped around her lower leg, supporting her ankle and extended halfway along the underside of her foot. Because she was experiencing difficulties with the orthotic she had been using, the neuro-physiotherapist had suggested a full orthotic which extended all the way along her foot rather than just half way, hoping it would stop her toes from clawing. It took a lot of persistence to get her to persevere when putting it on.

'Look Colls, I have marked with texta where you connect the Velcro strips. If you do this you'll be laughing,' I said. But within a couple of days everything had altered and the marks did not line up. I threw up my arms. It was still a few months until her appointment with Dr. Cunningham.

But it wasn't all doom and gloom in our lives. Colls was thrilled when she was invited after her friend Jackie's wedding ceremony, to travel with her to the wedding reception in the limousine. What an amazing friend. We already had an outfit for her to wear and with the tan done she looked oh so glamorous. We had another wedding on the horizon with Shaun and Laura announcing their engagement, and our family was expanding. Christine and Rachael had both given birth to little boys.

In an attempt to distract Colleen from the trouble she was having with her foot we joined her up with Technical Aid to the Disabled Australia (TADAust. Connect). This is a national body which was developed to give access to the internet for people with disabilities. It was created when it was found that people on a pension were having difficulty paying for commercial internet services, and were therefore denied access to the internet. This gave Colleen the ability to travel the world from in front of the computer, without it affecting her foot.

Not all of her activities at this time needed to be sedentary. We participated in the Scope interchange programme, which co-ordinated by local government, organizes three to four outings in a ten week term. You choose activities of interest such as a visit to the Melbourne Aquarium or an outing to Federation Square and participants are supervised by carers to a level required by their individual disability. Scope is a not-for-profit organization caring for children and adults with physical, intellectual and multiple disabilities. Colleen goes along and has a good time but does not talk about the other participants. In fact acquired brain injury people do not mix with those with an intellectual disability. Scope is committed to overcoming attitudinal barriers which prevent those with disability from participating in community life. It is a wonderful organization and we are pleased that Colleen is able to join in and get enjoyment from its activities.

As far as it was possible, we wanted Colleen to keep active. Her weight loss wasn't happening and she was continuing to snack. I often found she had raided my pantry.

'Colls, where's the packet of Tim Tams?' I'd asked when I returned home from work one day.

'Um…..I ate them,' she sheepishly replied.

'What all six of them? Really Colleen. They were not yours to eat, this is not your pantry. If you want Tim Tams you buy them.'

But of course she would not think to put them on her list for when she went shopping with her carer. Shaun got really cross with her because of her weight.

He would challenge her with, 'What have you pigged out on today?'

She would not get offended if she hadn't been eating, but if she had been up the street she would confess.

'Well I have no sympathy for you,' he would admonish her. 'Get down on the floor and do some top to toes.'

Colleen adores her brothers, especially Shaun. I kept telling them to put their arms around her and give her a hug. The only male she has in her life is her father and she needed more.

Finally on the 8th November we saw Dr. Cunningham. Colleen had a collapsed metatarsal. The metatarsal bone ends are cushioned in the ball of the foot. A lot of metatarsal pain can be caused by undue pressure on this region. These bones absorb the weight during walking, and if they are put under stress, they can be fractured. This can be caused by activities such as jogging, wearing ill-fitting shoes that put pressure on the bones of the feet, and for women, wearing high heel shoes which throw the weight onto the ball of the foot. For Colleen, the way she walked because of the stroke ultimately caused the middle metatarsal bone to collapse. In trying to avoid the pain this was causing her when walking, she would tense up her toes which in turn would cause them to curl and her leg to spasm. Dr. Cunningham discussed the alternatives with us. He does a lot of work with acquired brain injury patients and special needs people and he wasn't quite sure which way to proceed with Colleen. After due consideration when he spoke I understood him to say that he thought surgery in which he would lengthen the Achilles and split the tendon would be the best way to go, but he wanted to think about it before he proceeded down this path. I was a bit disappointed because we had hoped he would move on it straight away. I expressed my concern about the pain and discomfort she was experiencing, but he said just to have her keep taking paracetamol. She had gone back to the half orthotic and he suggested that we return to the full one to hopefully keep the toes straight.

  We lasted a couple of weeks. I rang again to say it was not working and that Colleen was very distressed. His secretary advised that Dr. Cunningham was booked out and we would not be able to see him until mid January so we had to be satisfied with making an appointment for then.

  So I'd thought perhaps now I had better make a conscious effort to tackle Colleen's weight. If she was lighter, the pressure on her foot would be less and hopefully the pain reduced. The problem with her foot had highlighted for me the concern I had generally for all her joints and the repercussions of her being overweight. I enrolled her in a course at Jenny Craig. It was disastrous. She was given a week's supply of food which was consigned to her fridge and freezer and we put some in my freezer. She ate three days' allocation of food in one day. It was not going to work. I did not want to have to stand over her and demand she follow the recommended regime. I was her mum, not the Gestapo. I rang the people at Jenny Craig and explained the situation to them. They were very understanding and gave me a refund. I decided it was no good using Colleen's pension money to pay for these programmes which did not work when we could spend half as much on good food and try yet again to tackle her binge eating.

The year was drawing to a close as was Colleen's three and a half year association with AFL Sportsready. At the beginning of December Colleen attended the Christmas party which was held at Moonee Valley Racecourse. She had completed the traineeship and was now ready to graduate. The time spent with the Sportsready people was a wonderful experience for her. We will always be grateful she was given this opportunity.

With Christmas festivities and activities all around us I had an inspired thought. We purchased a second hand motorized scooter for Colleen. She was now unable to walk any distance. We did not want her to miss out on all the excitement of this special time of the year, and being able to put the scooter in the boot of the car enable us to take her anywhere, even Christmas shopping which had always been difficult for her with the general rush and bustle of the other shoppers. Also instead of walking, she could now hop on her scooter and ride up to the local shops. It was the best thing we ever did. The weight was off her foot and she had regained her independence.

We had hoped when Colleen finished with AFL Sportsready we would be able to actively seek employment for her. Unfortunately the problem with her foot and the likelihood of surgery meant we would have to sort this problem out first. It would be unfair to expect an employer to take her on in her existing condition. Still 2008 promised to be if nothing else, interesting. We would get Colleen's foot sorted, find her employment, and move into a whole new phase of seeking her independence. But, as it turned out, we would have to jump a few hurdles along the way.

Chapter 23

MARKING TIME

'It is not a pre-existing condition,' I said. I could feel the heat rising up my neck as I tightly gripped the phone. I had rung Medibank Private and advised them that Colleen had a foot problem and was likely to require surgery. I explained that this may occur before the twelve month's qualifying period had expired and enquired whether there were any exceptions to the rule. They suggest I write a letter explaining the extenuating circumstances and this phone call from them was the result of my approach. I had been told that as they considered it was a pre-existing ailment, Colleen would not be covered. I was livid.

'The collapsed metatarsal was not present when she had the stroke nine years ago. It is a result of but was not in existence then,' I argued. They agreed to review my claim: then.

'They've knocked us back again, Peter,' I said with disgust. 'I'm not giving up.'

First I had to get Mr. Cunningham to fill out forms. When I received them from him he had written that it was a pre-existing condition. Back I went. His secretary was very angry.

'Well Mrs. Clancy, it is a pre-existing condition,' she argued.

'Glennis, you and I can argue until the cows come home. I'm telling you it's not pre-existing, and I'm going to the Ombudsman with my case. I'm not paying Medibank Private one hundred and fifty dollars a month to be told it's pre-existing. I have a person dealing with a foot she cannot walk with and I need to get it fixed. I'm not backing off until it happens, so end of story,' I'd said. She was not impressed. Eventually I got forms from Mr. Cunningham stating that it wasn't a pre-existing condition. By now I was totally focused on my goal. Off my documentation went to the Ombudsman.

After many weeks my persistence paid off. I rang through to Mr. Cunningham's rooms.

'Glennis, we need an appointment for surgery for Colleen please,' I requested.

'What! Well, I never heard the likes of it,' she said in amazement.

'Yes, we won,' I'd said more than a little gloatingly. 'You don't know who you're dealing with,' I told her. I recalled using those very same words years ago when Colleen had been so desperately ill.

From the outset of Colleen's illness I had been passionate about the outcome of her treatments. I thought to myself, it's because of whom they've been dealing with that Colleen is where she is today. I'll never stop fighting for what I believe will be in her best interests. Colleen's surgery was scheduled for the 26th June, her thirty-first birthday.

While we had been marking time awaiting resolution of the Medibank Private battle, we had been continuing in our quest to keep Colleen in the best physical shape we could. Locally there had been exercise classes where machines were employed to stretch muscles, but these classes were no longer available in our area and I was at a loss to know where to source this facility. As Colleen was unable to exercise because of her foot I was anxious that her muscles were activated in an endeavour to keep her supple and prevent them from wasting. I needed to know where these classes were now being held. I'd had a brain wave and rang Ernie Sigley on 3AW. Could anyone help me in my quest? Not two minutes later a woman rang in and I was directed to Box Hill a couple of suburbs away where this exercise regime was being run. I enrolled Colleen and she attended classes right up until she had her operation.

Through the local Council, Colleen was eligible for the services of a housekeeper. She loved the girl who came in once a fortnight and worked with her as she mopped the floors, cleaned out the fridge and microwave, polished the glass sliding door and cleaned the toilet and vanity. Sometimes I worked with her cleaning the venetian blinds and other more onerous tasks. I found this facility stopped me from becoming bitter because of all the things I needed to do for Colleen. It was at this time that we found out that Colleen had funding available to her from Uniting Care Community Options which is operated by the Uniting Church. The funding from the Slow to Recover programme, for which we had been truly grateful, had finished in 2004 and this alternative source of funding had been available to her since then. Here it was March 2008 and we had never used the one thousand dollars per annum allotted to Colleen. We were also eligible for a disability parking sticker which greatly assisted us while she was incapacitated with her foot.

Sometimes I couldn't help thinking perhaps I was expecting too much financial assistance. After all there are a lot of people out there much worse off than Colleen. She receives a pension and the quarterly insurance payments. Any money she earns reduces the pension by that amount. The Department of Human Services pays fifteen thousand dollars per annum to cover carers. Up to this point of time we had been accessing carers from Australian Home Care which charged a thirty per cent administration fee. Then through Living Distinctive Lives we changed to Melba Support Services. Melba is a not for profit organization supporting individuals with a disability by helping them to lead everyday lives and be valued and contributing members of their community. We found it charged only ten per cent meaning we could access a further twenty per cent of the fifteen thousand dollars for Colleen. I was determined to use the money to the best advantage, and to try and source someone who could be creative with moving Colls out into the community. I'd thought to myself it is a huge task but the important thing is to keep your eye on the vision and not get bogged down with everyday tasks. This is where Living Distinctive Lives (L.D.L.) helped me keep focused.

'Mum, I've meet this woman, Deb Rouget. What she told me sounds too good to be true,' Shaun had said enthusiastically. 'I think we should give it a go.'

He went on to tell me about Living Distinctive Lives (L.D.L.) which is hosted by Melba Support Services. It is a small family governed group focused on supporting individuals with a disability to have a life entwined with the community, and to allow them to participate in all facets of community life, including work, recreation and housing. Each person involved in Living Distinctive Lives makes decisions about their home and lifestyle.

'We need to have a meeting inviting everyone we think may be interested in setting up a structure to support Colleen,' he continued.

'But Shaun, won't people think it is our problem and why should they be there to prop us up?' I'd queried. I found the thought of opening up to people daunting and quite scary.

Finally Shaun convinced me that we had nothing to lose by giving it a go and I agreed to him setting up the meeting. I did not invite anyone. Who would I invite? I left it to the kids. They're the ones who will have to be progressive in their thinking, I thought to myself. It will fall on them if it doesn't work. So they sent out all these emails. Family and friends were rallied and thirty people attended at Jim's office to hear what Deb had to say. For me it was a nerve wracking experience. Colleen thought she was pretty important. Hey, this is all about me!

'We need to have a structure in place so that if anything happens to Bernadette and Peter, Colleen can continue to live without upsetting her routine too much,' Deb had said.

This was something I had been struggling with for a while. Just what would happen if Peter and I were killed in a car accident? Would she be able go and live with another family member? Anyway Deb was very clear and precise about how it could work. In addition to the immediate family, it just meant that everyone involved would have to make a commitment to be involved in Colleen's life if she were living independently by filling in the gaps when a carer could not be present or when she was not occupied with her regular activities like work and therapies. The more people who were involved, the less turns they would have to take in being there for Colls. This group of people would be called "Colleen's Circle of Friends". The meeting brought to the group's attention how successfully this could work and in the weeks following, Colleen was invited to join in activities of the various group members, including attending a concert and art exhibition, and an overnight stay and a day's outing. This sort of support would be invaluable for Colleen's siblings if they were in trouble and could ring around for someone to help them out even if only for a few hours. This might really work, I thought to myself. Colleen thrived on the additional attention she was receiving and her view was that she would be living independently within twelve months. At least we were all working towards a common goal. We had a long way to go but at least it was a start. I wanted to learn a lot more about L.D.L.

Meanwhile the A.F.L. Sportready graduation dinner came and went. Colls received her certificate with Peter proudly looking on. But it did not lead anywhere. After all the training Colleen had received I think we were a bit disappointed that her Disability Employment Action Centre (D.E.A.C.) mentor was not able to channel Colls into some sort of employment. It looked like it would be up to us to pursue Colleen's career path.

We continued to look at alternatives for Colleen. We arranged an interview for her at the Glen Iris branch of Eastworks, an organization which helps people with disabilities realize and achieve their vocational goals by finding employment for them in the community. Its approach is to have their clients compose a wish list of where they would like to work. In Colleen's case we looked at different retail situations, like the photo department at Harvey Norman, positions at local shops and as she was still keen on child care, local child care centres. She did help out at Little Paddington Care Centre in a voluntary position. Unfortunately she felt in danger. The little tables and chairs and other equipment dotted around the room proved to be a mine field for Colleen to navigate with her bad leg, and she freaked out. It was just too cluttered for her.

Meanwhile, our next door neighbour who told us he would often hear Colleen yelling to us from her Unit, told Peter he thought he knew of a job for her. So we started to transport her to Crown Street, Richmond where she was employed as the quality control officer in a women's clothing factory. Wow, we thought, how good is this? She was required to check to see if there were any threads hanging on the garments, that the buttons were sewn on properly, then sort the clothes into the different sizes. She quite liked it but I don't think these people had dealt with an acquired brain injury person before and they found it a bit tricky, especially when Colleen could not do a lot of the things they required and when they discovered she had no attention to detail. Anyway the job came to an end when there was a bit of a downturn in the industry and the work sort of dwindled, but it had kept her occupied for a couple of months.

During this time I had read about a local theatrical/drama group run through the Boroondara Shire community centre. I hesitated. Was I looking for a babysitter for Colleen or trying to find something that she would like doing? The latter came to the fore and I met two of the loveliest girls who were only too delighted to have Colleen join the group, the members of which all had disabilities, most more so than Colls. Well I thought, it's up to Colleen whether or not she wants to be involved. She loved it. They made a film, did some improvised acting and performed some ABBA songs. For two terms Colleen eagerly participated, but unfortunately all the time having trouble with her foot. When I went to pick her up she would be sitting on a chair holding the offending appendage. Then suddenly her interest waned. I think it had something to do with one of the male members of the group who had Down Syndrome.

'He just stares at me all the time, Mum,' she'd said. She refused to go back. They were very sad to see her go.

Then as a result of the first circle meeting Coll's friend Jackie organized a voluntary job for her with 'S.I.D.S.

(Sudden Infant Death Syndrome) Kids', work she could take on while waiting for her foot problem to be sorted. Each year the surplus red nose day badges had been put in a storeroom, and the question arose, what were they going to do with them? It would be irresponsible to throw them into landfill. So they needed volunteers to separate them. The paper would be recycled and the metal melted down to make more pins. We could handle that!

'Gee this will be a good job, Colls,' I'd said when the first six boxes arrived at our home by courier. She looked a bit doubtful and I shot Peter a warning glance before he could make any comment.

So every night the three of us would set up our production line, removing the pin from the card, separating the front from the pin and sorting into separate piles. It worked fantastically, even though it was a bit chaotic in the family room.

'What on earth have you got yourself into here, Mum,' Christine asked indicating to the boxes, piles of discarded cards, and pins heaped on every available surface of the family room .

I shrieked with laughter. 'This is Colls' new job,' I said.

'Did she make all this mess by herself?' Christine replied also chuckling.

'This is the second lot we've done,' I told her. 'When we'd finished the first six boxes, Peter returned them and collected another six.'

'How many more boxes,' Christine asked in amazement.

'I don't know. Until there're finished,' I replied.

When we got to the last three boxes, I decided I would take Colleen with me to deliver them instead of Peter so we could meet the girls he had told me were so fantastic.

'Oh, you must be Bernadette and Colleen. We're so grateful you have done all those pins. We are absolutely delighted.' they all said enthusiastically. Colleen beamed. They then went on to say that they would love to give Colleen a job putting names and addresses into a data base. They were desperate because they could not send out their appeal letters as the data base was not up to scratch and they were losing money all the time. I thought to myself, we really need to do this for them. I told them Colleen was not brilliant on the computer but if someone sat with her it might work, but once again we would have to get her foot sorted first. Perhaps next year.....

We had still not accessed the funding Colleen had available to her from Uniting Care Community Options and the end of the financial year was approaching when I had a phone call.

'Mrs. Clancy, I'm just letting you know there's money left for Colleen if you need anything,' the girl told me.

'What do you mean if I need anything? How long's a piece of string! Her shoes are three hundred dollars a pair. Which angle do you want me to come from?' I'd retorted.

'Well, would she like a holiday?' she asked.

Would she like a holiday? Wouldn't we all like a holiday? So I suggested she send me a list of the places available for us to choose from. Frankston on Port Phillip Bay at five hundred dollars a night sounded absolutely beautiful so I booked for Colleen and her cousin to go with her as her carer. But then when making final arrangements and I advised the establishment that Colleen would be in plaster, I was told that they could not take anyone in plaster as there were twenty stairs and no balustrade. So after all the research and phone calls I had been wasting my time and all the arrangements fell over.

All was not lost though, for at short notice Peter and I were able to have a weekend away at Wangaratta in central Victoria. I was so looking forward to having champagne on the train and just completely switching off for a couple of days. We arrived at Southern Cross Railway Station, the interstate terminal in Melbourne, and with great anticipation I had stood in line to collect our pre-booked tickets while Peter guarded our two cases. As I was leaving the ticket box someone went charging past with their wheeled case and clipped the end of my shoe, spun me around like a top and I landed flat on the ground on my face, banging my brow on the pavement. Peter came running over and after he had ascertained there appeared to be no broken bones and that I was just badly shaken announced, 'Well that does it. We're going home.'

'Oh, no we're not,' I retorted. 'We're getting on that train.'

'You can't,' Peter replied.

'Oh yes we can. We're going away. I don't care. We may as well be pampered for the weekend anyway.' I'd said adamantly.

So we'd got on the train and spent the weekend being indulged, even though I was black and blue and sore all over. But I was devastated. I felt so miserable on the train journey that I did not even get to have my champers. I vowed and declared I would make sure I used the funding for Colleen before the end of the financial year in the future.

Colleen spent three days in hospital when her foot was operated on. A month after the surgery she was able to walk without pain. The foot was stiff and tight but not painful. Hydrotherapy was helping her with her recovery. With the surgery behind us I thought it would be a good time to launch the Young Stroke Group. I wrote to the Brain Foundation and the Victorian Stroke Foundation and received positive feed back from them. In turn I wrote to about fifty young stroke victims and made just as many phone calls. Jenny Chang the coordinator of the older group of stroke people that Colleen had been associated with assisted me sourcing catering at the right price, platters of food and jugs of cordial (on the day I was dying for champers), and we booked a room at The Hawthorn Hotel for 3.00 p.m. The Council disability support officer and the disability services officer from the Eastern Recreational Leisure Services came on board and we got in touch with young people with a disability with whom Colleen had come into contact over the years. It turned out a really nice afternoon, except mostly older people attended. We had photos taken and a little article appeared in the local paper. Not discouraged, after all this was just the launch, I went ahead and locked in bi-monthly dates for other activities, the next being a film and pizza afternoon. I had plans for going to the 20/20 cricket, jazz at the zoo and ten pin bowling. All the dates were put on the calendar and I notified everyone I could by email of the next event. The activities I had in mind were only suggestions. I thought it is really up to the group to decide what they wanted to do, not for me to dictate. I was fortunate to have the promise of some funding to be channeled our way through the City of Boroondara so I forged ahead with my planning.

Colleen was still getting about on her scooter. One day she'd returned from the local shops.

'I can't add up Mum. I didn't know my change,' she said quite distressed.

We had discontinued the Kumon course at the time we shifted to Ashburton. It was very beneficial but I think she found the work difficult, and she never did the homework that was required. Also the kids she was with were in the seven to ten year age group and she probably felt she was old enough to be their mother, and although she did not say it, probably realized that she was different and that she had something wrong with her. I thought she felt inadequate, even humiliated.

She went on, 'I can't read properly and I can't spell either.'

'Well, let's see what we can do about this,' I'd said. So I found a numeracy and literacy course which was being run locally and enrolled her for one day a week of the final term of the year. Colleen loved it and we continued on in the new year, and at the suggestion of one of the teachers, enrolled her in a "back to the work place" computer based programme on another day.

At this stage I had a bit of time to myself to think about the L.D.L. concept with a new job I had taken on. I had become part of a team of carers who were rostered to spend the night with an elderly woman recently widowed. She lived in a lovely old home in Malvern (although she called it Toorak). My night was Monday. I had to arrive at 8.00 p.m. by which time my charge had consumed a little drop of wine and was quite talkative. (I could've done with a drop myself). I would spend the next hour and a half chatting until it was her bed time. From then on the evening was my own. I would've loved a laptop to work on but still I was able to put quite a few ideas together otherwise. Alternatively, I would just read until time for bed. In the morning I would have the kitchen ready for my lady; table set, open the drapes, kettle on, bring in the paper, and then as she required, stay silent while she ate her breakfast. While waiting for her to be ready to have her shower I would strip the bed of my sheets ready for the next carer to make up the bed with their own sheets when they came that night. I would then sit on a chair outside the bathroom. Or, not one to waste an opportunity, would use this time to do my exercises. Crash.

'Oh dear, did I hear you knock my chandelier,' I heard her call from behind the closed bathroom door.

'Yes, yes, but it's OK,' I called back. Boy you're as sharp as a tack I thought to myself.

It was a bit of a shock to Colleen and Peter having me out of the house overnight. Mind you I don't think they did anything, probably just watched television. The ironing certainly didn't get done. I had thought of taking my ironing with me but I think my lady would have been a bit horrified. I think the noise would've annoyed her. I was not even allowed to turn the light on if I needed to go to the toilet during the night. I had been doing the job for quite some time and thought she had mellowed. I asked if I could swap my night with one of the other carers on just one occasion so I could take Colleen to a special church choir practice.

'Oh no, you can't do that. I couldn't cope with different people coming,' was the quick reply. So, I thought to myself, I haven't got you eating out of my hand yet. I'll have to work on you. In any event, it really was a very easy job and I really did enjoy our interesting chats.

The time for the second "Circle of Friends" meeting arrived. No-one turned up. A breakdown in communication was blamed, but no-one was admitting anything. Perhaps those who had been so enthusiastic with their ideas at the first meeting had gone away and thought this is too hard. After all I found it daunting and Colleen was my daughter.

The second meeting of the young stroke group for a movie and pizza afternoon was also poorly attended. Only one of the young people turned up with her mother. I had taken the young woman I cared for and of course Colleen. In the end the funding did not eventuate and I ended up paying for all the pizza, but more disappointing was the lack of interest. We tried again attending a local production of "Doctor in the House", but subsequently I just did not hear from anyone before the designated dates. I was disappointed but thought well, I just can't continue and the whole thing just fell flat.

Although the operation on Colleen's foot had been successful and she was no longer experiencing a great deal of pain, it became necessary in October for her to have rods inserted in her toes to solve a further problem which had occurred. Thank goodness she had the scooter on which to get around.

Meanwhile I had been successful in securing a volunteer position for her at Highgate Childcare Centre, close enough to home for her to take herself there on her scooter. One day I had walked in with Colleen and introduced ourselves. I explained that Colleen had worked in the industry and would now like to try and connect back into life and asked if we could give it a go. They were delighted to have her on board. Initially though, Colleen was hanging back. She lacked the confidence to take part in activities. We were anxious that the position was beneficial for them as much as for Colleen. After lots of chats in which we explained that we did not want it to be a hassle and they must let us know if it was not working, things settled down to everyone's satisfaction, and this association continued until the end of June the following year.

The year was drawing to a close and there was the regular round of Christmas activities for Colleen to attend one of which was the Craig Family Centre party. I'd thought to myself perhaps it's time for her to move on from her five year association with this group. She had not really connected with any of the people, but she still seemed to enjoy being there. Besides, sitting in front of a video and eating popcorn and chocolate slices that they had made was one very good reason alone for her not to be at the Centre. I could see where the Living a Distinctive Life (L.D.L.) people were coming from when they said you don't mix people with a disability with people with a disability. When I looked back at all the positions Colls had had with ordinary people, like Safeway at Lara, the mail room at the Alfred and the opportunity shop, I couldn't help but agree with them that people like Colls where possible should be integrated into the community. When I observed her conduct when she was with people with a disability I believed there was an interesting shift in her manner that I needed to monitor. We'd had an interesting experience when we'd visited Waverley Industry earlier in the year. This industry employs hundreds of people with a disability and I took Colleen along to see what it was like and to my surprise she immediately asked if she could start work the next day.

'Let her go Mum,' Paul said. 'It doesn't matter if it fails. See what happens.'

At the time I'd thought she probably could've sat down and not had to worry about her foot, and in hindsight with the length of time it took for us to sort her foot problem, perhaps I should've let her. But it wasn't the environment into which I had wanted to put her.

The third circle meeting had a much better attendance. This time twelve people were very constructive with their thinking. This number was much more manageable than the first meeting; less daunting. Still, I found the process mind boggling; all those people wanting to help and me having no idea how I could get them to help. It was nerve wracking because you were asking people to volunteer their time and energy for you and your daughter. But those in attendance were very supportive and in fact commented on how much better Colleen was communicating. They said they thought there had been a huge step forward as she was speaking fluently in that social atmosphere. I was surprised as she still became tongue tied at home and often her brain and mouth did not seem to be synchronizing. I would have to say hang on a minute, start again, and then she would say it better. Someone at the meeting said that the message was coming through loud and clear that the problem with Colleen's foot was much more debilitating than anyone realized. I could've cried.

'Oh, yes! You've hit the nail on the head,' I said with tears in my eyes. 'It is affecting Peter's and my life so badly and until it's sorted we are just having to put everything on hold.'

From that meeting Colleen was included in further outings and activities were arranged. I still had the vision of purchasing a house or unit for Colleen and putting carers in place to assist her, and with her "Circle of Friends" this was beginning to seem more like a possibility. Colleen would need to have someone living with her, say a student, perhaps studying to become a carer in disability services, to point her in the right direction with her daily tasks without necessarily having her dependent on them. Deb told us of families where this had been successful, one in a country town and the other with a flat below the family home where a live-in flat mate made it possible for the disabled person to live independently with the help of their circle of friends. As usual Peter's siblings and mine were enormously supportive. They were right when they said the houses in the price range I was looking at were falling down. Their suggestion that I was not to let money be an obstacle to my plans because they were happy to pool resources, brought tears to my eyes.

Then we were faced with a dilemma. Colleen received a wedding invitation, and as quick as a flash she'd ticked the box and sent off her acceptance. It was to be the day before Peter was admitted to hospital for his knee operation and on the day I had a workshop. Colleen had rung around to the only mutual friends she knew who were attending but they were bridesmaids and unable to assist in getting her there and making arrangements for her after the wedding.

'How are we going to do this Pete?' I asked anxiously.

'Perhaps one of the kids could take her,' he suggested, then, 'but that would be difficult. They would have to hang around to bring her home.' I agreed with him. It was a big ask especially as Christine and Rachael's families had increased, each having given birth to little boys the previous year.

'If I took her we would have to leave here at one, you could do the workshop instead of me, or we'll have to give that a miss completely. We could go to the church, take Colls to the reception, go somewhere for dinner and wait until midnight to bring her home. Then we have to be at the hospital at sparrows the next day. No Pete, it's just all too hard,' I'd said despondently.

In the end I wrote the bride a letter and said unfortunately Colleen had accepted but it was now too difficult for her to attend and very briefly explained our dilemma and left it at that. Colleen was massively heartbroken.

Here I thought is a perfect situation where Colleen's "Circle of Friends" when properly structured would kick in. On this occasion it was beyond Peter and I to overcome the insurmountable obstacles, but given sufficient notice and the structures being in place with her circle of family and friends, surely something could have been organized. I became even more determined to explore in 2009 what L.D.L. was advocating.

More importantly, I wanted to further my push to have Colleen established in an independent living arrangement. I just knew it would work given the right set of circumstances. It was time for Colleen to move on and I was sure L.D.L. was the right organization to help us achieve this goal. I was going to make 2009 a year of change.

Chapter 24

LIVING A DISTINCTIVE LIFE

By the end of 2008 I really thought we were moving in the right direction. There were so many positives on which to build.

Through Living Distinctive Lives (L.D.L.) I went to a conference at the Salvation Army Citadel at Doncaster which was organized by Deb Roget and attended by families who are in the L.D.L. group. It was an expensive weekend, but not to be deterred I'd written away and was successful in obtaining funding. One of the purposes of the conference was to reinforce the view that people can have a life even though they have a disability, and for us to look outside the square. Guest speakers, one from America, were promoting setting up independent living for people with a disability. Wasn't this what I had been advocating for Colleen? The instances where this had been put into practice were very encouraging. I listened with rapt attention as we were told of the success stories.

One family had cared for their twenty-eight year old daughter all her life. She is confined to a wheel chair, is mentally impaired, unable to verbally communicate and requires twenty-four hour care. They had just moved her into a house and had a network of carers to cater for her needs, even though at great personal expense. She is a mad keen drummer and they have found a group for her to join and she is as happy as Larry. Another family have a young guy who is a part-time chef living in a flat underneath their house with their disabled son Warren. Warren attends lots of community activities during the day and at night the fellows cook the meals together and occasionally go out socially. It is just working beautifully. Then a real success story, is where a young disabled fellow lives with a house sharer. The local community is aware of his weekly routine and if he hasn't been up the street someone checks up on him. He has been a guest speaker at some of our L.D.L. functions. With his Mum beside him, he delights us with his great sense of humour, and he just seems to keep on improving.

Examples like these gave me the drive to keep going. Sometimes I'd think, this is all too hard and I'd just want to crawl under my blanket and not come out. Some days I'd just want to walk away from it and felt I didn't have the emotional energy to deal with it. On these occasions I'd think, Colleen will survive, why let it get to me. Given my family history I don't want to get struck down by a stroke with the stress of this. But sometimes I'd have to force myself to continue; a bit of a guilt thing I suppose. I didn't want to be in control but had to be because she made a mess of everything, but all the time I felt I should be trying to let go. But I'd have to be reinforcing even the simple things all the time.

'I went across the road with no lights,' Colleen had declared one day when she came back from an expedition to the shops on her scooter.

'Why didn't you cross over at the lights? Why?' I asked incredulously.

''Cause I wanted to come home,' she replied and then continued 'this guy said to me you might get run over.'

'Colleen, that is so dangerous,' I said.

'I know. I've done it twice now,' she said sheepishly.

She knows what is right and wrong but does not always stop to think of the consequences of her actions. Thinking about it, how often have you and I done things which in hindsight we have thought have been a bit careless but would be reluctant to admit to having done. Is Colleen any different other than she feels obliged to own up to her transgressions? Still this was something I would have to work on if Colleen was to live independently.

Just shortly prior to Christmas it was time to visit Mr. Cunningham. I'd kept up a constant stream of inane patter as each of the skewer like rods was removed from her toes and dropped with a clang into the waiting bucket. Colleen although she did not look, did no more than flinch. I was surprised when in answer to my questions, the doctor said physio or hydro therapy would not be needed, the tendon had been cut and the Achilles lengthened: job done. Even so, a couple of months later we found both these therapies very beneficial in helping her mobility, especially when she discarded the scooter in February.

Pilates also helped her tremendously. Her teacher advocated that if she removed the artificial foot orthotic and did the exercises in bare feet this would help to stimulate her muscles. This seemed to make sense to me. He was so pleased with her progress that he only accepted payment every second week. Unfortunately at one of the lessons, she had a fall, bruised her foot, lost her confidence and her enthusiasm, so we had to discontinue the lessons. It was good while it lasted.

Not all arrangements we made for Colleen proved to be satisfactory. The third circle meeting giving me the confidence, I advertised locally and secured the services of a drama teacher for Colleen. She had shown great enthusiasm when she had been involved in local productions, so we thought it would be a good idea to explore this avenue further. She loved her private lessons and the best part was she could ride her scooter and not have to rely on us to transport her. At Christmas time the students put on a little play at someone's home, and for the next couple of months all went well. Then an incident shook us all.

'He touched me on the breast, Mum,' Colleen said when she returned from one of her lessons.

'Are you sure, Colleen. Was he not just turning the page of the script and brushed against you accidently?' I'd asked skeptically. Colleen is very big in the bust and I thought this was a likely explanation. 'This is a very serious accusation Colleen.'

'No! I'm telling you, it wasn't an accident,' she said adamantly.

'We'll have to talk with Dad about this Colleen, for he will have to ring your teacher and tell him you are not going back or whatever you want to do,' I said.

'Well, I'll tell you right now, I won't be going back,' she said determinedly.

When we discussed it further when Peter came home, she said he had put his hand on her breast and said, oh you're big. She became very distressed and reiterated that she would not be returning for lessons. Peter went to the Police Station to ask for advice about how to handle the situation. He was told it was very dangerous if he made an accusation and it hadn't happened. After a lot of agonizing, Peter rang the teacher and advised Colleen's lessons would have to stop and the reason why. The teacher said there was no way he would do such a thing, and that it wasn't true. Peter said he was really sorry but he would have to take Colleen's word. It was just awful. What had been a lovely association had to come to an end, but we had to believe what Colleen said.

Meanwhile I had been anxious that Colleen's music skills be cultivated. I had been investigating bands. I tried three but they were all a bit too advanced. It was hard work. Sometimes I thought, oh I can't make yet another phone call, I'll go crazy. The kids are wonderful but they don't live with it. I think they think oh, you'll be right, and what's she carrying on about? They have their little children and my situation is way down on their radar. They just accept it for what it is whereas I am dealing with an adult child, adult physically, child mentality, day in and day out. Also I worry about Colleen's health if I'm not there to drive the bus. It makes me wonder. My father always said "you have to go to the extreme to achieve half way results". Is that why I expect so much and drive myself as hard as I do? I was not going to give up on doing the very best I could for Colleen.

Our L.D.L. group consisting of eight families, all with an adult special needs person, decided that Colleen and one other in the group would become their priorities. So we applied for and were successful in obtaining a grant from the Scanlon Foundation through my brother Peter, allowing us to employ for eight hours a week a community inclusion facilitator. Theresa's job would be to help these two connect into the community. I always thought I was a very good community connector but I found that Colleen knew more people in the community than me through all the programmes she had been involved with over the years. In consultation with Jo Walters, our L.D.L. coordinator, it would be Theresa's job to source meaningful employment and assist us in making independent living arrangements for Colleen. The sooner the better for all of us I'd thought. Sometimes I would just lose it when I would pop into her unit to see her.

'Colleen, you're an absolute disgrace. You just leave your clothes where you step out of them. Everything here is a big mess. You say you want to move on from here but you will never get anyone prepared to live with you. You are so untidy. I despair!' I said, and with that I'd spun around, tangled my feet in her pajamas stumbled forward, knocked my head on the bed post, then cracked it again on the open wardrobe door before I hit the floor. I dragged myself up onto bed and sat, face buried in my hands, close to tears. I thought to myself, you're a bloody shit Colleen. I've had this. I can't stand it any longer. I just felt so exhausted. But what could I do? I just had to move on.

For about eighteen months I had been noticing a change in Colleen's attitude and she had been expressing her frustration with the structure of her life. She did not want to be told that today was swimming and what was on the agenda for the rest of the week. Although at first she had been thrilled to have her own space in the granny flat now at the end of five years, she was becoming disgruntled. I would watch as she sat on the couch in front of the television, hands on knees leaning forward like a contained spring ready to uncoil, three empty coffee cups in front of her,.

'Sit back, relax Colls. Perhaps you could turn the telly off and play your flute or get your paints out.'

'No!' she would shout at me. 'Oh, I want to leave. When can I go?'

'Well Colls, the case is in the garage. Would you like me to pack it now?' I would jokingly reply.

'Yeah. Whatever.' She'd say sarcastically.

'One day , darl. We've just got to do it gradually,' I'd reply gently.

I'd sighed to myself and thought I would become very bitter if I was to keep doing this for another ten years. Peter was also becoming more negative.

'She can't do that,' he would admonish me when I suggested some task for her to do.

'Yes she can,' I would retort, 'and don't you suggest otherwise to her.'

'Gosh you're tough,' he replied.

'No, I'm just moving forward. You have to be tough. You just won't survive otherwise.'

This dissatisfaction with her life was also exacerbating her problem with food too. I had got to the stage where I thought there were a lot of negative vibes surfacing between the three of us; niggling and sarcasm flowed through our conversations.

I still today draw on my religion daily. If I miss Mass it doesn't trouble me. I say to myself that my lot in life is my Mass. This is the little bit of sacrifice you have chosen to give me God, but I'm finding it hard today, You'll have to help me through this. I used to go to Mass as a habit, now I go because I need that quiet prayer time. I prayer every day and thank God that I awake in the mornings, that I was able to get up to do a wee during the night. There are people in nursing homes who wear a nappy because they can't. I could've given up so many times but I thank God for having kept me strong and focused, and pray, dear God keep me safe. I need to be here.

Peter has struggled with it all. Most men would've gone. Many marriages with a special needs person don't survive. Perhaps we would struggle when we arranged independent living for Colls, but I guess we'll have to hang in there. The alternatives are not much chop. Besides, I could not do it to the kids. They've been through enough. But Peter needed to work; he needs the people; he needs the connection and stimulation. And it would be really good to find something to reconnect us.   Well I guess that's something else to pray for I'd think to myself.

The times Colleen spent away from us gave us all a bit of breathing space. A weekend was again arranged for her to visit her friend Danny at Mulwala on the Victorian/New South Wales border. Off she went on her journey. Unfortunately she had boarded the wrong bus and was heading for Wangaratta. I had a call from a complete stranger.

'This lass is looking very worried,' a lady said, 'just checking for her to see if she is on the right track.'

Discovering the mistake I began to try and find a solution. I didn't have to solve the problem.

'We're going to Yarrawonga. Give us the address where she is going and we'll take her there,' Colleen's rescuer declared.

I was dumbfounded. I rang Danny to tell her Colls would be a bit late and to fill her in on the details. I requested she obtain Colleen's good Samaritan's name and address, so I could write a thank you note: how precious this act of kindness was and way above the call of duty.

A more adventurous expedition was arranged for Colleen to fly to Queensland accompanied by her cousin Edwina. An incident the night before the trip highlighted how important it was for us to have time out from each other. I had had an exhausting day. I was looking after the twins, shopping for last minute items to be packed in the suitcase, keeping an appointment for Colls to have her hair cut, and the day just disappeared. Colleen was tired too and because I wanted her to be adequately prepared for the journey which was to begin at 4.00 a.m. the next day, I wanted to ensure that she had a good dinner that night;

cutlets with veggies and a desert to complete the meal, even though I was dog-tired.

'Hello! Did anyone in this room have a nice tea? Did you enjoy your rhubarb and apple and custard? Well you both need a kick up the backside. Neither of you said that was yummy or thanks for the tea,' I said angrily. It just wasn't good enough. I didn't like being taken for granted.

Not long after this holiday in June, Danya came into our lives. This beautiful eighteen month old Labrador/golden retriever cross became Colleen's new companion. The previous Christmas we had looked after my brother Terry's dog Rollo. It was a real eye opener, watching Colleen interact with the dog. She loved taking her for walks, and I was delighted as this was giving her the exercise necessary for the rehabilitation following her surgery as well as burning kilojoules. Then we had Shaun's dog Lenny, while he and Laura were honeymooning, and once again Colleen enjoyed the experience. Although Lenny was too strong for her to walk him, she loved feeding him and throwing the ball for him to chase. I took some photos.

'Pete, I'm going to ring tomorrow to see about getting a companion dog for Colls,' I had said after Shaun had collected Lenny.

'What happens when we go away if we get a dog?' Peter queried.

'Go away! Go away!' I said my voice rising. 'Hello! When do we go away? That doesn't happen too often, and if it's only once a year we'll put it in a kennel.'

Unfortunately we were told there was a waiting list a mile long and we may have to wait eighteen months. Anyway I filled in the application form and posted it off with some photos. Not long after we were visited to check out our suitability and to ensure that our yard was secure. I was heartened when I was told we would bolt it in. Then not even six months later Danya arrived, fully house trained and beautifully behaved.

Initially Colleen panicked.

'She's following me everywhere, Mum,' she said.

'Well she's your dog, Colls. Give her a pat, tickle her ear. Let her know that you love her.' I'd replied.

For the first few days Danya looked really sad and I'd thought, oh dear, she doesn't like us. Soon Colleen got into the routine of feeding her, although sometimes she would have to be prompted, but the best thing was taking the dog for a walk. Going to the shops took on a whole new meaning.

'Mum, everyone says what a beautiful dog,' Colleen said on her return from one such excursion. 'I told them, yes, and it's mine,' she said proudly, her eyes shining.

In addition to working for my brother Terry at Lifestyle and Rehabilitation, I was still doing home care. I had Tania my wheelchair bound young girl, my overnight stay job Monday and Thursday nights and I had one day caring for a T.A.C. patient and his wife who had suffered a stroke. Also I had commenced working at a local nursing home. Initially I was employed as a personal carer on the shower shift seven until eleven, but within a couple of weeks I was asked whether I would like to be the activities lady. I agreed to take on this new roll even though I thought I was not qualified. I loved it.

The oldies, loved the activities I arranged for them, including bingo. Not ever having been a fan of this activity, I could not have imagined that I would ever be calling the numbers for this popular game. I bought little gifts which I wrapped and would spend hours on the internet looking for games and jokes, and then making gift cards and other aids for the activities. I found I was spending more and more time on preparations, outside of the hours for which I was being paid. One day I was running late. I had stopped at the shopping centre to buy some balloons for the table centres for the Melbourne Cup Day celebrations, and I nudged one of the cars in the car park. There did not seem to be any damage to what I thought was the bank manager's expensive model. I'd looked at my watch and thought, I'll have to keep going. I'll come back later in the day before the bank is closed and give my name and address, and off I dashed. I didn't give it another thought.

'Mum, the police have been here,' Colleen said anxiously when I arrived home, 'about some accident?' she queried.

The phone rang. 'Guilty, your honour,' I said flippantly to the constable. 'I didn't leave my name and address. What do you want me to do?'

'Well you'll be hearing from the insurance company. A claim's going to be lodged,' I was told.

'Right-o, constable, there's no damage anyway,' I replied. Still I thought it wise to go and take some photos and to see the owner of the car. I could not see a scratch or mark or anything. So I went and introduced myself. On inspection together, we had to agree to disagree on the issue of damage to the vehicle. I would have to wait and see what if anything eventuated. Ultimately the first quote of $1,800 was rejected by my insurance company and one for $800 was settled on. But as it turned out this was not to be the end of the matter.

But I was not going to let this incident spoil my delight at the turn for the better in our lives. Peter had a job.

Across the road from where we lived a couple of enterprising young women had set up "Lunchbox Cuisine" providing healthy food for primary school children. Lunch orders are taken and paid for on the internet, packaged and then delivered by Peter. He now had his first paid job since we shifted to Ashburton. More importantly, he loves it. He's out there mixing with people, driving around, keeping alert. It is just fantastic to see him actively involved in a worthwhile occupation.

Meanwhile, my work arrangements were about to change. I knew my job with my brother at Lifestyle and Rehabilitation was to finish at Christmas time which was OK, but in November I had decided I would challenge the nursing home which had been more than pleased with my performance.

'Oh Bern, the patients love you and the activities you arrange for them. We have never had eighteen in the activities room, ever, you're wonderful,' I had been told.

'You know, you're getting a pretty good pound of flesh from me. I think you should be able to pay me for at least another hour, preferably two for all the additional time I spend out of work preparing activities,' I'd suggested. I also requested that boards be purchased to enable jigsaw puzzles to be left set up and for individual clip boards for word games to be bought, both at minimal expense. They refused all these requests.

Around this time I was asked if I knew of anyone who would be a nanny to four children one and a half days a week.

'You're looking at her,' came my quick reply and I immediately wrote out my resignation for the nursing home.

'You can't do this!' was the horrified response.

'Oh yes I can. You were not honouring what I did. You have to look after good staff,' I replied. This was the most courageous thing I had ever done.

I also needed some courage for next challenge with which I was presented. My little 'accident' in the car park was to have its repercussions. A week before Christmas I received a letter to say my driving licence would be suspended unless I had an eye test. So off I went to my doctor and then the ophthalmologist to obtain the necessary reports which I quickly sent with a letter to VicRoads. The next correspondence I receive was to say my licence had been suspended. They never received my letter. So Peter this time hand delivered a copy of my letter. Then I received a further letter to say I needed a driving assessment because they believed I may not be competent. Why were they doing this?

'Mum, you'll never slow down, and now the bloody law can't slow you down,' my family laughingly said. They thought it was a huge joke.

I was humiliated, even more so when I received my examiner, Vavek's, assessment.

'I've been driving for forty years and never had an accident, and you're failing me?' I'd asked.

'That's right,' came the smug reply. 'I reckon you did five kilometres over in the sixty zone.'

'I never did!' I declared. I was devastated especially at having to front up to everyone. It felt like I had failed my John and Betty grade one reader. I had another four weeks without driving. The next guy said I was perhaps a bit over cautious but that my driving was perfect. All this was so ridiculous and very stressful. While I was without my licence, as my chauffer, Peter found out just how much I crammed into a week. Especially as during all this turmoil, to our delight, and Colleen's great excitement, on the 10th November, 2009 she had moved on to an independent living arrangement. Consequently I had needed to be mobile to ensure that things in her world continued to go smoothly.

Chapter 25

INDEPENDENCE

The independent living arrangements we made for Colleen turned out to be a steep learning curve for all of us; the family, Colleen and most of all for her housemate, Wen.

For several months we had been actively trying to secure independent accommodation for Colleen. We'd ploughed through the papers and visited the advertised two bedroom flats, all the time thinking, how are we going to afford this? We had prerequisites: it had to be within walking distance of us, transport, the pool and the shops. We put in application after application always thinking, this will be the one, but were unsuccessful. I looked at a three bedroom flat. It would be easy to sublet, wouldn't it? Then a family from our church was going overseas vacating their four bedroom house around the corner and I put in an application for that.

'You've done what, Mum?' asked Christine incredulously.

'How on earth do you think we are going to fill a house?' chimed in Paul.

'You must be mad!' declared Shaun.

So I panicked. I realized that the kids probably had reason to be wild and angry. I thought to myself, well we'll just have to put this in God's hands. He'll have to work it out. We weren't accepted. Problem solved. Then:

'This two bedroom one would be perfect, Mum,' Paul said, unable to contain his excitement. 'It's one kilometre from here, a short distance from the pool, and near where Colleen was going to school last year.'

So we put in an application and lo and behold, were successful in securing this back unit in a block of four. Now all we needed was a housemate. Living Distinctive Lives (L.D.L.) had been advertising for us and was communicating with Wesley Home Share which had only recently branched out from aged care into this area of care. Wen was the only one on their books. A friend of hers had returned to Bejing after having been a housemate to a young man with multiple sclerosis who had died. His family offered Wen accommodation until she got her own home sharing situation. We met her about three times, and with no other prospects on the horizon, decided to give it a go. If it didn't work, then either party could give the other one month's notice to terminate. In the coming days we were to wonder if we had done the right thing. Wen had no experience with disabilities or caring as such.

Colleen right up until the time she shifted into the unit, was still binge eating and as a consequence would sometimes be in the foulest of moods because she felt crap after her splurge. On one particular occasion I found the reason for her bad temper revealed by an entry in her diary. She had bought and snacked on a pie, can of coke, two dim sims and a packet of potato chips.

Calling in on Colleen and Wen one lunch time I found they were each devouring a huge bowl of pasta. I took Wen out for coffee the next day.

'What would your thinking be on that?' I quizzed her. 'You know Colls is getting fatter. You have to make sure she has a very small serving. And if you had that for lunch, what would you have for tea?'

'I did not know. I know nothing about disabilities. I not know how she can get all muddled up. I haven't lived with anyone like her. I have no idea,' Wen said in her stilted English.

We've found that Wen would be happy to survive on two minute noodles. Where our culture has been one of nurturing, sharing of a meal at the end of the day, for Wen food is a very insignificant part of her routine. We had lots of conversations about what we expected and how we thought the living arrangement would work. In exchange for free board, Wen has a commitment of ten hours per week, which is to include providing an evening meal on four nights, doing the shopping and keeping the house in order. Also we told her she needed to be there to prompt Colleen where necessary, and more importantly to give her the security to enable her to cope with everyday situations. Paul and Rachael called in one night.

'I don't know how to handle this. It's not working,' I said. 'Colleen has told me she is too scared to have a shower. Petrified.' Apparently we had not said directly to Wen that she needed to be around when Colls had her shower. Also she had no idea how to clean out the shower, or to sweep the floor. She'd leave for university before Colleen was up in the morning. There was no interaction between them.

'Well, let's sit down and work out how we can break the ten hours up to be constructive.' Rachael replied. 'We need to have a programme to cover Colls showering times and to have her up in the morning in time for her to be ready to leave for her day's activity.'

So we devised a timetable. Colleen's carers would prepare Monday and Thursday nights veggies with Wen providing the protein component of those meals. Colleen with her carer would together cook Friday evening's meal. I would prepare Tuesday's meal, and Wen would take care of the evening meal on Wednesday, Saturday and Sunday. Wen is to prompt Colls to have her shower at 8.00 o'clock and to help solve the shower problem, we took the door off, had hand rails installed and put in a shower seat. We've asked Wen to check that Colleen is awake before she leaves in the morning and to remind her what time she has to leave home. We now print out a weekly plan and because there have been a couple of occasions when Colleen has left an hour early for her destination and been absolutely exhausted at the end of the day, I have been texting Wen to reinforce the arrangements. Once we have perfected the timetable I should not have to do this. Otherwise, Colls may just as well be living here. On Saturday mornings Colls and Wen do the housework. Together they are to vacuum, wash the towels, sweep the floor and dust, just basic stuff. Colleen's participation is to be limited to her capabilities. Wen is then to do the shopping with the fifty dollars they each put in per week. This routine has yet to be perfected. We found Wen is not good at cleaning out the fridge, disposing of scraps and stale food, nor at keeping Colleen in line.

I went in one day and found the place in absolute chaos. The couch was covered in clothes, dirty dishes and mess all over it.

'This is not good enough. I'm not buying good furniture to have it ruined. It's expensive and has to be looked after. You're not helping her, Wen. You must say this is not allowed. You have our authority to growl and say "Colleen, pick that up, put it away, pack the dishwasher, fix your mess!" You have to reinforce what we expect of her,' I said.

Poor Wen. She was petrified and was probably thinking "who is this mad woman?"

'Oh, but I don't like doing it,' she meekly said. 'I have no attention to things as you have.' We'd found we had to spell out everything in minute detail for this pleasant mannered thirty-five year old Asian student.

Well, I thought to myself, now I've blown it. I should've taken the matter up with Kieran, the C.E.O. of Wesley Home Care. Gone in and said, look here, Wen's on a bloody good wicket. She's going to have to pull her finger out because it ain't good enough. I should've gone in to see him and done my stack. But I didn't. I just flew off the handle at Wen. Perhaps Wen complained to Kieran. I don't know. Anyway since then things have improved.

Colls is loving the space. I have had to grit my teeth when I've seen her down the street, untidy, with an awful mix of clothes, and her hair not done. We cannot expect Wen to fix that. We will just have to work harder to achieve improvement there.

We were still hopeful that we would find employment which would further integrate Colleen into the community. Teresa, the Living Distinctive Lives Community Inclusion Facilitator, has been successful in finding a volunteer position for her. On Friday mornings she catches the train to Camberwell where she meets a support worker and together they attend a preschool children's music session. There Colleen hands out the music instruments to the children, sings along with them and generally helps organize the littlies as they become familiar with sound and movement. She has a real rapport with some of the kids. Once again she is back in the child care environment which had meant so much to her.

Then, the first week in March 2010 was amazing. All of a sudden Colleen's work arrangements fell into place. I had been scanning the voluntary work page in the local paper.

'How would you like a job at the local toy library, Colls? Let's give them a ring and see what they have to say,' I suggested. I was told about the very simple computer operation to sign the toys in and out, just like a book library. Apparently it had not had appeal for anybody else. I said we were very interested and when we went to check it out Colleen was rostered on for Tuesday and Saturday shifts. Just like when she used to work in the newsagency business in Broadford, she was in her element. Then out of the blue, Eastworks employment agency rang. Earlier, Colleen had done a ten week course and then a four hour trial at Dimmeys store in Heidelberg with a support worker, but until this point in time we had had no follow up.

'Mrs. Clancy, Colleen has been allocated a position at Coles in Chadstone,' I was told. I was ecstatic. Colleen would be paid to work three, four hour shifts, initially with a support worker, then on her own, bringing stock from the back of the shelves forward when the ones at the front had been taken. I did the bus training travel with her, checking that she knew how the ticketing system worked, where to get off, how to negotiate her way to Coles on two buses, and then the reverse for the trip home.

At last things seemed to be falling into place. Colleen was very excited. Now her week seemed fully allocated with meaningful occupations, and with her other activities her time completely taken up. She loves her swimming twice a week, attends drama on a Monday night, on a Wednesday morning travels to Blackburn for Peer Support for stroke winners, and attends pilates fortnightly on a Thursday evening.

We now seem to have struck the right balance with her carers. They are wonderful. I have always advocated that they need to be there not just because they want a job, but to see that the goal posts are shifted and Colleen extended. We will always have to have a team of carers to assist Colleen. But who knows as time goes by her capabilities might improve and she may become less dependent on them, and with her "Circle of Friends" to step in and lend a hand, be more independent.

We invited Wen to the fourth circle meeting and she was amazed by the concept and the support Colleen receives from her family and friends who were present. We are hopeful that the "housemate" arrangement will work for the benefit of both of them.

'I'm Wen's teacher,' Colleen proudly told the circle meeting.

'Colleen very good to me. She teaches me words. I now know what a tea towel is,' Wen said, her face lighting up with her beautiful smile.

My sister Pat rang me following this meeting.

'I think that meeting was unbelievably beautiful. You must feel so proud of how far you have come,' she said. I could not speak.

At times it had been incredibly hard. Christine had been worried that I was being drowned by it all and had come with me when I had attended a clinical psychologist appointment some time ago. I felt I was just being bombarded. Do this, do that, attend doctor's appointments, get injections, be here, go there, check on Colleen's movements. God, give me strength, this is such hard work, I would whisper to myself. I felt I was slipping into a big hole.

Over the years my sister Pat has not had to say anything about the issues she knew I'd been facing. She's just known I have struggled with it all. Her support over the years has been invaluable.

In a conversation with her I said, 'I sometimes think people are thinking, why aren't you out playing golf, Bern? If only they knew the time…….but I can't say that…..I don't want to say that. Colls is a good patient ….imagine others.'

I am not one to say woe is me. I'm not a me person. But sometimes I feel I am running out of energy. Colleen's illness has controlled my life for twelve years. I want to put those years behind me, lighten up. All along the way I have been lifting the bar. I don't want to be in control. I must let go.

Hopefully as time goes by and Colleen becomes a little less dependent on me, it will be time for my life to come off hold. The saddest part is that we have let a lot of friendships go. It's been tricky. Now we will have the time to make re-connections, not only with friends but Peter and I. My busyness drives him insane. There was a tiny spark of enthusiasm from him on a recent excursion to a rock and roll festival in Geelong. I was talking to a woman there and discovered there was such a group activity just two kilometres from our home.

I think to myself I just need to get Peter's knee more flexible, and this bloody knee of mine working and we can go and do some living. I've been looking to purchase a bike. A girlfriend of mine rides everywhere while waiting for two hip replacements and a knee job, and I only have one crook knee. Perhaps I'll even get Peter on a bike too!

'There's a hell of a lot of living to do out there, Pete,' I tell him. 'And I have no intention of not working, even past retirement age.'

My quest to have Colleen participating in main stream activities and living independently away from us, seems no longer to be a dream but a reality. Her siblings treat her very normally. They do not play down to the disability. They see her as an adult and look past the disability. They will always perform a very important role in her life.

I know that the arrangements we have made for Colleen will not last for ever. Nothing in life ever stays the same, but hopefully we will be able to organize other meaningful activities along the way and put in place whatever other living arrangements are required to meet her very special needs.

Our darling Colleen turned thirty-four on the 28th June, 2010. We don't know what the future holds for her. I can only hope that with her network circle of family and friends she will be able to live a happy fulfilled life.

Christmas 2010

Colls celebrates with her nephews and nieces

Colls cuddles "Harper Grace", Shaun & Laura's little daughter

POSTCRIPT

As I look back over the years of this journey we have travelled with Colleen, I marvel at the incredibly large hurdles we have had to vault, sometimes stumbling along the way. From that very first moment when I was gripped with fear by what had befallen my daughter and what the future would hold for us, and through all the stages of her recovery, I have held steadfastly to the belief that Colleen would recover.

Even now I cling to the hope that our beautiful child, who was so full of the love of life, will one day be completely restored to me. Even though this is probably a vain hope, after having come so far, why would I give up now? If having read the account of the past twelve years of our lives you think I am being overly optimistic, to you I say, "You don't know who you are dealing with!"

The issue of Young People In Nursing Homes has been around for far too long. The journey taken by the families of young people, who find themselves either living in nursing homes or risking placement there, is unexpected and often arduous. Yet it demonstrates the tenacity and determination that individuals can find when faced with deeply distressing circumstances.

The courage these young people and their families display in the face of often overwhelming odds is an inspiration to others.

Dr Bronwyn Morkham
National Director
Young People In Nursing Homes National Alliance

www.ingramcontent.com/pod-product-compliance
Lightning Source LLC
Chambersburg PA
CBHW050623300426
44112CB00012B/1636